SATHER CLASSICAL LECTURES

VOLUME FIFTY-ONE

Virgil's *Aeneid*
and the Tradition of
Hellenistic Poetry

WENDELL CLAUSEN

Virgil's
Aeneid
and the Tradition of
Hellenistic Poetry

UNIVERSITY OF CALIFORNIA PRESS / Berkeley Los Angeles London

University of California Press
Berkeley and Los Angeles, California

University of California Press, Ltd. London, England

© 1987 by The Regents of the University of California
1   2   3   4   5   6   7   8   9

Library of Congress Cataloging-in-Publication Data
Clausen, Wendell Vernon, 1923–
  Virgil's Aeneid and the tradition of Hellenistic poetry.

  Bibliography: p.
  Includes index.
  1. Virgil. Aeneis. 2. Aeneas in literature.
3. Hellenism in literature.   4. Greek poetry,
Hellenistic—History and criticism.   I. Title.
PA6825.C53   1987   873'.01   86–1356
ISBN 0–520–05791–0 (alk. paper)
Printed in the United States of America

MARGARITAE MEAE

CONTENTS

Preface   ix

I. A NEW POET'S EDUCATION   1

II. TWO SIMILES AND A WEDDING   15

III. THE WOODEN HORSE   26

IV. DIDO AND AENEAS   40

V. ARCADIA REVIEWED   61

VI. THE DEATH OF TURNUS   83

Appendixes   101

1. Notes on *Eclogue* 6.47–60   101
2. The White Tents of Rhesus   103   3. Black Memnon   105
4. How Old Is Dido?   106   5. Iopas   108
6. Sudden Departure from Carthage   111
7. A Note on *Aeneid* 6.30   113   8. The Shield of Turnus   115
9. The Exclusiveness of Hercules   117
10. The Kinship of Evander and Dardanus   119
11. Mulciber   121

Abbreviations   123   Notes   125   General Index   167
Index of Passages Cited   173

PREFACE

The chapters of this book were conceived as lectures and delivered as the Sather Lectures at Berkeley in the spring quarter of 1982. I have revised all six for publication, I, V, and VI extensively, and added notes and appendixes; I have not, however, attempted to change their original character, and something of the lecturer's tone and manner no doubt remains.

It was impressed upon me by the then Chairman of the Classics Department, John Dillon, when I received the invitation to give these lectures, and again later, and somewhat more firmly, by his successor, Charles Murgia, that they should be intelligible to a literate general audience. Taking their advice to heart, I provided translations of the passages of Greek and Latin I quoted and confined scholarly argument to the notes and appendixes. The translations are my own, although in a very few places I have borrowed a word or phrase from another translator.

For the most part I have chosen to present my own opinions without dissecting or criticizing the opinions of others—on the shield of Aeneas, for instance, or on the final scene of the poem. I have, however, occasionally criticized recent commentators for their neglect of Hellenistic poetry, since those using a commentary will naturally assume that it contains what is necessary for an understanding and appreciation of the text. From this prejudice against Hellenistic poetry Virgil's earlier commentators and readers were happily free; for them (as for Virgil) there was no discontinuity in Greek poetry, for them Callimachus was a poet comparable with Pindar. Thus Milton,

The Reason of Church Government: "Or if occasion shall lead to imitate those magnifick Odes and Hymns wherein Pindarus and Callimachus are in most things worthy."

It will be objected, I suppose, that I have turned Virgil into a Hellenistic poet while disregarding other aspects of his poetry. Any new or strong emphasis almost inevitably involves some distortion. But Virgil was a Hellenistic poet, a poet educated and writing in that tradition. Of course he was widely read in earlier Greek poetry; so too were the Hellenistic poets. Of course the main reference of the *Aeneid* is to Homer, but Virgil imitates Homer (whatever the deeper resonance of his own poetry) as a Hellenistic poet would, as Apollonius did. Virgil may be described as a New Poet of the second generation, with a literary technique, and hence a literary sensibility, formed by a close and unremitting study of the Hellenistic poets and their Roman descendants, the New Poets of the first generation.

When I recall Berkeley and my pleasing anxious existence there as Sather Professor I am conscious of a sense of gratitude to more people than I can possibly thank for their abundant hospitality. I am particularly grateful to Anthony Bulloch, Charles Murgia, Thomas Rosenmeyer, and Danuta Shanzer, and to my Sather assistant Stephen White. I owe a debt of gratitude also to two of my colleagues at Harvard, David Mitten and Emily Vermeule, and to Henry Rosovsky, then Dean of the Faculty of Arts and Sciences; to my former colleague Richard Thomas; to Lorna Holmes, Lenore Savage, Ann Hawthorne, and Norbert Lain; and to Doris Kretschmer and Mary Lamprech of the University of California Press. My chief and abiding debt is recorded more prominently elsewhere.

I

A NEW POET'S EDUCATION

Fuit enim hic poeta ut scrupulose et anxie, ita
dissimulanter et quasi clanculo doctus.

Macrobius, *Saturnalia*

With the posthumous publication of the *Aeneid* in 19 B.C., which
Virgil on his deathbed had sought to prevent, it was inevitable that
his literary career should be regarded as a progression from the lesser
to the greater work, from the *Eclogues* to the *Georgics* to the su-
preme achievement of the *Aeneid*. And the *Aeneid* so imposes itself
that the figure of the younger poet, sporting with Amaryllis in the
shade, tends to be obscured. This view of Virgil's literary career is
already represented—indeed, insisted upon—in the *Culex*, an exquisitely bad little poem written some years after his death.[1] The
poetaster, pretending to be the adolescent Virgil, apologizes for the
slightness of his effort and promises to honor Octavius (as he calls
him) with a weightier poem in the future, "posterius grauiore sono
tibi Musa loquetur / nostra" (8–9); thus unintentionally (he intended
quite the opposite) unmasking his impersonation. For the younger
Virgil—the true younger Virgil, that is, the poet of the *Eclogues*—
had explicitly rejected the idea of epic; a rejection already implicit
in his cultivation of Theocritean pastoral.

> Prima Syracosio dignata est ludere uersu
> nostra neque erubuit siluas habitare Thalea.
> cum canerem reges et proelia, Cynthius aurem
> uellit et admonuit: "pastorem, Tityre, pinguis
> pascere oportet ouis, deductum dicere carmen."
> nunc ego (namque super tibi erunt qui dicere laudes,
> Vare, tuas cupiant et tristia condere bella)
> agrestem tenui meditabor harundine Musam.

(*E.* 6.1–8)

My Thalia condescended to amuse herself with Syracusan verse, nor did she blush to dwell in the woods. When I was singing of kings and battles, the Cynthian god tweaked my ear and warned me: "A shepherd, Tityrus, ought to feed his sheep to be fat but sing a fine-spun song." Now I—for you will have many eager to sing your praises, Varus, and recount grim wars—will practice the rural Muse on a slender reed.

This passage, introducing the second half of the Book of *Eclogues* and therefore emphatic, can now[2] be read for what it is: not an autobiographical statement, as ancient scholiasts thought,[3] but a literary allusion—Virgil's pastoral translation of Callimachus' famous rejection of epic in the preface to the second edition of his *Aetia*, written when Callimachus was an old man looking back on his literary career.[4] His critics, Telchines as Callimachus wittily styles them, ill-natured literary dwarfs, complained that he had not written a continuous poem of many thousands of lines about kings and battles. Judge poetry by its art, he says, not by its length, and don't expect a great rattling song from me: thunder is not my business but Jove's:

καὶ γὰρ ὅτε πρώτιστον ἐμοῖς ἐπὶ δέλτον ἔθηκα
γούνασιν, Ἀπόλλων εἶπεν ὅ μοι Λύκιος·
". . . . . . .]. . .ἀοιδέ, τὸ μὲν θύος ὅττι πάχιστον
θρέψαι, τὴ]ν Μοῦσαν δ' ὠγαθὲ λεπταλέην·
πρὸς δέ σε] καὶ τόδ' ἄνωγα, τὰ μὴ πατέουσιν ἄμαξαι
τὰ στείβειν, ἑτέρων ἴχνια μὴ καθ' ὁμά
δίφρον ἐλ]ᾶν μηδ' οἶμον ἀνὰ πλατύν, ἀλλὰ κελεύθους
ἀτρίπτο]υς, εἰ καὶ στεινοτέρην ἐλάσεις."

    (fr. 1.21–28 Pf.)

For when first I set a writing-tablet on my knees, Lycian Apollo spoke to me: "Poet, feed your victim to be as fat as possible, but your Muse, my friend, keep her slender. And I bid you this besides: Where no wagons pass, walk there; don't drive your chariot in the common tracks of others or on a broad way, but on roads unworn, even though you drive on a narrower one."

The idea of a pastoral translation may have been suggested by the original preface to the *Aetia* (of which only a fragment is preserved):

ποιμένι μῆλα νέμοντι παρ' ἴχνιον ὀξέος ἵππου
Ἡσιόδῳ Μουσέων ἑσμὸς ὅτ' ἠντίασεν . . .

    (fr. 2.1–2 Pf.)

When the bevy of Muses met the shepherd Hesiod feeding his
sheep by the hoofprint of the spirited horse . . .

The reference is to Hesiod's encounter with the Muses on Mt. Helicon, which symbolized for Callimachus (as Virgil knew) a higher
source of poetic inspiration.[5]

"Agrestem tenui meditabor harundine Musam": an attentive
reader will not fail to hear the echo of the first *Eclogue*:

Tityre, tu patulae recubans sub tegmine fagi
siluestrem tenui Musam meditaris auena.

    (1–2)

Tityrus, reclining under the cover of a spreading beech, you
practice the woodland Muse on a slender oat.

Although the intricate word order of line 2 is suggestive of Alexandrian elegance, a reader might not, given the context, perceive a
special literary sense in "tenui" and might take it merely as contrib-
uting to the shape and balance of the line. In *E.* 6.8, however, there
is no mistaking its sense: "tenui" is not merely ornamental; it involves a concept of style, the Callimachean concept, being the equivalent of λεπταλέην.[6] Furthermore, the god who admonishes the
poet-shepherd is himself an elegant Callimachean, Cynthian Apollo.
The epithet "Cynthius" as applied to Apollo seems to be Callimachus' invention, a literary epithet unhallowed by cult or tradition;
and as such it was recognized by Virgil, who uses it only here and
once elsewhere, in an intensely Callimachean context.[7] His Syracusan
verse, Virgil subtly asserts, is Callimachean in nature.

Virgil was born in 70 B.C. near Mantua in the Po Valley. His father
was a landowner, whatever the truth of the information supplied by
Donatus' *Life*.[8] Certainly he was not a peasant,[9] the social gulf between peasant and middle class being then as now in Italy profound;
a man, rather, with ambition and money enough to send an extraor-
dinarily gifted son away to school. Apparently Virgil's father was
aware of the inadequacies of education in Mantua, one of those small
and insignificant towns that loom large in imagination because
of a famous son.[10] Virgil went first to Cremona, a flourishing
municipality[11] some forty miles away—unhappily, in the time of the
land confiscations, not far enough away: "Mantua uae miserae nimium uicina Cremonae" (*E.* 9.28)—studying there until he assumed

the *toga uirilis*, the dress of manhood, probably when he was seventeen;[12] then to Milan; and then, probably when he was eighteen,[13] to Rome.

What sort of education had Virgil had by the time he arrived in Rome? The sort then available, with some managing, to the son of a fairly prosperous family:[14] mainly literary, devoted to the study of "classical" Greek and, to some extent, early Latin poetry (prose was neglected), and concentrating on grammar and rhetoric. The truth is we know very little in detail about education in Virgil's day.[15] We know that Horace was made to memorize the *Odusia* of Livius Andronicus (*Epistles* 2.1.69–71); but that may have been a matter of personal taste on the part of his teacher, the irascible Orbilius. The anonymous *Vita* of Horace is silent about his education,[16] as the *Vita Donati* is silent about Virgil's, presumably because no information was wanted: Roman education did not change in any essential way with the passage of time, and no one would have been curious.

Not surprisingly, contemporary poetry had no place in the curriculum; still, Virgil must have read privately during his school years, and with particular interest, as we may imagine, the new poetry of two fellow Transpadanes: Catullus of Verona and Cinna of Brescia. (According to Suetonius, the first teacher of contemporary poetry in Rome was Q. Caecilius Epirota, a man of bad character. After the suicide of Cornelius Gallus, with whom he had lived on terms of intimacy, in 26 B.C., he opened a small school and began to lecture on Virgil and other new poets.[17]) Yet only in Rome can Virgil have experienced the enthusiasm of this new movement in poetry, discovering there a select group of very self-conscious young poets—the New Poets, "poetae noui," as Cicero called them[18]—with definite, passionately held ideas about poetry, and a literary environment in which poetry flourished as it had not in Rome for a hundred years.

In the ninth *Eclogue* the pastoral illusion is momentarily shattered when the irrepressible young Lycidas compares himself with two "real" poets:

nam neque adhuc Vario uideor nec dicere Cinna
digna . . .

(35–36)[19]

For as yet my singing seems worthy neither of Varius nor of Cinna . . .

Similarly, the illusion is shattered in Theocritus' seventh *Idyll* (the mysterious goatherd Lycidas is speaking):

οὐ γάρ πω κατ' ἐμὸν νόον οὔτε τὸν ἐσθλόν
Σικελίδαν νίκημι τὸν ἐκ Σάμω οὔτε Φιλίταν
ἀείδων . . .

(7.39–41)

For to my mind I cannot as yet vanquish in song either the
excellent Sicelidas from Samos or Philitas . . .

Virgil's imitation is intensely self-conscious.[20] Asclepiades, whom Lycidas calls Sicelidas, was a contemporary of Theocritus (Virgil may
have imagined that he was also a friend) and of Philitas,[21] an older
poet and scholar much respected by the Alexandrians. Varius was a
contemporary and close friend whose poetry Virgil admired and imitated,[22] and Cinna an older poet, the associate of Catullus and Calvus. But why Cinna? Why not rather Calvus ("nec dicere Caluo /
digna"), whose Io Virgil imitates in the sixth Eclogue (47–52)? Presumably because Virgil had known Cinna (in the intimate literary
society of Rome it would be surprising if he had not), and it is characteristic of Virgil that he should involve his personal experience in
an imitation of Theocritus. Catullus and Calvus had died not long
before Virgil's arrival in Rome,[23] but Cinna was still alive, living on
until 44 B.C., when he was mistaken for one of Caesar's assassins
and killed by the angry mob.

According to Macrobius,[24] the poet Parthenius, Cinna's mentor,
instructed Virgil in Greek. But Virgil was already well read in classical Greek poetry by the time he met Parthenius; what we are to
understand from Macrobius—what Macrobius can scarcely have
understood himself—is that Parthenius initiated Virgil into the mys-
teries of Hellenistic, and especially Alexandrian, poetry. The case of
Varro of Atax is not dissimilar. Born in 82 B.C. in Gallia Narbo-
nensis, the Province, Varro wrote a Bellum Sequanicum, an epic in
Ennian style, to celebrate Caesar's victorious campaign against the
Sequani in 58 B.C., and, no doubt, to attract favorable attention to
himself. In this latter respect at least, his poem seems to have been
a success; he made his way to Rome, where he discovered the New
Poetry and produced a version of Apollonius' Argonautica.[25] According to St. Jerome,[26] Varro did not learn Greek until he was thirty-
five years old. But Varro must have received a good Roman education, including Greek, in the Province. Nor is it likely that so late
a scholar could have dealt with Apollonius' difficult, composite
Greek.[27] It is far more likely that Jerome's note is confused and that
Varro published his Argonautae when he was thirty-five.

Parthenius[28] had been established in Rome for a number of years by now; a zealous Callimachean, a poet and scholar in a tradition extending back to Philitas, ποιητὴς ἅμα καὶ κριτικός,[29] and—to judge by the results—an exciting and influential teacher. He had not, however, come of his own free will: he had been taken prisoner when the Romans defeated Mithridates, given as a prize to a certain Cinna (not further identified but presumably an older relative of Cinna the poet), and later freed because of his learning, διὰ παίδευσιν.[30] Parthenius therefore arrived in Rome sometime after 73 B.C., the year the Romans captured Nicaea, and possibly as late as 65 B.C., when Mithridates was finally defeated. And with him he brought Callimachus; that is, he introduced the poetry of Callimachus to some young poets in Rome—the New Poets, as they were to become— and made it an effective part of their education. Literary young men in Rome at the time may have been minded to read Callimachus without prompting; but if so the suddenness and intensity of their interest would be hard to explain, and it is doubtful whether a Cinna or a Calvus or a Catullus could have read and appreciated Callimachus without a Parthenius at his elbow.[31]

Cinna labored for nine years to be as obscure as Euphorion[32] and succeeded brilliantly: his *Zmyrna* required a commentary. Catullus greeted the appearance of Cinna's miniature epic, or epyllion,[33] with Callimachean enthusiasm:

Zmyrna mei Cinnae nonam post denique messem
   quam coepta est nonamque edita post hiemem,
milia cum interea quingenta Hortensius uno

. . . .

Zmyrna cauas Satrachi penitus mittetur ad undas,
   Zmyrnam cana diu saecula peruoluent.
at Volusi annales Paduam morientur ad ipsam
   et laxas scombris saepe dabunt tunicas.

     (95)

My Cinna's *Zmyrna* is at last out, nine summers and nine winters after it was conceived, while in the meantime Hortensius . . . five hundred thousand . . . in one. . . . *Zmyrna* will be sent all the way to the Satrachus' curled waves, gray centuries will long peruse *Zmyrna*. But the *Annals* of Volusius will perish by the Padua itself, supplying many a loose wrapper for mackerel.

The technique of the poem is minute.[34] A polemical poem in the Callimachean manner was not intended merely as a confutation; it was to be at the same time a demonstration of how poetry should be written. (Catullus wrote another such poem vilifying Volusius and his *Annals*, "Annales Volusi," which has not quite been recognized for what it is.[35]) Catullus pays Cinna an artful compliment: his poem will be read even by that far distant river which it celebrates.[36] There is a piquancy, also, in the implied comparison of the two rivers: the broad familiar Po, sluggish and muddy, and the imagined Satrachus, flowing clear and fast.[37] Callimachus had used a similar metaphor for long and short, or bad and good, poetry at the end of his second *Hymn*: Envy (Φθόνος) whispers an anti-Callimachean opinion into the ear of Apollo; Apollo gives Envy a kick and replies:

"Ἀσσυρίου ποταμοῖο μέγας ῥόος, ἀλλὰ τὰ πολλὰ
λύματα γῆς καὶ πολλὸν ἐφ' ὕδατι συρφετὸν ἕλκει.
Δηοῖ δ' οὐκ ἀπὸ παντὸς ὕδωρ φορέουσι μέλισσαι,
ἀλλ' ἥτις καθαρή τε καὶ ἀχράαντος ἀνέρπει
πίδακος ἐξ ἱερῆς ὀλίγη λιβὰς ἄκρον ἄωτον."

(108–12)

"Great is the flood of the Assyrian river, but it drags much filth of earth and much refuse on its water. No common water do the bees bring to Demeter, but that which seeps up pure and undefiled from a sacred spring, a tiny rill, the crest and flower of water."[38]

What was the *Zmyrna* about? The incestuous passion of Zmyrna for her father Cinyras, her metamorphosis into a tree, and the birth of Adonis from her trunk: precisely the kind of story that Parthenius liked—erotic, morbid, grotesque—as may be inferred from the fragments of his poetry and from the handbook Περὶ ἐρωτικῶν παθημάτων, *Love Stories*, which he compiled for his pupil Cornelius Gallus.[39] "I have put them together and set them out as briefly as possible. These stories not being related fully as they are found in the poets, you will have here a summary of each" (Preface). One of these (11) tells of the incestuous passion of Byblis for her brother Caunus, about which Parthenius himself had written a poem. And he quotes, for example, some of his own lines:

ἡ δ' ὅτε δή ῥ' ὀλοοῖο κασιγνήτου νόον ἔγνω,
κλαῖεν ἀηδονίδων θαμινώτερον, αἵτ' ἐνὶ βήσσῃς

Σιθονίῳ κούρῳ πέρι μυρίον αἰάζουσιν.
καὶ ῥα κατὰ στυφελοῖο σαρωνίδος αὐτίκα μίτρην
ἁψαμένη δειρὴν ἐνεθήκατο. ταὶ δ' ἐπ' ἐκείνῃ
βεύδεα παρθενικαὶ Μιλησίδες ἐρρήξαντο.

When she knew her brother's cruel heart, she wept more loudly than the nightingales that in the glens make a myriad lament for the Sithonian boy. Then to a rough oak she fastened her headband and therein laid her neck. For her the virgins of Miletus rent their garments.

As in Catullus 95, so also in these lines a concern for symmetry and intricate detail is evident.[40] And a comparison with the passage in Apollonius which Parthenius is imitating (the death of Cleite)[41] will show how deliberate and self-conscious his concern was:

κακῷ δ' ἐπὶ κύντερον ἄλλο
ἤνυσεν, ἁψαμένη βρόχον αὐχένι. τὴν δὲ καὶ αὐταὶ
Νύμφαι ἀποφθιμένην ἀλσηίδες ὠδύραντο.
          (*Arg.* 1.1064–66)

To the evil done she added a worse evil, fastening a noose about her neck. For her dead even the Nymphs of the groves wept.

Not only has Parthenius shaped his imitation with much care,[42] he has defined it, by introducing two exquisitely rare words, σαρωνίδος and βεύδεα, as Callimachean.[43]

Virgil admired the delicacy and restraint of Parthenius' narrative (the death of Byblis is only suggested, not described[44]) and imitated it twice. In the *Georgics*:

"illa quidem, dum te fugeret per flumina praeceps,
immanem ante pedes hydrum moritura puella
seruantem ripas alta non uidit in herba.
at chorus aequalis Dryadum clamore supremos
impleuit montis . . ."

          (4.457–61)

"She, as she fled headlong from you by the river, did not see before her feet in the deep grass—the doomed girl—a monstrous watersnake guarding the bank. But the band of her Dryad companions filled the mountain-heights with their cries . . ."

And in the *Aeneid*:

> multaque per maestum demens effata furorem
> purpureos moritura manu discindit amictus
> et nodum informis leti trabe nectit ab alta.
> quam cladem miserae postquam accepere Latinae . . .
>
> (12.601–4)

Flinging out wild words in her sorrow and pain, the doomed woman rends her purple robes and fastens the noose of hideous death to a high rafter. The wretched Latin women when they learned of their calamity . . .

The central figure of the Hellenistic period, the all-important literary "fact," for the New Poets was Callimachus, although Apollonius, himself a Callimachean, was nearly as important, and to Virgil writing his *Eclogues* Theocritus obviously more important. Still, Callimachus remained the ideal of Alexandrian elegance. Without his poetry and his poetics, as interpreted by Parthenius, the New Poetry would have been inconceivable.

It is impossible to read much of Callimachus—apart from his *Epigrams*, which belong to an old tradition—and not be impressed, or perhaps depressed, by the scope and detail of his erudition. It would be a mistake, however, to wish that his poetry might somehow be separated from his scholarship. Callimachus was not a poet and a scholar; he was, or rather could be, a poet precisely because he was a scholar, a γραμματικός, a man whose business was with literature. Earlier Greek literature had now been collected in the great library at Alexandria, where it was catalogued by Callimachus,[45] and men came to know the refined pleasure of writing books from books. Callimachus was that rarity—a poet of genius whose imagination was nourished almost wholly on books: "nothing unwarranted sing I," ἀμάρτυρον οὐδὲν ἀείδω.[46] Again and again Callimachus reminds his reader that what he is telling him is true; that it can be found (he means) somewhere in a book. His extreme antithesis, in English poetry, is Wordsworth:

> The sounding cataract
> Haunted me like a passion; the tall rock,
> The mountain, and the deep and gloomy wood,
> Their colours and their forms, were then to me

An appetite; a feeling and a love,
That had no need of a remoter charm,
By thought supplied, nor any interest
Unborrowed from the eye.

(*Tintern Abbey* 76–83)

For Callimachus it was not the eye but the ear (it should be remembered that the ancients read aloud) that mattered.[47]

Now Callimachus—to take him as an exemplar—could study and compare any number of texts; choose a word or phrase he liked and incorporate it, subtly modified, in his own poetry; adapt a metaphor or simile with a view to improving it (imitation ideally implied emulation); recall a poetic presence, a context, with a word or two; ostentatiously pursue a remote version of a myth or legend while incidentally referring to the usual version; and so on, to the limits of verbal sophistication.[48]

Above all, Callimachus cared passionately for style—for a poetry that should be elegant, terse, new. Hence his rejection of old-fashioned epic. Not that Callimachus condemned Homer, whose text he studied assiduously and minutely imitated;[49] rather, he condemned the Homerizing poets of his own day (some of whom, apparently, had criticized him for not writing an epic poem)—poets who inertly reproduced Homer's language and attempted to continue the epic tradition by applying it to contemporary history, to Hellenistic kings and battles, not perceiving that it had long since been exhausted.

Virgil's response to the New Poetry is everywhere evident in his *Eclogues*, but especially in the sixth, in the song of Silenus.

Silenus is unknown to the pastoral world of Theocritus, nor is he found elsewhere in Theocritus. Callimachus mentions him once, in describing the virginal loveliness of Cydippe—no girl with more of dawn in her eyes came to the spring of shaggy old Silenus.[50] Traditional features remain:[51] he is the ancient drunkard still, the lover of nymphs and music, a forest seer gifted with mysterious wisdom. Yet Virgil's Silenus—and he seems to be mostly Virgil's[52]—has suffered a wondrous change: he has become a literary critic, a New Critic, as it were.

Virgil's song of Silenus originates in Apollonius' song of Orpheus.[53] Like Orpheus, Silenus begins with the creation of the world and the emergence of living things, primeval figures, Pyrrha, Prometheus. But unlike Orpheus, who "stayed his lyre and his ambrosial voice" with

Zeus still a child, still thinking childish thoughts in the Dictaean
Cave, Silenus sings on, singing as if, in the plenitude of song, there
would be no end of song, singing "till the Evening Star advanced in
the unwilling sky," "inuito processit Vesper Olympo" (87). He seems
to sing distractedly, almost casually, as a pastoral singer might,
touching on various themes. His song is, however, a neoteric *ars
poetica* artfully concealed, with but a single subject: poetry, as defined and practiced by Callimachus (and poets after Callimachus) and
now by Gallus. That Pasiphae's perverse passion, her ἐρωτικὸν
πάθημα (45–60), and an appreciation of Gallus' miniature epic on
the Grynean Grove (64–73) occupy much of the song can only be
a reflection of contemporary taste, Virgil's and that of his friends.

> et fortunatam, si numquam armenta fuissent,
> Pasiphaen niuei solatur amore iuuenci.
> a, uirgo infelix, quae te dementia cepit?
> Proetides implerunt falsis mugitibus agros,
> at non tam turpis pecudum tamen ulla secuta
> concubitus, quamuis collo timuisset aratrum
> et saepe in leui quaesisset cornua fronte.
> a, uirgo infelix, tu nunc in montibus erras:
> ille latus niueum molli fultus hyacintho
> ilice sub nigra pallentis ruminat herbas
> aut aliquam in magno sequitur grege. "claudite, Nymphae,
> Dictaeae Nymphae, nemorum iam claudite saltus,
> si qua forte ferant oculis sese obuia nostris
> errabunda bouis uestigia; forsitan illum
> aut herba captum uiridi aut armenta secutum
> perducant aliquae stabula ad Gortynia uaccae."

> (E. 6.45–60)[54]

And he consoles Pasiphae (happy if herds had never been) with
her passion for the snow-white bull. Ah, wretched woman,
what madness seized you? Proetus' daughters filled the fields
with their mimic lowing, and yet not one sought intercourse so
depraved, although she feared the plow's yoke on her neck and
often felt for horns on her smooth forehead. Ah, wretched
woman, you roam the mountains now, while *he*, pillowing a
snow-white flank upon soft hyacinths, under a dark holm-oak
chews the pale grass or follows some heifer in the great herd.
"Close, you Nymphs, Dictaean Nymphs, close now the glades
of the forest, if by any chance his wandering hoofprints may

present themselves to my eyes. Perhaps he has been attracted by green grass or followed the herds, and some cows are leading him home to the barnyards of Gortyna."

These lines constitute Virgil's perfect miniature of a miniature epic: 45–46, elliptical narrative, assuming the familiar story; 47, the poet's sympathetic apostrophe; 48–51, Proetus' daughters, hysterical girls who imagined that they had been turned into cows—a story within the story, as in Callimachus' *Hecale* (Erichthonius), Moschus' *Europa* (Io), Catullus 64 (Ariadne); 52, a repetition of the apostrophe to "frame" the interior story; 52–55, the poet's feeling comment; 55–60, the heroine's lovely, sad, and disproportioned speech.

"A, uirgo infelix, quae te dementia cepit?" (47). "A, uirgo infelix" is a quotation from the *Io*, Calvus' miniature epic, of which scarcely six lines survive: "a, uirgo infelix, herbis pasceris amaris,"[55] "ah, wretched woman, you will feed on bitter grass." A celebrated line, apparently. Calvus sympathizes with his poor bewildered heroine, so lately the loved of Jove but now turned into a cow and obliged to eat grass—bitter, as the poet fondly imagines, to her dainty human palate. "Quae te dementia cepit?" is also a quotation, from the second *Eclogue* (Virgil likes to quote or imitate himself), and thus indirectly an imitation of Theocritus: "a, Corydon, Corydon, quae te dementia cepit?"—shepherd Corydon's self-reproach as he awakens from his dream of love to sober reality (2.69). Your vine is only half-pruned on the leafy elm; why not weave a basket, something useful at any rate? (Abandoning former occupations is a symptom of love-sickness in Hellenistic poetry.) Compare Theocritus 11.72: ὦ Κύκλωψ, Κύκλωψ, πᾷ τὰς φρένας ἐκπεπότασαι;, "O Cyclops, Cyclops" (dear old Polyphemus, no longer Homer's grisly monster but Theocritus' Sicilian neighbor, hopelessly in love with the fickle sea-nymph Galatea)—"O Cyclops, Cyclops, where have your wits flown?" You would show more sense if you would go and plait cheese-crates or gather green food for the lambs.

Clearly, the poet of the sixth *Eclogue*—of the *Eclogues*—had no intention of ever writing an epic. Silenus cannot spare the time of day for kings and battles.

Yet Virgil did write an epic, did sing of kings and battles. That the same poet who wrote "cum canerem reges et proelia" could write, some years later, "Arma uirumque cano" is, or ought to be, one of the major surprises of literature. Not that Virgil proceeded directly from the *Eclogues* to the composition of the *Aeneid*; the

Georgics intervenes, his most perfect if not his greatest poem, written (he declares) at the command of Maecenas, "tua, Maecenas, haud mollia iussa" (3.41)—an understood form of flattery by which a poet attributes to his patron's order the poem he would have written anyway.[56] Still, the *Aeneid* may have been written under some compulsion: not the compulsion of an order—a poet can hardly be ordered to write a great poem, certainly not a poem so peculiar and personal as the *Aeneid*—but the subtler compulsion of interest and desire, on the part of Augustus himself,[57] to which Virgil could not remain indifferent.

At the beginning of the lengthy proem to the third Book of the *Georgics*, which formally balances that to the first (and both proems are concerned with the poet's relation to Augustus), Virgil rejects mythological themes as being too hackneyed now for serious poetry. The themes he mentions are nonheroic and notably Hellenistic: "Who has not told the tale of the boy Hylas, of Latona and Delos?" "cui non dictus Hylas puer et Latonia Delos?"[58] Now he will venture on a path by which he can rise from earth and fly triumphant on the lips of men, "uictorque uirum uolitare per ora," recalling Ennius' proud self-epitaph.[59] "I will be the first," he continues, Roman-fashion:

> primus ego in patriam mecum, modo uita supersit,
> Aonio rediens deducam uertice Musas;
> primus Idumaeas referam tibi, Mantua, palmas,
> et uiridi in campo templum de marmore ponam
> propter aquam, tardis ingens ubi flexibus errat
> Mincius et tenera praetexit harundine ripas.
> in medio mihi Caesar erit templumque tenebit.
>
> (G. 3.10–16)

I will be the first returning, if only life lasts, to bring the Muses home with me from the Aonian Mount; the first to carry palms of Edom, Mantua, back to you; and in a green meadow I will build a temple of marble by the water, where broad Mincius wanders slowly winding and fringes his banks with tender reeds. In the center will my Caesar be and keep the temple.

Virgil proceeds to embellish this monumental conceit in lavish detail. Like the declaration of dependence on Callimachean principles at the beginning of *E.* 6, the proem to *G.* 3 is placed to advantage and must have been composed with extreme care. But whereas the brief declaration is, properly understood, unequivocal, the proem seems, for all its detail—possibly because of its detail—ambiguous, unclear; or perhaps, as clear as Virgil meant it to be. Is Virgil engaging to write an epic in honor of Augustus? or grandly refusing? or hesitating still?[60]

The trouble is that these lines are necessarily read *ex post facto*: not, that is, with an epic only vaguely if at all in prospect, but with the *Aeneid* sublimely *there*, imposing its presence. Let the critic not be wise after the fact; let him consider, rather, how he would read these lines if Virgil had not written the *Aeneid*, or had somehow failed. (How could Virgil know in advance that he would succeed? In a letter to Augustus he writes almost despairingly "about my Aeneas."[61]) And what in 29 B.C. would a reader, not otherwise informed, make of these lines—make of a poet who announces that he will gird himself to sing of Augustus' fiery battles someday, "mox tamen ardentis accingar dicere pugnas / Caesaris" (46–47), meanwhile turning to the poem in hand, a didactic poem in Hellenistic style, however else it may be qualified, which ends with an epyllion, the story of Aristaeus the legendary beekeeper and of Orpheus and Eurydice?

When he had nearly finished with the *Georgics*, sustained, as we may imagine, by that high success, Virgil decided, with some misgiving, to write an epic—an epic of a kind largely unprecedented, Homeric in form, Callimachean in style;[62] a prolonged literary allusion to Homer[63] in the manner of Apollonius, whose *Argonautica*, while attempting less, served as a model for the *Aeneid* in that it realized certain possibilities and indicated others. So viewed, the *Aeneid* represents not an abandonment but an extension of Callimachean poetics by Virgil, greatly daring, into an area of poetry precluded by Callimachus. The composition of the *Aeneid* cannot have been easy (if composition was ever easy for Virgil), and, having once committed himself to Homeric magnitude and continuity, he may occasionally have felt some aesthetic strain—a Callimachean scruple perhaps—especially in the latter books.

> dicam horrida bella,
> dicam acies actosque animis in funera reges . . .
>
> (7.41–42)

I shall tell of grim war, tell of embattled squadrons and kings rushing valiantly upon their death . . .

II

TWO SIMILES AND
A WEDDING

Vor allem aber ist Vergil auf dem
Umwege über Apollonios Nachahmer
Homers geworden.

Ulrich von
Wilamowitz-Moellendorff
Hellenistische Dichtung

"Arma uirumque . . .": the shape and content of the proem; Juno's
inveterate malice and the sudden storm at sea, with Aeneas' despair-
ing first utterance; the magnificent natural harbor on the coast of
North Africa, that unforeseen and dangerous landfall—these and
other passages which follow in quick succession, as if Virgil were
concerned at the outset to establish a fundamental Homeric reference,
have long been recognized for what they are: imitations, beautifully
realized, of the *Odyssey*.

To consider one example, but in some detail: the morning after
the Trojans' arrival in North Africa, Aeneas rises at daybreak and,
with his faithful Achates, sets out to explore the countryside. They
are soon met, in the middle of a wood—a darksome wood, that place
of strange encounters in European literature and folklore—by his
mother, emphatically if not quite effectively disguised as a huntress,
"*uirginis* os habitumque gerens et *uirginis* arma" (1.315). From her
face and voice Aeneas suspects that she is a goddess and addresses
her accordingly, in the language of prayer, "o dea certe" (1.328).
She tells him where he is: "You see a Punic kingdom, Tyrians and
the city of Agenor; but the land is Libya, a people stubborn in war,"
"Punica regna uides, Tyrios et Agenoris urbem; / sed fines Libyci,
genus intractabile bello" (1.338–39). She tells him, further, of Dido's
dark Phoenician past, of a dear husband murdered and her daring

15

escape from Tyre—"leader of the exploit, a woman," "dux femina facti" (1.364)—and of the new city she is now building, Carthage.

In *Od.* 7.14–77 Odysseus is met, as he approaches the city of the Phaeacians, by Athena in the guise of a young girl carrying a pitcher. He speaks to her courteously, as an older man might, ὦ τέκος, and asks her to show him the house of Alcinous. She answers in kind, πάτερ, and guides him there; then, unsolicited, urges him to throw himself on the mercy of Queen Arete, whose illustrious ancestry and high place of honor in the household she proceeds to describe. "As she finished speaking bright-eyed Athena disappeared," ὡς ἄρα φωνήσασ' ἀπέβη γλαυκῶπις Ἀθήνη (78).[1] Odysseus registers no emotion; he seems hardly to notice.

Not so Aeneas. As the huntress turns away she reveals an unearthly beauty, to her son's dismay, who cries out after her as she flees: "Why mock your son so often (you too are cruel) with false appearances? Why may I not join hand to hand, hear true words spoken and answer?" "quid natum totiens (crudelis tu quoque) falsis / ludis imaginibus? cur dextrae iungere dextram / non datur ac ueras audire et reddere uoces?" (1.407–9). To this impassioned plea for communion, converse as between mother and son—to his "O, answer me!"—there is no answer.

Aeneas and Achates continue on their way to Carthage. Venus encloses them in a protective cloud of invisibility, then herself repairs, with the sublime unconcern of deity, to her beloved Paphus, where a hundred altars breathe Sabaean odors.

In the middle of Carthage—let us boldly transport him there— Aeneas finds a grove, a strange and ominous place. Here Sidonian Dido was building a great temple to Juno, a temple enriched with offerings and the divine presence; and here, where it might least have been expected, Aeneas first dares to hope for salvation. For while waiting for the queen to appear, admiring the great work in detail, the hands of rival artisans, he sees in the portico a series of murals depicting incidents of the Trojan War,[2] already known by report throughout the world. He stands still, weeping; he had not expected to be reminded, so suddenly and so violently, of the past. "Look!" he cries to Achates as the figure of the aged king catches his eye, "Look, Priam!" "en Priamus!" (1.461). Then follow the pathetic lines "sunt hic etiam sua praemia laudi, / sunt lacrimae rerum et mentem mortalia tangunt" (461–62), "even here valor has its due reward, even here. . . ." (And now I can hardly translate. Line 462 is not, in context, a general comment on "the human condition," though it may be that as well. Aeneas means that even here, in Carthage, there is compassion for human suffering.³) He falls silent, feeding his heart with the insubstantial pictures, "sic ait atque animum pictura pascit inani" (1.464).

This whole passage is, technically speaking, an ecphrasis: the description, for literary purposes, of an imaginary work of art.⁴ The earliest example, much imitated by later writers of epic, as by Virgil in Book 8, is the Shield of Achilles in the *Iliad* (18.478–608): the only major ecphrasis in Homer. Ecphrasis, as offering scope for ingenuity and display, became a feature of Hellenistic poetry: notably Theocritus 1.27–56 (the shepherd's carved drinking-cup), Apollonius 1.721–67 (Jason's mantle),⁵ Moschus *Europa* 37–61 (Europa's golden flower-basket), and, by derivation, Catullus 64.50–264 (the coverlet on the marriage bed).

But we have no sense, as we read these splendid ornamental passages, that anyone in particular is looking at the objects; that cup or mantle or basket or coverlet is described from an interested point of view. Description is elegantly matter-of-fact and undramatic; the three scenes on the cup, like the seven on the mantle, have no individual shape or emphasis. In the *Aeneid*, however, ecphrasis serves a dramatic purpose. In the three major ecphrases of the poem—here, in Carthage, gazing at the temple wall; in 6.20–33, gazing at the temple doors in Cumae; and in 8.626–728, gazing at Vulcan's great shield—Aeneas is present as spectator, completely absorbed, the various scenes viewed as through his eyes, colored by his passion.⁶

Standing here, on alien ground, confronting his ghosts, Aeneas is all but overwhelmed by a sense of displacement and loss. Nowhere else is his grief so powerfully expressed.⁷ As he begins to examine the scenes, his view—after a shocked first impression—is fairly neutral; but soon it becomes partial to the Trojans. He sees, in the battles around the city, here Greeks fleeing, Trojan warriors attacking; here Trojans fleeing, plumed Achilles in his chariot pursuing, "hac fugerent Grai, premeret Troiana iuuentus; /hac Phryges, instaret curru cristatus Achilles" (1.467–68).⁸ The white tents of Rhesus⁹ (he recognizes them through his tears) plundered with great slaughter during his first night at Troy (469–73). And Troilus fleeing without his armor,¹⁰ a boy—no match for Achilles, "impar congressus Achilli" (475). In Athena's temple, Trojan women beating their breasts, "tristes et tunsae pectora palmis" (481), the goddess grim and averse. Then, with a convulsive outburst of grief, "tum uero ingentem gemitum dat pectore ab imo" (485), he sees Achilles selling Hector's mangled body for gold; the chariot, his friend's body, Priam's outstretched helpless hands. A brutal, ignoble scene, deliberately un-Homeric.

Aeneas is, by now, emotionally exhausted. He recognizes himself, almost absently, fighting in the front ranks (488); the bright armor of Memnon the Ethiop (489);[11] and a figure even more exotic, Penthesilea, queen of the Amazons—vividly represented yet evoking no response from Aeneas—the warrior maid who dares battle with warriors.[12] The purpose of these closing scenes is to reduce the extreme pitch of emotion to manageable terms; and of the last in particular, to prepare for the entrance of Dido.

Aeneas now loses himself in contemplation, gazing silently, fixedly, at the temple wall—as on a later occasion, in Cumae, he would have gone on scanning the temple doors had not the Sibyl interrupted him with a brusque reminder that his business lay elsewhere. So now, his somber reverie is interrupted by the entry of the queen, Dido in all her beauty, with a throng of men crowding around her.

> qualis in Eurotae ripis aut per iuga Cynthi
> exercet Diana choros, quam mille secutae
> hinc atque hinc glomerantur Oreades; illa pharetram
> fert umero gradiensque deas supereminet omnis
> (Latonae tacitum pertemptant gaudia pectus):
> talis erat Dido, talem se laeta ferebat
> per medios instans operi regnisque futuris.
>
> (1.498–504)

As by the banks of the Eurotas or on Cynthus ridge Diana leads the dance, and a thousand Oreads follow, thronging from every side; with a quiver on her shoulder she advances, excelling all the goddesses (joy pervades Latona's quiet heart): such was Dido, such in her happiness as she moved among them, pressing on with her work, the kingdom that would be.

This simile is modeled, as ancient readers recognized,[13] on one of the most exquisite similes in the *Odyssey*: the comparison of Nausicaa, playing ball with her handmaids on the seashore, to Artemis rejoicing in the hunt, with her nymphs playing around her.

> οἵη δ᾽ Ἄρτεμις εἶσι κατ᾽ οὔρεα ἰοχέαιρα,
> ἢ κατὰ Τηΰγετον περιμήκετον ἢ Ἐρύμανθον,
> τερπομένη κάπροισι καὶ ὠκείῃς ἐλάφοισι·
> τῇ δέ θ᾽ ἅμα νύμφαι, κοῦραι Διὸς αἰγιόχοιο,

ἀγρονόμοι παίζουσι· γέγηθε δέ τε φρένα Λητώ·
πασάων δ᾿ ὑπὲρ ἥ γε κάρη ἔχει ἠδὲ μέτωπα,
ῥεῖά τ᾿ ἀριγνώτη πέλεται, καλαὶ δέ τε πᾶσαι·
ὡς ἥ γ᾿ ἀμφιπόλοισι μετέπρεπε παρθένος ἀδμής.

(6.102–9)

As Artemis the huntress crosses the mountains, lofty Taygetus
or Erymanthus, delighting in the wild boar and swift deer;
around her play the rural nymphs, daughters of aegis-bearing
Zeus (and Leto's heart is glad); she is easy to recognize, head
and forehead above all where all are beautiful: so did the chaste
girl stand out among her handmaids.

As they are packing up to leave, Nausicaa, with an invisible assist
from Athena, accidentally tosses the ball into the water. A great
shriek ensues; and Odysseus, sleeping in the bushes nearby, wakes
up with a start.

Virgil was not the first to imitate Homer's simile; Apollonius had
already done so, thus rendering it more accessible to Virgil. In a
context intimately recalling Nausicaa's adventure, Medea—not the
disillusioned older woman, nor yet the witch of popular imagination,
but the enamored young princess—is compared to Artemis. Medea
drives out of the city, followed by her handmaids, to meet Jason in
the temple of Hecate, bringing with her the magic ointment that will
protect him from the fire-breathing bulls.

οἵη δὲ λιαροῖσιν ἐν ὕδασι Παρθενίοιο
ἠὲ καὶ ᾿Αμνισοῖο λοεσσαμένη ποταμοῖο,
χρυσείοις Λητωὶς ἐφ᾿ ἅρμασιν ἑστηυῖα
ὠκείαις κεμάδεσσι διεξελάῃσι κολώνας,
τηλόθεν ἀντιόωσα πολυκνίσου ἑκατόμβης.
τῇ δ᾿ ἅμα νύμφαι ἕπονται ἀμορβάδες, αἱ μὲν ἀπ᾿ αὐτῆς
ἀγρόμεναι πηγῆς ᾿Αμνισίδος, αἱ δὲ λιποῦσαι
ἄλσεα καὶ σκοπιὰς πολυπίδακας, ἀμφὶ δὲ θῆρες
κνυζηθμῷ σαίνουσιν ὑποτρομέοντες ἰοῦσαν·
ὡς αἵγ᾿ ἐσσεύοντο δι᾿ ἄστεος, ἀμφὶ δὲ λαοὶ
εἶκον ἀλευάμενοι βασιληίδος ὄμματα κούρης.

(3.876–86)

As after bathing in the warm waters of the Parthenius or the
Amnisus, Leto's daughter mounts a golden chariot and drives
her swift deer through the hills, coming from afar to enjoy a
steaming hecatomb; and the nymphs her companions follow,

some gathering from the Amnisus' very source, others leaving behind the glens and many-fountained peaks; and on either side wild beasts whimper and fawn, cowering as she passes: so they swept through the city, and on either side the people gave way, avoiding the eye of the king's daughter.

Virgil's commentators have neglected Apollonius.[14] But that Virgil should have neglected Apollonius, in such circumstances, is all but inconceivable. Almost as a matter of principle, a Hellenistic poet—and by now it should be abundantly clear that Virgil is a Hellenistic poet, writing in that tradition—will choose, where conveniently possible, to imitate two, or even more, poets simultaneously, or to add to his imitation of one poet from another. (And unlike the Greek poet, the Latin poet had two literatures, however unequal, available to him.) Thus Virgil incorporates his earlier imitation of Theocritus (*E.* 2.69) in his imitation of Calvus (*E.* 6.47): "a, uirgo infelix, quae te dementia cepit?"[15] Thus Apollonius here adds to his imitation of Homer from Callimachus' *Hymn to Artemis*,[16] as Virgil doubtless noticed, for he also adds to his imitation of Homer (and Apollonius) from the same *Hymn*.[17]

What, then, did Virgil add or adapt from Apollonius to his imitation of Homer?

To begin with, there are two mountains in Homer, Taygetus and Erymanthus; two rivers in Apollonius, the Parthenius and the Amnisus; but in Virgil a river and a mountain, the Eurotas and Cynthus. The Parthenius is subsequently ignored,[18] as is the Eurotas, though like the Parthenius named first. Thus subtly Virgil imitates both Homer and Apollonius.

The Eurotas, by which, at Amyclae, Apollo had a famous sanctuary, may have been suggested by Callim. *Aet.* fr. 75.24–26 Pf.: οὐδ' ἐν Ἀμυκλαίῳ θρύον ἔπλεκεν οὐδ' ἀπὸ θήρης / ἔκλυζεν ποταμῷ λύματα Παρθενίῳ, / Δήλῳ δ' ἦν ἐπίδημος, "nor was Artemis weaving reeds[19] in Amyclae's precinct nor washing away the stains of the hunt in the Parthenius; she was at home on Delos." If so, Virgil was thinking also of his favorite Latin poet, of Ariadne falling desperately in love at first sight of Theseus—the young girl, like the myrtle trees that grow by the Eurotas, "quales Eurotae progignunt flumina myrtus" (Catull. 64.89).[20]

In Homer, Taygetus and Erymanthus are mountains on which Artemis hunts, not cult-places. But Apollonius' Medea-simile implies ritual observance, and his Jason-simile—to be considered presently—

is explicit. (Medea is a priestess of Hecate, of Artemis, that is, in her infernal manifestation, and busies herself daily with the temple cult.) Artemis descends from the hills with a train of nymphs to visit an appointed sacrifice. In Virgil, Diana leads the dance, with a thousand mountain-nymphs following, by the Eurotas or on Cynthus, places where her cult was celebrated—Callim. *Hymn* 3.170–73: ἡνίκα δ᾽ αἱ νύμφαι σε χορῷ ἔνι κυκλώσονται / ἀγχόθι πηγάων Αἰγυπτίου Ἰνωποῖο / ἢ Πιτάνη, "when the nymphs encircle you in the dance by the springs of Egyptian Inopus or at Pitane." The Inopus was a river of Delos, reputedly derived from the Nile; Pitane a town on the Eurotas where Artemis had a sanctuary.

Is there any precise verbal reminiscence of Apollonius in Virgil's simile? Compare τῇ δέ ϑ᾽ ἅμα νύμφαι in Homer (105) with τῇ δ᾽ ἅμα νύμφαι ἕπονται ἀμορβάδες in Apollonius (881). ἀμορβάδες is one of Apollonius' countless innovations, the effect of which Virgil reproduces with the metrical and, in part, phonetically equivalent "Oreades";[21] and "secutae" is the semantic and very nearly the metrical equivalent of ἕπονται. The rhythm of Virgil's line—feminine caesura with bucolic diaeresis, as in Apollonius—is unique in the *Aeneid*.[22] Further, Apollonius (882) read not ἀγρονόμοι, "country-haunting," but ἀγρόμεναι[23] in his text of Homer: whence apparently "glomerantur," with "hinc atque hinc" being suggested by αἱ μὲν ... αἱ δὲ. Finally, therefore: "quam mille secutae / hinc atque hinc glomerantur Oreades"—a twofold imitation, verbal and metrical, contrived with much art.

Apollonius compares Jason as he leaves home to Apollo:

οἷος δ᾽ ἐκ νηοῖο ϑυώδεος εἶσιν Ἀπόλλων
Δῆλον ἀν᾽ ἠγαϑέην ἠὲ Κλάρον ἢ ὅ γε Πυϑώ
ἢ Λυκίην εὐρεῖαν ἐπί Ξάνϑοιο ῥοῇσι.
τοῖος ἀνὰ πληϑὺν δήμου κίεν·

(1.307–10)

As Apollo advances from his fragrant temple in holy Delos or Claros, or Pytho or broad Lycia by Xanthus stream: so Jason moved through the crowd of townspeople.

For this simile, in contrast with his Medea-simile, Apollonius had no model, unless indeed it was his Medea-simile. Although there is no verbal or structural correspondence between the two, an attentive reader—and Hellenistic poetry discourages inattention[24]—might well recall, on reading the Medea-simile in Book 3, the Jason-simile in

Book 1. Certainly Virgil did, and constructed two elaborate and intricately related similes of his own. Highly self-conscious art implies concern, and Virgil was concerned, obviously, that no reader of the Aeneas-simile in Book 4 should forget the Dido-simile in Book 1.

The fatal hunt begins at dawn. From the city gates issues a profusion of huntsmen, nets, snares, broad-bladed spears, Massylian riders, and bloodhounds. The queen, lingering in her chamber,[25] with the Phoenician nobles waiting, her courser, splendidly caparisoned with purple and gold, prancing and champing the bit—the queen at last appears, Dido in a golden radiance:

> cui pharetra ex auro, crines nodantur in aurum,
> aurea purpuream subnectit fibula uestem.
>
> (4.138–39)

> Of gold her quiver, her hair is bound up in gold,
> a golden brooch fastens her purple dress.

Here again, for want of serious attention to Hellenistic poetry, Virgil's commentators fail.[26] For here is not merely a repeated emphasis,[27] a threefold repetition,[28] but an allusion to Callimachus, to the golden epiphany of Artemis—her debut—as huntress:

> Ἄρτεμι Παρθενίη Τιτυοκτόνε, χρύσεα μέν τοι
> ἔντεα καὶ ζώνη, χρύσεον δ᾿ ἐζεύξαο δίφρον,
> ἐν δ᾿ ἐβάλευ χρύσεια, θεή, κεμάδεσσι χαλινά.
>
> (Hymn 3.110–12)

> Artemis, Virgin, Slayer of Tityos, golden
> thy weapons and belt, golden the chariot thou didst yoke,
> golden, goddess, the bridles thou didst put on thy deer.

Golden, too, is the epiphany of Callimachean Apollo:

> χρύσεα τὠπόλλωνι τό τ᾿ ἐνδυτὸν ἥ τ᾿ ἐπιπορπὶς
> ἥ τε λύρη τό τ᾿ ἄεμμα τὸ Λύκτιον ἥ τε φαρέτρη,
> χρύσεα καὶ τὰ πέδιλα· πολύχρυσος γὰρ Ἀπόλλων . . .
>
> (Hymn 2.32–34)[29]

> Golden the tunic of Apollo and the brooch
> and the lyre and the Lyctian bow and the quiver,
> golden, too, the sandals; for all-golden is Apollo.

The implied comparison of Dido to Artemis (4.138–39), recalling the explicit comparison in 1.498–504, is especially apt here as preceding the simile in which Aeneas is compared to Apollo:

qualis ubi hibernam Lyciam Xanthique fluenta[30]
deserit ac Delum maternam inuisit Apollo
instauratque choros, mixtique altaria circum
Cretesque Dryopesque fremunt pictique Agathyrsi;
ipse iugis Cynthi graditur mollique fluentem
fronde premit crinem fingens atque implicat auro,
tela sonant umeris: haud illo segnior ibat
Aeneas, tantum egregio decus enitet ore.

    (4.143–50)

As when Apollo leaves winter Lycia and Xanthus stream to visit
Delos, his mother's isle, and renews the dance; around his altar
Cretans and Dryopes and tattooed Agathyrsi[31] make a din; the
god himself paces Cynthus ridge, his flowing hair bound with
laurel leaves and entwined in gold; and his arrows ring on his
shoulders: no less swiftly did Aeneas move, such the beauty
that gleams from his princely face.[32]

Dido and Aeneas are thus beautifully paired. Aeneas is described as
"ante alios pulcherrimus omnis" (4.141),[33] and Dido, at the beginning of her simile, as "forma pulcherrima Dido" (1.496).[34] Nowhere
else is Aeneas so described. In fact the phrase occurs only once again,
in 7.55, of Turnus suing for the hand of Lavinia. So Homer describes
Odysseus after his bath in the river, *Od.* 6.237: κάλλεϊ καὶ χάρισι
στίλβων, "gleaming with beauty and grace"; Nausicaa, looking on,
wishes that she might have such a husband. And so Apollonius describes Jason in the palace of Aeetes: ἐν πᾶσι μετέπρεπεν Αἴσονος
υἱὸς / κάλλεϊ καὶ χαρίτεσσιν (3.443–44), "among them all Aeson's
son stood out for beauty and grace"; to which qualities Medea, holding her veil aside and watching, passionately responds: κῆρ ἄχεϊ
σμύχουσα· νόος δέ οἱ ἠύτ᾽ ὄνειρος / ἑρπύζων πεπότητο μετ᾽ ἴχνια
νισομένοιο (446–47), "her heart smoldering with pain; her soul, like
a dream, went creeping and fluttering after him as he left."

    Look, where they come in the early morning light, equal in state,
equal in beauty, Dido and Aeneas, to join the hunt—the hunt that
will end so abruptly, so incomprehensibly for the mortal participants,
in storm and rout and a dark consummation. Their coming together
in the selfsame cave had been engineered the night before by Juno,
with the amused assent of Venus (4.124–28); but Dido, the urgent,
passionate woman—as, from now on, she will show herself—seems
to take the lead, "speluncam Dido dux et Troianus eandem / deue-
niunt" (4.165–66), "to the selfsame cave come Dido and the leader

of the Trojans"—"Dido dux," the willing woman, the not-unwilling man.[35] For a moment, the reader construes "dux" with "Dido"; the effect is untranslatable. Ambiguity in Latin poetry is circumscribed and tends to be, as here, momentary and evanescent; but it does exist.[36] *Deuenio* is a rare verb in Virgil. Apart from 4.124–25, "speluncam Dido dux et Troianus eandem / deuenient," repeated here in Homeric fashion—perhaps to lend dignity to the goddesses' Hellenistic conversation[37]—it occurs only once earlier, 1.364–65: "dux femina facti. / deuenere locos."[38] They came to this place; came, that is, "Didone duce." Aeneas is not elsewhere styled "dux Troianus."

The vaguely felt, unobtrusive reference of this scene is to the wedding of Medea and Jason on Corcyra, Homer's Phaeacia, in the sacred cave of Macris, Ap. Rhod. 4.1131: ἄντρῳ ἐν ἠγαθέῳ; consummated under duress, at night. On the marriage bed the Golden Fleece glitters with a supernatural brilliance, kindling a sweet desire in the eyes of the flower-bearing nymphs who long to touch it, modesty forbidding. Spears in hand, foreheads garlanded, the Argonauts sing a wedding song to the music of Orpheus' lyre. The darkly splendid scene evokes from Apollonius, who intervenes as an epic poet will in his own fiction, a melancholy[39] reflection on the nature of human happiness:

> ἀλλὰ γὰρ οὔποτε φῦλα δυηπαθέων ἀνθρώπων
> τερπωλῆς ἐπέβημεν ὅλῳ ποδί, σὺν δέ τις αἰεὶ
> πικρὴ παρμέμβλωκεν εὐφροσύνῃσιν ἀνίη.
> τῶ καὶ τούς, γλυκερῇ περ ἰαινομένους φιλότητι,
> δεῖμ' ἔχεν εἰ τελέοιτο διάκρισις Ἀλκινόοιο.
>
>   (4.1165–69)

Miserable race of men that we are, never do we set foot securely on the path of joy, for always some bitter care accompanies delight: so even they, melting with love's sweetness, yet feared the verdict of Alcinous.

Virgil's cave is unhallowed and nondescript,[40] the celebration of the wedding uncanny.

>   prima et Tellus et pronuba Iuno[41]
> dant signum; fulsere ignes et conscius aether
> conubiis; summoque ulularunt uertice nymphae.
>
>   (4.166–68)

Primal Earth and bridesmaid Juno give the sign; lightning flashes in the heavens, witness of the wedding; and the nymphs wail on the mountain-top.

So wailed the women of Troy when Priam's innermost palace was violated:

> at domus interior gemitu miseroque tumultu
> miscetur, penitusque cauae plangoribus aedes
> femineis ululant.
>
> (2.486–88)[42]

And now Virgil, like Apollonius, intervenes to comment:[43]

> ille dies primus leti primusque malorum
> causa fuit; neque enim specie famaue mouetur
> nec iam furtiuum[44] Dido meditatur amorem:
> coniugium uocat, hoc praetexit nomine culpam.
>
> (4.169–72)

> That day first was the cause of death,
> that day first, of sorrow;
> for Dido is unmoved by appearances or rumor
> nor thinks now of a secret love:
> marriage she calls it, with this name veiling her sin.

III

THE WOODEN HORSE

Of Troy am I, Aeneas is my name.

Marlowe, *Dido, Queene of
Carthage* 1.1.216

Still enclosed in his mother's cloud, invisible—we return now to the
scene in Juno's temple—Aeneas observes Dido and her court. Suddenly a group of Trojans enters—his own men, whom he had believed drowned, Antheus,[1] Serestus, the brave Cloanthus, and others.
They had been swept away by the storm to a distant part of the coast
and there set upon by the Carthaginian defenders. They now demand
hospitality of Dido, the common hospitality of the shore, in order
to refit their battered ships. Her response is quick and generous: she
regrets the harsh necessities of her situation and offers them, should
they so wish, a share in her new and endangered kingdom;[2] meanwhile she will send scouts along the coast to look for their lost leader.
All of a sudden the cloud parts and dissolves into pure light and
Aeneas stands revealed, head and shoulders radiant, like a god's:
"restitit Aeneas claraque in luce refulsit[3] / os umerosque deo similis"
(1.588–89).

> namque ipsa decoram
> caesariem nato genetrix lumenque iuuentae
> purpureum et laetos oculis adflarat honores:
> quale manus addunt ebori decus, aut ubi flauo
> argentum Pariusue lapis circumdatur auro.[4]
>
> (1.589–93)

For his mother had shed a grace upon her son's hair and the
bright light of youth about his person, and on his eyes had
breathed joy and beauty: such grace as an artist's hand imparts
to ivory, or when silver or Parian marble is enchased in yellow
gold.

These lines recall a scene, or rather two scenes, in the *Odyssey*, in Books 6 and 23. In Book 6 Odysseus bathes himself in the river (for he is ashamed to show his brine-soaked body to Nausicaa's handmaids), then anoints himself with oil and puts on the new clothes she has given him.

τὸν μὲν Ἀθηναίη θῆκεν, Διὸς ἐκγεγαυῖα,
μείζονά τ᾽ εἰσιδέειν καὶ πάσσονα, κὰδ δὲ κάρητος
οὔλας ἧκε κόμας, ὑακινθίνῳ ἄνθει ὁμοίας.
ὡς δ᾽ ὅτε τις χρυσὸν περιχεύεται ἀργύρῳ ἀνὴρ
ἴδρις, ὃν Ἥφαιστος δέδαεν καὶ Παλλὰς Ἀθήνη
τέχνην παντοίην, χαρίεντα δὲ ἔργα τελείει,
ὣς ἄρα τῷ κατέχευε χάριν κεφαλῇ τε καὶ ὤμοις.

(6.229–35)

But Athena, daughter of Zeus, made him taller and stronger to the eye, and caused the locks to hang clustering from his head, like the hyacinth in flower. As when a craftsman pours gold around silver, a craftsman whom Hephaestus and Pallas Athena have taught all his art and whose work is graceful: such a grace did Athena pour upon his head and shoulders.

Nearly the same lines are repeated in 23.156–62: the old housekeeper Eurynome bathes and anoints Odysseus, and Athena glorifies him as he emerges to face a still incredulous Penelope.

Nausicaa witnesses the transfiguration undismayed. "Before he seemed to me ugly," she says to her handmaids, "but now he resembles the gods who inhabit wide heaven," and wishes that he might be her husband and stay with her always.

Odysseus follows Nausicaa into town, at a discreet distance, meeting on the outskirts a girl with a pitcher (Athena in disguise) who guides him to the house of Alcinous.[5] He passes swiftly through the great hall, where the Phaeacian elders are pouring their nightly libations to Hermes, and throws his arms about the knees of Queen Arete—as the girl with the pitcher and, earlier, Nausicaa had advised him to do. The cloud enclosing him dissolves, to the general astonishment, and Odysseus, his brief supplication made, sits down by the hearth among the ashes (7.133–54). Here there is no epiphany, no glorification of the hero, because there is no reason for a heightened awareness on Arete's part: for her Odysseus can be neither husband nor lover.

"I stand before you, the man you seek, Trojan Aeneas," "coram, quem quaeritis, adsum, / Troius Aeneas" (1.595–96). Aeneas first addresses Dido, amid the general consternation, acknowledging a debt of gratitude that can never be repaid, either by themselves or by the Dardanian race now outcast on the great world. As for himself, he will remember always (words that will come back later to haunt him): "while rivers run into the sea, while cloud-shadows move across the mountains, while heaven feeds the stars, always your fame and name and praise will remain, whatever lands call me away," "in freta dum fluuii current, dum montibus umbrae / lustrabunt conuexa, polus dum sidera pascet, / semper honos nomenque tuum laudesque manebunt, / quae me cumque uocant terrae" (1.607–10).

Of Arete's response to Odysseus we hear nothing: she "disappears" from the scene without a word.[6] The Phaeacian elders sit silent and bewildered; at last, the oldest and most eloquent of their number addresses Alcinous, to remind him of the courtesy due a suppliant. Arete presently reappears, in an intimate domestic scene: she and Alcinous are left alone in the hall with Odysseus; she recognizes the clothes he is wearing and asks him where he got them; did he not say he came from the sea? Dido, by contrast, is struck dumb at first sight of Aeneas, "obstipuit primo aspectu Sidonia Dido" (1.613). These words suggest, but only suggest, love-at-first-sight, a motif of Hellenistic poetry.[7] For Virgil, ever mindful of epic decorum, defers to Dido's state and person: she is a queen, Sidon's high-descended daughter, not a Medea or an Ariadne[8] who will succumb instantly to the glamor of a prince from over the sea—although at times, it must be admitted, a strong family likeness is noticeable.

Dido immediately regains her composure and, with a gracious speech, welcomes Aeneas and his men. Aeneas, whose father's heart is anxious, sends Achates back to the ships to fetch Iulus (Ascanius) and gifts for Dido—precious things saved from the wreckage of Ilium (so Virgil informs his reader), rich garments that Argive Helen had brought with her from Mycenae when she sought Troy and unhallowed wedlock, "Pergama cum peteret inconcessosque hymenaeos" (1.651). In the evening Dido holds a banquet; first come the Trojans, then the Carthaginians in crowds, eager to see the strangers but not, it seems, to mingle with them. The Carthaginians marvel at the gifts, marvel at Iulus, at the glowing features—not, as they suppose, of Iulus but of Cupid, whom Venus, fearful of Punic treachery, had substituted in his place.[9] Dido, the destined victim of love, cannot be satisfied, gazing ardently, charmed alike by the boy and by the gifts, "pariter puero donisque mouetur" (1.714).[10] Her Carthaginians, however, while admiring the false Iulus, attend principally to the gifts, "mirantur dona Aeneae, mirantur Iulum" (1.709). Dido presses the boy to her breast, unmindful of the god besieging her heart, "gremio fouet inscia Dido / insidat quantus miserae deus" (1.718–19).[11]

When they have finished eating and the tables are removed, Dido calls for an ancestral cup, heavy with gems and gold—the cup of Belus (Baal)[12] and of all the kings descended from him; she fills it with wine and, in the hushed hall, prays to Jupiter, prays that the day may be joyful for Carthaginians and Trojans alike, and that their descendants may remember it. (A sense of fatality, of history foredoomed, pervades and informs the *Aeneid*.) She pours a libation, barely touches the cup to her lips, then hands it to Bitias, one of her courtiers, with a challenge. He drains it impulsively, swilling himself with wine, "ille impiger hausit / spumantem pateram et pleno se proluit auro" (1.738–39).[13]

Now appears a traditional figure, the long-haired poet or singer,[14] to entertain the banqueters. But it is a strange song that Iopas sings.

hic canit errantem lunam solisque labores,
unde hominum genus et pecudes, unde imber et ignes,
Arcturum pluuiasque Hyadas geminosque Triones,
quid tantum Oceano properent se tingere soles
hiberni, uel quae tardis mora noctibus obstet.

    (1.742–46)

He sings of the wandering moon and the sun's labors,
Whence humankind and animals, whence water and fire,
Of Arcturus and the rainy Hyades and the twin Bears,
Why winter suns so hasten to bathe themselves in Ocean,
Or what hindrance retards the slow nights.

What kind of song had the Trojans expected to hear? A traditional song, of the famous deeds of men and gods—in the words of Penelope, *Od.* 1.338, ἔργ' ἀνδρῶν τε θεῶν τε, τά τε κλείουσιν ἀοιδοί. A song such as one of their own, Cretheus the Muses' friend, always used to be singing, of war-horses and warriors and battles, "semper equos atque arma uirum pugnasque canebat" (9.777). Possibly a song of some exploit in the late war (the fighting had not gone all one way)—as Demodocus sings of the Wooden Horse before Alcinous and his guests, causing the anonymous stranger to weep (8.485–534). The Carthaginians, however, are delighted; the song is familiar, or of a kind familiar, to them. They redouble their applause, and the Trojans politely follow suit, "ingeminant plausu Tyrii, Troesque sequuntur" (1.747).[15]

The intemperance of Bitias is amusing; but Virgil was not concerned simply to amuse. He alludes to a scene in Apollonius. On the eve of sailing, Jason is visibly despondent. One of the company, Idas, notices and taunts him with cowardice, then seizes a beaker full of unmixed sweet wine and drains it, drenching his lips and beard.[16] The Argonauts are indignant and the seer Idmon speaks out; Idas answers threateningly, and their quarrel would have gone further had not Jason and the others intervened. At this juncture Orpheus picks up his lyre and sings of the mysterious workings of the universe.

> Ἤειδεν δ' ὡς γαῖα καὶ οὐρανὸς ἠδὲ θάλασσα,
> τὸ πρὶν ἔπ' ἀλλήλοισι μιῇ συναρηρότα μορφῇ,
> νείκεος ἐξ ὀλοοῖο διέκριθεν ἀμφὶς ἕκαστα·
> ἠδ' ὡς ἔμπεδον αἰὲν ἐν αἰθέρι τέκμαρ ἔχουσιν
> ἄστρα σεληναίης τε καὶ ἠελίοιο κέλευθοι·
> οὔρεά θ' ὡς ἀνέτειλε, καὶ ὡς ποταμοὶ κελάδοντες
> αὐτῇσιν νύμφῃσι καὶ ἑρπετὰ πάντ' ἐγένοντο.
>
>   (1.496–502)

He sang how earth and sky and sea had been joined together of old, but separated, each apart, the result of a deadly quarrel; and how forever in heaven the stars and the paths of the moon and sun have their steadfast place; and how the mountains rose up, and how sounding rivers with their nymphs and all the beasts of the earth came to be.

Harmony is restored by the enchantment of Orpheus' song. The Argonauts pour their accustomed libations to Zeus and lie down to sleep on the seashore.[17]

Virgil's indebtedness is evident.[18] But simply to point out an imitation, in Virgil's case, is insufficient; rarely if ever are his imitations inert. Why, then, does Iopas sing Orpheus' song? Or what literary problem did Virgil face?

The Phaeacians belong, if only marginally, to the heroic world; they are in fact Greeks, notable for their luxurious living and fantastic seamanship. Demodocus sings easily of the Trojan War—as if, Odysseus tells him, he had been there himself or heard of it from someone who had (8.491). The Carthaginians, on the other hand, are aliens; they have heard of the War—who in the world had not (1.456–57)?—and scenes from it adorn the walls of their great new temple, but they have no share in the heroic world of the Trojans. How then can Iopas sing one of the songs of Troy? Troy and all that befell there lie far outside his competence. Great Atlas was his teacher, "docuit quem maximus Atlas" (1.741)—a rooted, indigenous figure, associated with the study of astronomy.[19] The strangeness of Iopas' song seems to accentuate the strangeness of this festive occasion with its undercurrent of discord.

Dido prolongs the night with talk, drinking deep of love, putting question after question to Aeneas, asking about Priam, about Hector, now about Aurora's son and his armor, now about Diomedes' horses, now about the mighty Achilles. Her mounting excitement is expressed, with beautiful precision, in lines 751–52: an inverted tricolon. A tricolon or threefold period disposed over two hexameters will ordinarily be of the form: half-line, half-line, full line. Here, however, Virgil writes:[20]

nunc quibus Aurorae uenisset filius armis
nunc quales Diomedis equi, nunc quantus Achilles.

Did Virgil expect his Roman reader (he envisaged no other) to notice and appreciate an effect so fine? Virgil's Roman reader, unlike his modern, read aloud, read slowly, and had been trained from boyhood in the discipline of rhetoric.

It can hardly be accidental, especially at the end of a book, where closeness and precision of form may be expected, that the five lines reporting Iopas' song (742–46) are followed, with a single line intervening, by five lines indicating Dido's emotional state (748–52). A contrast seems to be implied between the calm, remote heavenly bodies and the immediate tumult in Dido's breast. (And is this not the implication of the scene in Apollonius?) Such a contrast is also implied in Virgil's description of the sack of Priam's palace: "at domus interior gemitu miseroque tumultu / miscetur, penitusque cauae plangoribus aedes / femineis ululant; ferit aurea sidera clamor" (2.486–88), "within the palace is a pitiful scene of confusion and woe, and vaulted chambers wail with the sound of women lamenting; the uproar strikes the golden stars."[21]

Tell us, Dido at last concludes, your story from the very beginning, tell us of the treachery of the Greeks, of your country's fate and your wanderings.

Aeneas tells of that fatal night and the wasted, fugitive years as, in similar circumstances, Odysseus tells of his adventures. But there is a difference—as, with Virgil, there always is. When Demodocus sings of the Wooden Horse Odysseus weeps (he had requested the song himself) and covers his face; Alcinous, who is seated beside him, cannot help noticing. Odysseus is finally ready to talk, at his own convenience, and it is a long and spellbinding tale that he has to tell. Aeneas tells his story reluctantly, out of gratitude to the queen and in response to her urgent questioning. He begins with a grave, almost pained courtesy: "infandum, regina, iubes renouare dolorem" (2.3). He shrinks from recalling a grief so terrible, and the hour is late; but, yielding to the force of her desire, he consents: "sed si tantus amor casus cognoscere nostros / et breuiter[22] Troiae supremum audire laborem" (2.10–11). And he speaks to her alone, it seems (for we hear no more of her Carthaginians)[23]—to "lovesick Dido's sad, attending ear,"[24] as the stars sink in the West.

Aeneas speaks as an eyewitness to events in which he claims to have had a large part: "quaeque ipse miserrima uidi / et quorum pars magna fui" (2.5–6). This prominence seems to be Virgil's innovation, for which he had two sufficient reasons: the hero's credit would be much diminished otherwise; and there was a variant tradition according to which Aeneas left the doomed city, with Greek assistance, before its fall.[25] Virgil's Aeneas must therefore be shown fighting to the bitter end, and only then leaving by his mother's command, when she unclouds his mortal vision and he sees the gods—shapes of terror, mighty presences—destroying the city.[26]

Although Aeneas figures prominently in Quintus of Smyrna, especially in Book 11, he is conspicuously absent from Book 12, the story of the Wooden Horse;[27] nor is he shown later fighting in defense of the city.[28] Aeneas has no part in the story of Troy's destruction as told by Triphiodorus, who merely mentions his escape, with a prophecy of Roman greatness (651–55). And it will be noticed that Virgil's Aeneas does not involve himself personally in the story of the Horse: he speaks in the first- or third-person plural only, more as a spectator than as a participant.[29] Virgil's awareness of the tradition enables him to relieve his hero of responsibility for the decision fatal to his city; but once the treachery is discovered Aeneas takes a leading part in the action (2.314–17, 347–434).[30]

No doubt Lucretius contributed to Virgil's peculiar sense of the Wooden Horse—that inevitable, unwieldy problem confronting a poet who wished to tell, once again, the immemorial story of Troy; the problem, that is, of convincing a sophisticated modern audience, Virgil's audience, that their ancestors could have been deceived by such a stratagem. Events of long ago, Lucretius argues, like the rape of Helen or the Trojan War, exist not in themselves but as accidents of the countries in which they occurred; for had there been no matter, no place or space—a somewhat obscure and crabbed refutation of Stoic doctrine illuminated by a sudden flash of poetry[31]:

numquam Tyndaridis forma conflatus amoris
ignis, Alexandri Phrygio sub pectore gliscens,
clara accendisset saeui certamina belli,
nec clam durateus Troiianis Pergama partu
inflammasset equus nocturno Graiiugenarum.

    (1.473–77)

Never had the fire of love, kindled by the beauty of Tyndareus' daughter, blazed beneath the Phrygian breast of Alexander and lighted up the famous struggles of cruel war, nor had the timber horse unknown to the Trojans wrapt Pergama in flames by its night-issuing brood of sons of the Greeks.[32]

Lucretius' language is studied, ambiguous. The Wooden Horse, "the timber horse," is presented as a thing alive and yet not alive, as giving birth to Greek warriors in the night[33] and setting fire to Troy. It is this delusive double sense that Virgil develops so carefully and consistently.

Aeneas begins with the Horse, huge and menacing on the deserted shore:

    fracti bello fatisque repulsi
ductores Danaum tot iam labentibus annis
instar montis equum diuina Palladis arte
aedificant,[34] sectaque intexunt abiete costas.

    (2.13–16)

Broken in war and repulsed by fate, with so many years now slipping away, the leaders of the Greeks build, by Athena's divine art, a mountainous horse, covering its ribs with planks of fir.

uotum pro reditu simulant; ea fama uagatur.
huc delecta uirum sortiti corpora furtim
includunt caeco lateri penitusque cauernas
ingentis uterumque armato milite complent.

    (17–20)

A vow for their return is the pretext; the rumor goes about.
Deep in its dark recesses they conceal picked men and fill the
vast cavern and womb with armed soldiery.

Virgil preserves the ambiguity with two nouns, first describing the
interior of the Horse as *cauernae* then as *uterus*, so that attention is
drawn equally to its inanimate and animate nature.

The Trojans throw open their gates and hurry out onto the beach
to see the sites: here camped the Dolopes, here savage Achilles, their
ships lay here, here they used to join battle. Through the ocean-roll
of the hexameter can be heard the excited rhythms of ordinary
speech: "hic Dolopum manus, hic saeuus tendebat Achilles, / classi-
bus hic locus, hic acie certare solebant" (29–30). Others gaze in awe
at the Horse, Minerva's deadly gift. What to do with it? drag it inside
their walls? burn it? or bore into it and probe the hollow hiding-
places of its womb ("aut terebrare cauas uteri et temptare latebras,"
38)? At this juncture the warrior priest Laocoon rushes down from
the citadel and, after a brief excited speech, hurls his spear into the
side, the belly, of the beast.

> uteroque recusso[35]
> insonuere cauae gemitumque dedere cauernae.
>
> (52–53)

Again, the same ambiguity: the womb trembles, the hollow interior
resounds, and groans. Virgil's art is exquisite, the line describing the
echo itself echoing: "insonu*ere cauae* gemitumque ded*ere caue*rnae."
Alexandrian cleverness merely? While Virgil never forgot what he
had learned as a young poet, he had, in constructing his Wooden
Horse so artfully, a serious literary purpose: to prepare his reader
for the climactic scene of the Book.

But first we must deal with Sinon, the resolute, cunning Greek who
imposes on the Trojans' humanity and persuades them to take the
Horse into the city.

Sinon appears in both Triphiodorus and Quintus of Smyrna, but
plays a more important part in Triphiodorus. While the Trojans are
debating what to do with the Horse, an unknown man appears, a
Greek, stripped and bleeding from the lash. He throws himself at
Priam's feet, groveling; then, to ingratiate himself, relates how his
fellow Greeks had beaten him (in fact his wounds are self-inflicted,
to arouse the Trojans' sympathy)[36] because he refused to flee with
them. He likens himself to other victims of Greek injustice, to

Achilles, Philoctetes, and Palamedes,[37] and declares that the Greeks
will rejoice if he perishes a suppliant at the hands of the Trojans.

In general, as in details, there is a similarity between the speech
of Sinon in Triphiodorus and the more elaborate speech of Virgil's
Sinon:[38] his disarming frankness (*A.* 2.77–78: Triph. 292–94); Palamedes, a famous victim of Odysseus (2.81–91: 272);[39] kill me and
you will be doing Odysseus and the sons of Atreus a service;[40]
Priam's kindly response and questioning (2.146–51: 283–90); the
Horse is sacred to Athena and may be either a curse or a blessing
(2.189–94: 296–99).

The Trojans are convinced, as they are in Virgil (2.195–96), and
drag the Horse into the city. Cassandra warns of the impending
doom; but Priam rebukes her and has her led away to her chamber
(Triph. 358–443).

Laocoon does not appear in Triphiodorus. Triphiodorus, a more
imaginative poet than Quintus,[41] recognized that since Laocoon and
Cassandra were both opposed to the Horse, dramatic economy required the exclusion of one or the other. He therefore excluded Laocoon, choosing the pathetic Cassandra, whom not even her own
father believed; Quintus excludes neither. Faced with the same problem, as we may surmise, Virgil chose Laocoon, who might have been
believed had not fate and human error determined otherwise
(2.54–56); but he alludes, in the Hellenistic manner, to Cassandra
(2.246–47).[42]

Sinon as conceived by Quintus is a bold and fearless man with a
settled purpose to deceive, but no orator. The Trojans at first question him, then proceed to threats and torture, finally lopping off his
ears and nose.[43] Yet he persists in his simple tale: weary of war, the
Greeks have fled; the Horse is a propitiatory offering to Athena;
Odysseus singled me out for sacrifice to the sea-gods, but I threw
myself at the Horse's feet, and there, fearing Athena's anger, they
reluctantly left me. A brief, manly utterance:[44] some of the Trojans
are convinced; others, suspecting treachery, are not[45]—among the
latter Laocoon, who urges them to burn the Horse.

And they would have done so and escaped destruction had not
Athena caused the earth to quake beneath their feet and blinded
Laocoon. Horrified, pitying Laocoon, whose blinding Quintus describes in grisly detail,[46] and afraid that they have offended the goddess by torturing Sinon, the Trojans drag the Horse into the city.
Still Laocoon continues to protest, urging them to burn it; whereupon Athena inflicts an even more hideous punishment on him: two

snakes, dreadful monsters from the island of Calydna, who kill his
sons while he stands helplessly by.

The speech of Virgil's Sinon (2.76–194) is the longest and most
elaborately rhetorical in the *Aeneid*. (Aeneas' narrative in Books 2
and 3 is not properly a speech, nor is Anchises' exposition of me-
tempsychosis in Book 6.) Sinon's speech consists of three parts, of
twenty-eight, thirty-seven, and forty-one lines respectively: an extensive tricolon crescendo with the three parts set off by Aeneas' inter-
jected comments, the first of three lines (105–7), the second of nine
(145–53, with Priam's reported questions to Sinon). But why so long
and calculated and calculating a speech? and why here, where, for
the modern reader, it seems to retard the action? Evidently to coun-
teract the powerful effect of Laocoon's irruption, to persuade the
Trojans to the contrary. And they were persuaded, as Aeneas ruefully
admits, "credita res" (196); persuaded by such deceit, by Sinon's
lying art, taken in by trickery and forced tears—we, whom neither
Tydeus' son nor Achilles of Larissa subdued, not ten years, not a
thousand ships.

> Talibus insidiis periurique arte Sinonis
> credita res, captique dolis lacrimisque coactis
> quos neque Tydides nec Larisaeus Achilles,
> non anni domuere decem, non mille carinae.
>
> (2.195–98)

Eloquent testimony to the terrible power of rhetoric. The ancients
believed that Persuasion (Πειθώ) hung upon the orator's lips; but
we have become suspicious of rhetoric, mistrustful of eloquence, to
the point of regarding verbal ineptness and even bad grammar as
evidence of sincerity in our public men. Hence, through no fault of
Virgil's, Sinon's speech may fail of its purpose for the modern reader,
who is more likely to be impressed by the monstrous irrationality of
the Horse.

We come now to the climactic scene of the Book, the taking of
the Horse into the city.

> diuidimus muros et moenia pandimus urbis.
> accingunt omnes operi pedibusque rotarum
> subiciunt lapsus, et stuppea uincula collo
> intendunt; scandit fatalis machina muros
> feta armis. pueri circum innuptaeque puellae

sacra canunt funemque manu contingere gaudent;
illa subit mediaeque minans inlabitur urbi.

    (2.234–40)

We breach the walls and lay bare the city. All set to work,
placing rollers under its feet or attaching hempen cables to its
neck. The deadly engine mounts the walls, pregnant with weapons. Unwed boys and girls surround it, singing hymns, and rejoice to touch the rope. It advances and glides menacingly into
the city.

Again, the insistent ambiguity: the deadly engine, pregnant.[47] Why
did Virgil invent so curious a phrase as *rotarum lapsus*?[48] Elsewhere
he has simply *rotae*. Because, I suspect, he wanted the arresting col-
location "pedibusque rotarum," which for a moment concentrates
the reader's general sense of strangeness; for the reader will momentarily construe, or be tempted to construe, "pedibus" with "rotarum," "feet of wheels."[49] Virgil had another reason too, but of
that presently.

As he relives the scene in memory, Aeneas can no longer contain
himself.

o patria, o diuum domus Ilium et incluta bello
moenia Dardanidum! quater ipso in limine portae
substitit atque utero sonitum quater arma dedere;
instamus tamen immemores caecique furore
et monstrum infelix sacrata sistimus arce.

    (2.241–45)

O my country! O Ilium, home of the gods! and walls of Dar-
dania famed in war! Four times it stopped in the very gateway,
four times from its womb came the sound of arms. Yet we press
on unheeding, blind and mad, and place the monster in our
holy citadel.

At this same point, as he describes the Horse being dragged into the
city, Triphiodorus interrupts his narrative with a passionate denunciation of human blindness and folly.

σχέτλιον ἀφραδέων μερόπων γένος, οἶσιν ὁμίχλη
ἄσκοπος ἐσσομένων· κενεῷ δ᾽ ὑπὸ χάρματι πολλοὶ
πολλάκις ἀγνώσσουσι περιπταίοντες ὀλέθρῳ.

οἵη καὶ Τρώεσσι τότε φθισίμβροτος ἄτη
ἐς πόλιν αὐτοκέλευθος ἐκώμασεν· οὐδέ τις ἀνδρῶν
ᾔδεεν, οὕνεκα λάβρον ἐφέλκετο πένθος ἄλαστον.

(310–15)

Wretched, heedless mankind! from whom an impenetrable mist
conceals the future. Through vain joy many men many times
stumble on death unawares. So then for the Trojans a mortal
doom came reveling into the city by its own will, and no man
knew he was drawing after him a fierce and unforgettable
sorrow.

Apparently a passage resembling that in Triphiodorus stood in the
common source of Virgil and Triphiodorus, which Virgil, with an
imitation of Ennius,[50] transformed into a dramatic outburst by
Aeneas.

Monstrum—the word is enormously satisfying when at last it appears, for it defines and completes what Virgil has been preparing
his reader to feel. The Latin word signifies far more than its English
derivative: *monstrum*, some abnormal creature or thing, uncanny,
insinuating disaster. The grammarian Festus, whose material is borrowed from the erudite Verrius Flaccus, the teacher of Augustus'
grandsons, defines *monstra* (p. 146.32 L.) as "naturae modum egre-
dientia, ut serpens cum pedibus," "things exceeding the limit of nature, like a snake with feet."

Laocoon's death[51] removes the only obstacle to bringing the Horse
into the city; but even more important, to Virgil's story, is the hideous way in which he dies.

Laocoon, ductus Neptuno sorte sacerdos,
sollemnis taurum ingentem mactabat ad aras.

(2.201–2)

Laocoon, chosen by lot as Neptune's priest, was sacrificing a
huge bull at the appointed altar.

Suddenly, across the water from Tenedos, where the Greek fleet is
lurking, come two immense snakes, breasting the sea and making for
the shore. They entwine his two sons and then Laocoon himself in
a scaly embrace, fouling his priestly fillets with gore and poison.
Laocoon shrieks horribly, bellowing like a wounded bull that has
escaped from the altar, shaking off the ax:

qualis mugitus, fugit cum saucius aram
taurus et incertam excussit ceruice securim.

(2.223–24)

The scene, with its stately opening ("sollemnis ... ad aras"), ends
in confusion and a monstrous inversion: the sacrificing priest becomes the slain victim.[52] The snakes glide swiftly away to the citadel,
to Minerva's temple, and take refuge at the goddess's feet beneath
her shield.

Then a strange fear insinuates itself into the stricken hearts of the
Trojans: "tum uero tremefacta nouus per pectora cunctis / insinuat[53]
pauor ..." (2.228–29). They imagine that Laocoon has been punished for violating the sacred Horse: bring it to Minerva's temple,
they cry, let the goddess be appeased. Cassandra warns of the ap-
proaching disaster, Cassandra by a god's command never believed.
And the Trojans, for whom that day would be the last, joyfully dec-
orate the temples of the gods throughout the city.

Night rises from the ocean,[54] involving earth and sky and the
treachery of the Greeks in its great shadow; in the city, from the
Trojans, no sound; sleep embraces their weary bodies, while the ships
advance through the moonlight from Tenedos.

IV

DIDO AND AENEAS

In such a night
Stood Dido with a willow in her hand
Upon the wild sea-banks, and waft her love
To come again to Carthage.

Shakespeare, *The Merchant
of Venice* 5.1.9–12

The tale of Troy and his wanderings told, Aeneas at length falls silent, "conticuit tandem factoque hic fine quieuit" (3.718). So ends the Book, and so, we may infer, the banquet ended.[1] But the queen cannot be quiet, cannot sleep, "nec placidam membris dat cura quietem" (4.5). Love-smitten, she feeds the wound with her heart's blood; an unseen fire consumes her:

At regina graui iamdudum saucia cura
uulnus alit uenis et caeco carpitur igni.

    (4.1–2)

With these abrupt, allusive lines Virgil prepares his reader for the story that follows: a love story in Hellenistic style (there being no other)—a miniature epic, so far as the larger decorum of epic permitted[2]—concentrating on the woman's emotions and ending unhappily. (Benevolent critics sometimes forget that such a story must end unhappily.)

Dido wounded by love, "saucia cura," recalls Ennius' Medea, "sick at heart, wounded by savage love,"

Medea animo aegro amore saeuo saucia.[3]

    (*Medea exul* 254 V.[2] = 216 J.)

But Virgil's reference here, as elsewhere, is twofold:[4] to Ennius and to Catullus in his miniature epic (64)—to Medea, that is, and especially to Ariadne lamenting on the lonely beach of Dia; like Medea, a princess seduced by an adventurer from over the sea and abandoned.⁵

quae tum prospectans cedentem maesta carinam
multiplices animo uoluebat saucia curas.

    (Catull. 64.249–50)

Then, gazing sadly after the receding sail, she revolved a multitude of sorrows in her wounded heart.

"Saucia curas": "saucia cura"—Virgil's imitation is exquisite, the implication unmistakable.⁶

The metaphor of love's burning wound (to be developed in the simile of the stricken deer in lines 67–73) is borrowed from Apollonius 3.280–87:⁷ Eros steals into Aeetes' palace, crouches at Jason's feet, takes aim at the unsuspecting Medea, and fires—and the arrow burned deep in her maiden's heart, like a flame:⁸

βέλος δ᾽ ἐνεδαίετο κούρῃ
νέρθεν ὑπὸ κραδίῃ, φλογὶ εἴκελον.

    (286–87)

Dido's passion, if less sudden, is no less intense: she thinks only of Aeneas, of his valor, of the glory of his race; his looks, his words are fixed in her heart, "haerent infixi pectore uultus / uerbaque" (4.4–5). Here Virgil uses *infigo* metaphorically;⁹ elsewhere he uses it in its proper sense of the stroke of an arrow or a spear (*A.* 5.504; 9.579, 699; 12.375) and, at the end of this Book, of Dido's death-wound, "infixum stridit sub pectore uulnus" (689). Less distantly, "haerent infixi pectore uultus" anticipates the simile of the stricken deer: "est mollis flamma medullas / interea et tacitum uiuit sub pectore uulnus" (4.66–67), "the flame meanwhile devours the marrow of her bones, deep in her breast lives the silent wound."

Dido is restless and frightened. "What dreams terrify me!" she exclaims to her sister Anna the next morning; "Anna soror, quae me suspensam insomnia terrent!" (4.9). "If it were not fixed and settled in my mind never to join myself with another in wedlock, since my first love deceived me by dying; if I were not sick of nuptial bed and torch, perhaps I might have yielded to this one—sin."

si mihi non animo fixum immotumque sederet
ne cui me uinclo uellem sociare iugali,

postquam primus amor deceptam morte fefellit;
si non pertaesum thalami taedaeque fuisset,
huic uni forsan potui succumbere culpae.

(4.15–19)

The intensity of Dido's barely suppressed emotion is evident in the intensity of her language, in the repetition "si mihi non . . . si non," in the alliteration and assonance "pertaesum thalami taedaeque," and especially in the line "huic uni forsan potui succumbere culpae." Since Dido has been speaking of Aeneas, the reader momentarily refers "huic uni" to him, then corrects this first impression on finding "culpae" at the end of the line. (The ancient reader, it will be remembered, read aloud, slowly.[10]) The slight syntactical ambiguity, with Dido's almost instantaneous "correction," mirrors her wavering constancy and sudden resolution as she thinks of Aeneas and then, guiltily, of her dead husband Sychaeus.[11] The idea of this remarkable line seems to have been suggested by Apollonius. In her desperation Medea wishes that she were dead:

$$\dot\omega\varsigma\ \ddot{o}\varphi\epsilon\lambda\acute{o}\nu\ \gamma\epsilon$$
Ἀρτέμιδος κραιπνοῖσι πάρος βελέεσσι δαμῆναι
πρὶν τόν γ᾽ εἰσιδέειν, πρὶν Ἀχαιίδα γαῖαν ἱκέσθαι
Χαλκιόπης υἷας. τοὺς μὲν θεὸς ἤ τις Ἐρινὺς
ἄμμι πολυκλαύτους δεῦρ᾽ ἤγαγε κεῖθεν ἀνίας.[12]

(3.773–77)

O that I had been killed by the swift arrows of Artemis before I saw this man, before Chalciope's sons reached the land of Achaea. Some god or Fury brought them here for our tears, our sorrow.

In *her* desperation—"I recognize the traces of the old flame," "agnosco ueteris uestigia flammae" (4.23)—Dido pronounces a curse, a pathetic and hauntingly beautiful curse on herself should she prove untrue to the memory of Sychaeus: "But may deep earth sooner swallow me up or the Father Omnipotent with his thunderbolt hurl me down to the shades, the pale shades in Erebus and profound night," "sed mihi uel tellus optem prius ima dehiscat[13] / uel pater omnipotens adigat me fulmine ad umbras, / pallentis umbras Erebo noctemque profundam" (24–26). Then, with renewed intensity: "he has stolen my love away, the man who first wedded me; let him have it and keep it with him in the grave," "ille meos, primus qui me sibi iunxit, amores / abstulit; ille habeat secum seru-

etque sepulcro" (28–29).[14] Whereupon she bursts into tears. All this
Virgil accomplishes in thirty lines.

Anna is a concerned and loving sister; like the amiable nurse-con-
fidante of tragedy, a woman of more warmth than sensibility. She
sees no difficulty; rather, a heaven-sent opportunity. Will you always
be grieving, she asks, and never know the joys of love and marriage?
Do you really believe the dead and buried care? True, you rejected
previous suitors; will you struggle now against a love that pleases
you? Think of your situation, of the wild tribes surrounding you.
Think of the glory and empire that will accrue to Carthage from
such a union. Only ask leave of the gods, "tu modo posce deos
ueniam" (50) (Anna has no fears or scruples)—only ask leave of the
gods and invent reasons for detaining him. Dido is only too willing
to be persuaded; Anna reassures her and dispels her shame, "so-
luitque pudorem" (55)—so simply and easily, in a phrase—the idealized *Pudor* Dido had so lately sworn to preserve inviolate ("ante,
Pudor, quam te uiolo aut tua iura resoluo," 27).

They visit the temples, praying for peace at altar after altar, and
sacrifice to various gods, but chiefly to Juno, guardian of the mar-
riage-bond; Dido, in all her beauty, pouring a libation between the
horns of a milk-white heifer. She sacrifices again and again throughout the day, gapes at the victims' opened breasts, and studies their
throbbing entrails. (Dido is no Roman matron, although she is sometimes judged by that severe standard; she is a Phoenician, "Phoenician Dido," as Aeneas reminds her in a terrible moment [4.348],
exotic and passionate—hence something of her fascination for the
father of the Roman people.)

Dido's inhibitions have now been removed. Virgil represents her
condition by comparing her to a mortally wounded deer:

> uritur infelix Dido totaque uagatur
> urbe furens, qualis coniecta cerua sagitta,
> quam procul incautam nemora inter Cresia fixit
> pastor agens telis liquitque uolatile ferrum
> nescius: illa fuga siluas saltusque peragrat
> Dictaeos; haeret lateri letalis harundo.
>
> (4.68–73)

She burns, unhappy Dido, and in her passion wanders throughout the city—like a deer pierced by an arrow, an incautious
doe that a shepherd hunting in the Cretan woods has shot un-
knowingly from a distance, leaving the winged steel in her: she

flees, scouring the forest and glades of Dicte, the fatal reed fixed in her side.

The two adjectives so artfully arranged are not merely ornamental, to embellish the picture; they confirm the Hellenistic character of the simile. *Cresius* first occurs here, a rare adjective used only by poets.[15] *Dictaeus* is somewhat less rare but equally poetic;[16] Virgil had already used it in *E.* 6.55–56: "Nymphae, / Dictaeae Nymphae, nemorum iam claudite saltus," "Nymphs, Dictaean Nymphs, close now the glades of the forest," of which there seems to be a reminiscence here.[17]

But why a shepherd?[18] And why hunting in the Cretan woods? Hunting is only incidental to pastoral life, but Virgil's shepherds (the shepherds of Theocritus appear to be less enterprising) do hunt, most notably the lovesick soldier and would-be shepherd Gallus in his fantasy of pastoral life:

> interea mixtis lustrabo Maenala Nymphis
> aut acris uenabor apros. non me ulla uetabunt
> frigora Parthenios canibus circumdare saltus.
> iam mihi per rupes uideor lucosque sonantis
> ire, libet Partho torquere Cydonia cornu
> spicula—tamquam haec sit nostri medicina furoris . . .
>
> (*E.* 10.55–60)

Meanwhile I will range over Maenalus with the Nymphs or hunt the wild boar. No frost will stop me from encircling the glades of Parthenius with my hounds. Now I see myself speeding over rocks and through echoing groves; what pleasure to shoot Cydonian arrows from a Parthian bow—as if this were a remedy for my madness . . .

The Cydones were an ancient people inhabiting northwestern Crete (*Od.* 3.292). Callimachus, in keeping with Alexandrian practice, extends their name to Cretans in general.[19] Since Callimachus twice applies Κυδώνιος to the bow,[20] the adjective here may be considered—as Virgil no doubt considered it—Callimachean. The Cretans enjoyed a literary reputation for archery from Homer onward;[21] of Parthian archery the Romans had had bitter experience.

Virgil's simile was probably suggested by the simile of Apollonius,[22] prominently placed at the beginning of Book 4, in which Medea is compared to a deer startled by hunters:

τρέσσεν δ᾽ ἠύτε τις κούφη κεμὰς ἥν τε βαθείης
τάρφεσιν ἐν ξυλόχοιο κυνῶν ἐφόβησεν ὁμοκλή.

(4.12–13)

She trembled like a nimble doe put to flight by the baying of
hounds in the thicket of a deep wood.

Virgil introduces his simile with a line enclosed by two verbs, "uritur
infelix Dido totaque uagatur," the second defining or explaining the
first: her extreme restlessness is an indication of the secret passion
which consumes her. For this detail of technique he is indebted to
Catullus 83.6, "uritur et loquitur" (the two verbs enclose the second
half of the pentameter): Lesbia burns and complains;[23] or to 5.1,
"Viuamus, mea Lesbia, atque amemus": to live, Catullus implies, is
to love.

So passes the long winter of love. At last, importuned by Iarbas, a
neighboring prince whom Dido had scorned, Jupiter looks down
from heaven on the reckless lovers ("oblitos famae melioris amantis,"
4:221) and decides that Aeneas must leave. On descending to convey
the peremptory command, Mercury finds Aeneas wearing foreign
dress—a mantle of Tyrian purple laced with gold thread, the gift of
Dido's own hands—and overseeing the construction of Carthage.
Aeneas submits instantly, speechless with dread and dazed by the
divine apparition. Now he yearns to be gone, to leave Africa's sweet
land behind, "ardet abire fuga dulcisque relinquere terras" (281).[24]

But how to manage? How get around the impassioned queen "reginam ambire furentem" (4.283)? After much anxious thought
Aeneas calls his captains together, bids them quietly ("taciti," 289)
equip the fleet, muster their comrades on the shore, and conceal
("dissimulent," 291) the reason for this sudden activity. In the meantime he will try to approach her in the easiest, gentlest way,[25] when
circumstances are right; for Dido, "optima Dido" (291), does not
know nor will she imagine a rupture possible in a love so strong,
"tantos rumpi non speret amores" (292). His men are glad to be
going ("laeti," 295) and swiftly obey his orders.

Virgil is too humane a poet, too scrupulous, to exculpate his hero.
But several of his commentators are embarrassed by Aeneas' behavior,[26] and in particular by two words he uses, "ambire" and "optima," which they would like to explain away.

Virgil's ancient commentators had no doubt about the meaning of
"ambire"; DServius: "blanditiis uel subdole circumuenire," "to cir-

cumvent by flattery or deceit."[27] Nor would his modern commentators have any were they not concerned to uphold the hero's character, at whatever cost.[28] The verb is found only in the *Aeneid*: here;
twice in its literal sense (6.550, 10.243), which is irrelevant here; and
in 7.333–34, "neu conubiis ambire Latinum / Aeneadae possint,"
where Juno fears that Latinus will be cajoled into a marriage alliance
by the Trojans.[29]

"How get round the impassioned queen?" On only four occasions
does Aeneas use the title *regina*: on that first night when, reluctantly,
he consented to tell her the story of Troy ("infandum, regina, iubes,"
2.3), not knowing that she was falling in love with him;[30] here, startled from his dream of love and perceiving not the woman but the
queen; in direct discourse, when he is on the point of leaving her
("numquam, regina, negabo," 4.334);[31] and in the Underworld ("in-
uitus, regina," 6.460). The hastily resumed formality of reference
here may be attributed to the fact that Aeneas is speaking to his
men; but the unemotional, respectful adjective is disturbing even
so. Suddenly Dido, "optima Dido," seems estranged and remote—
as in his parting speech, when, for the first time, he uses her old
Phoenician name: "nec me meminisse pigebit Elissae" (4.335).[32] Elsewhere in the poem *optimus* is applied to Anchises, Evander, Latinus,
and to Aeneas himself.[33] Again, Virgil's commentators and transla-
tors are embarrassed and offer various improbable interpretations of
"optima."[34]

But who can fool a woman in love ("quis fallere possit amantem?"
4.296)? Dido, fearing her own happiness,[35] senses the deception and
realizes that Aeneas intends to leave her.

> saeuit inops animi totamque incensa per urbem
> bacchatur, qualis commotis excita sacris
> Thyias, ubi audito stimulant trieterica Baccho
> orgia nocturnusque uocat clamore Cithaeron.
>
> (4.300–303)[36]

> Raging and desperate, she wanders wildly throughout the city,
> inflamed with passion—like a Maenad roused by the commo-
> tion of the sacred emblems, when the triennial orgies goad her
> with the cry of Bacchus and Cithaeron's clamor calls her into
> the night.

But she collects herself and, not waiting for him to speak, confronts
Aeneas.

"dissimulare etiam sperasti, perfide, tantum
posse nefas tacitusque mea decedere terra?"

(4.305–6)

"And did you hope, traitor, to conceal such wickedness and leave my land without a word?"

She begins abruptly, with an angry question,[37] repeating two words, in chiastic order, from Aeneas' own instructions to his men ("taciti," 289; "dissimulent," 291) and echoing the forsaken Ariadne.[38]

"sicine me patriis auectam, perfide, ab aris,
perfide, deserto liquisti in litore, Theseu?"

(Catull. 64.132–33)

"Have you then, traitor, carried me away from my father's house to abandon me, traitor Theseus, on this lonely shore?"

Angry as she is, Dido soon relents and begins to plead with Aeneas, imploring him not to leave her. Suppose you were not seeking a strange land, an unknown home—suppose Troy were standing as of old; would you seek Troy across a wintry sea? Then, assailed by a sudden doubt: Is it *me* you flee?[39] If I have pleased you at all, or if anything of mine was sweet to you, have pity: "si bene quid de te merui, fuit aut tibi quicquam / dulce meum, miserere" (317–18). Because of you, she continues, the tribes of Libya and the Nomad lords hate me, my own people are hostile; because of you, my honor is lost, my reputation. Will you leave me here to die? She ends by wishing that she had borne a child by him, a little Aeneas to play in her palace, whose features at least would bring Aeneas back to her: "si quis mihi paruulus aula / luderet Aeneas, qui te tamen ore referret" (328–29) ("paruulus" is the only true diminutive—and infinitely pathetic—in this long heroic poem).[40]

Aeneas is powerfully affected—who could not be? We know, for Virgil tells us, but Dido does not: "He held his eyes motionless, at Jove's command, and, with an effort, repressed the love in his heart," "ille Iouis monitis immota tenebat / lumina et obnixus curam sub corde premebat"(331–32).[41]

But why does Aeneas never tell Dido of his love? Because he cannot: he is inhibited by the tradition in which he has his being. Love, passionate love, on the man's part may be expressed in comedy, elegy, or pastoral, but not in epic (only the foolish Coroebus, who fell madly in love with Cassandra and came to Troy in those last days, is so described, 2.343: "insano Cassandrae incensus amore").[42] A modern reader will be surprised that Virgil reveals so little of Aeneas' passion, and may even be inclined to doubt its existence; an ancient reader would have been surprised at how much Virgil reveals, for he goes further in this respect than any previous epic poet.

Dido's passionate outpouring is met with a constrained, chill response.[43] This is Aeneas' only speech to Dido in Book 4, and only his second speech to her in the poem; his third, and last, will be in the Underworld. Dido, on the other hand, speaks nine times;[44] only Evander speaks more lines in a single book.[45] But the loquacity of Dido and of Evander proceeds from quite different causes: Evander represents Nestor, the garrulous old hero of the *Iliad*; Dido the Hellenistic woman in love, excitable, histrionic, giving rein to her emotions.

"I shall never"—Aeneas begins, after a pause—"never, Queen, deny the many claims to gratitude which you can enumerate, nor shall I be sorry to remember Elissa while I am mindful of myself, while I live and breathe": "ego te, quae plurima fando / enumerare uales, numquam, regina, negabo / promeritam, nec me meminisse pigebit Elissae / dum memor ipse mei, dum spiritus hos regit artus" (333–36). Here, for the first time, he uses her old Phoenician name, creating an impression of distance and estrangement.[46] Now, suddenly, it is "Queen" and "Elissa"; before (but how long before it seems) it had been "Dido"—as it will be once again, in the Underworld, "infelix Dido" (6.456). He did not intend to steal away, he says (appearances to the contrary), nor did he promise marriage (true, but he seems to have let her think of their relationship as marriage, 4.172, 316, 431). Left to himself, if fate allowed, he would rebuild the city of Troy.[47] But now Apollo's Lycian oracle (of which we have heard nothing) bids him seek Italy, great Italy, "sed nunc Italiam magnam Gryneus Apollo, / Italiam" (345–46). There is his love, there his country. Why should she, a Phoenician,[48] with her own city of Carthage in Libya, begrudge him his destiny? Night after night his father's troubled ghost disturbs his dreams (of which, again, we have heard nothing).[49] And there is the wrong done his son, whom he defrauds of a kingdom in Hesperia, the land of fate. Now, too, the messenger of the gods has come from Jove himself; he has seen him, he swears he has seen him, and heard his voice. Cease, he cries— cease inflaming yourself and me with your complaints.[50] Unwillingly I seek Italy, "Italiam non sponte sequor" (361).

Aeneas is a Homeric hero, and as such treats with gods; Dido only a woman, and to her no visions come.[51] Her experience of the supernatural is confined to the dubious practices of haruspicy and witchcraft; naturally she disbelieves him, and is scornful, when he tells her of Apollo's oracle, of the visitation of Mercury. "Now it's prophet Apollo, now the Lycian oracle, now the messenger of the gods come from Jove himself" (mockingly, it seems, she repeats his own words) "flying through the air with the dread command. No doubt this is the business of the gods above, the concern that troubles their peace," "scilicet is superis labor est, ea cura quietos / sollicitat" (379–80). (There is an ironic allusion to Lucretius here, and to the remote, passionless Epicurean gods.[52] Dido, it seems, is an Epicurean, Aeneas a Stoic—a Roman Stoic.) Dido's nature is passionate, impulsive; her life here and now. What is she to make of this driven wanderer, with his obsessive, Troy-centered grief, his talk of gods and fate and a kingdom in the West? How can she understand him? how accept what is happening to herself?

Dido is, by the end of Aeneas' speech, aflame with anger;[53] her speech agitated, almost incoherent. (Which is not to say that Virgil's rhetoric is incoherent: note the tricolon, with anaphora, in 369–70.) She lapses into the third person, as if turning away from Aeneas and appealing to an imaginary audience, as characters in drama occasionally do in moments of intolerable exasperation or anger.[54] "Why should I pretend? Or for what greater outrages should I wait? Did he groan at my tears? Did he move those hard eyes? Did he yield and weep, or pity the woman who loves him?" "nam quid dissimulo aut quae me ad maiora reseruo? / num fletu ingemuit nostro? num lumina flexit? / num lacrimas uictus dedit aut miseratus amantem est?" (368–70). She disdains to argue: let him go, let him sail for Italy, seek his kingdom. Yet she hopes, if the gods in their goodness have any power, that he will be shipwrecked, and imagines him, in distress, calling and calling her name: "spero equidem mediis, si quid pia numina possunt, / supplicia hausurum scopulis et nomine Dido / saepe vocaturum" (382–84) ("if the gods in their goodness have any power"—bitterly recalling his first, heartfelt words to her, 1.603: "di tibi, si qua pios respectant numina," "may the gods reward you, if any powers divine regard human goodness"). Though far away, she will pursue him in black fire and, when the chill of death has parted soul from body, be present everywhere to haunt him. He will be punished and she will know—word of it will reach her, deep among the dead, "Manis . . . sub imos" (4.387).

With these words Dido faints dead away, leaving Aeneas baffled: there had been so much he feared to say, so much he wanted to say, "multa metu cunctantem et multa parantem / dicere" (390–91).[55]

(But what could he have said?) Her women support her to her marble chamber and lay her on her bed, "suscipiunt famulae conlapsaque membra / marmoreo referunt thalamo stratisque reponunt" (391–92). In Virgil *conlapsus* (the only form he uses, and the only form used by most writers) is always associated with death.[56] And this sense determines the sense of "marmoreo."[57] Marble is mentioned only twice in this book, here and in 457: the marble temple of her dead husband, "de marmore templum / coniugis antiqui" (457–58), from which, in the night, she seems to hear his voice calling, "hinc exaudiri uoces et uerba uocantis / uisa uiri, nox cum terras obscura teneret" (460–61).

Dido's thoughts now turn toward death; however, she resolves on a last attempt, not to win Aeneas back (she has no hope of that) but to persuade him to wait for a little: mere time is all she asks, a respite, a breathing space for her passion, "tempus inane peto, requiem spatiumque furori" (433). Anna acts as go-between, for Dido is aware that she enjoys a special relationship with Aeneas and will know how to approach him. Poor Anna—again and again she conveys the tearful appeal. Fate withstands, and a god stops up his ears; Aeneas is as intractable, as stubborn under pressure, as an ancient oak.[58]

> ac uelut annoso ualidam cum robore quercum
> Alpini Boreae nunc hinc nunc flatibus illinc
> eruere inter se certant; it stridor, et altae
> consternunt terram concusso stipite frondes;
> ipsa haeret scopulis et quantum uertice ad auras
> aetherias, tantum radice in Tartara tendit:
> haud secus adsiduis hinc atque hinc uocibus heros
> tunditur, et magno persentit pectore curas;
> mens immota manet, lacrimae uoluuntur inanes.
>
>   (4.441–49)

As Alpine winds, blowing now from this side, now that, strive with one another to uproot an old and sturdy oak; its trunk creaks and shakes, and the high foliage strews the ground; yet the tree clings to the rocks, for its root descends as far toward Hell as its crown ascends heavenward: even so the hero is buffeted from every side by an incessant storm of words and, deep in his mighty heart, feels love's anguish; but his mind remains fixed, and tears flow in vain.

The simile is of a traditional kind: the age-old simile between men and trees, in which the Homeric hero falls as naturally as a tree falls;

although in Virgil's simile neither tree nor hero falls. It is also one of the more elaborate similes in the poem, elaborate in itself and in its relation to a previous simile: the comparison of Troy, the ancient doomed city ("urbs antiqua ruit," 2.363), to an ancient tree:[59]

ac ueluti summis antiquam in montibus ornum
cum ferro accisam crebrisque bipennibus instant
eruere agricolae certatim, illa usque minatur
et tremefacta comam concusso uertice nutat,
uulneribus donec paulatim euicta supremum
congemuit traxitque iugis auulsa ruinam.

(2.626–31)

As on a mountain-top farmers strive with one another to up-root[60] an ancient ash, attacking its battered trunk with blow upon blow of their iron axes; the tree continues to nod and threaten, leaves trembling, crest tossing, until gradually over-come with wounds, it gives a loud last groan and, torn from the ridge, crashes down.

In dealing with such descriptive passages in Latin poetry, and in Virgil especially, the critical question is not, What had the poet seen? but, What had the poet read? For even personal observation will have been transformed by literary reference.[61] Here again Virgil's reference is twofold, to Homer:

ἤριπε δ' ὡς ὅτε τις δρῦς ἤριπεν ἢ ἀχερωΐς,
ἠὲ πίτυς βλωθρή, τήν τ' οὔρεσι τέκτονες ἄνδρες
ἐξέταμον πελέκεσσι νεήκεσι νήϊον εἶναι.

(*Il.* 13.389–91 = 16.482–84)

He fell, as when an oak falls, or a white poplar or a tall pine, which woodsmen have cut down in the mountains with their sharp axes to make a ship-timber.

And (for Virgil recognized Apollonius' imitation of Homer) to Apollonius:

ἀλλ' ὡς τίς τ' ἐν ὄρεσσι πελωρίη ὑψόθι πεύκη,
τήν τε θοοῖς πελέκεσσιν ἔθ' ἡμιπλῆγα λιπόντες
ὑλοτόμοι δρυμοῖο κατήλυθον, ἡ δ' ὑπὸ νυκτὶ
ῥιπῆσιν μὲν πρῶτα τινάσσεται, ὕστερον αὖτε
πρυμνόθεν ἐξαγεῖσα κατήριπεν.

(4.1682–86)

As high in the mountains a giant pine, which woodcutters, returning homeward, have left half hewn by their sharp axes—
at first it trembles with the force of the night wind, then, snap-
ping at the stump, crashes down.

What is the reader to make of the correspondence, so carefully de-
signed, of these two similes? Briefly, he is to be aware of a contrast.
Troy, like a battered ancient tree, falls; but Aeneas heroically resists.
The tree-simile in Book 2 is uniquely memorable in that a city, and
not merely a single warrior, is compared to a felled tree.[62] And the
reader's previous experience of such matching similes—the Diana-
and Apollo-similes in Books 1 and 4, the similes of the stricken deer
and the Maenad in Book 4—will have prepared him to notice and
appreciate the correspondence of the two tree-similes, as will also,
perhaps, Dido's speech to Anna, which precedes the tree-simile in
4.425–26: "non ego cum Danais Troianam exscindere gentem / Au-
lide iuraui," "I did not swear with the Greeks at Aulis to extirpate
the Trojan race."

Now (for Virgil's similes, unlike those of Homer, advance the action) Dido grows weary of gazing at the eternal sky; she longs for
death.[63]

It was night . . .

Nox erat et placidum carpebant fessa soporem
corpora per terras, siluaeque et saeua quierant
aequora, cum medio uoluuntur sidera lapsu,
cum tacet omnis ager, pecudes pictaeque uolucres,
quaeque lacus late liquidos quaeque aspera dumis rura
tenent, somno positae sub nocte silenti.
at non infelix animi Phoenissa . . .

    (4.522–29)

It was night, and all the world over, weary creatures enjoyed
peaceful slumber; the woods and the wild seas were quiet; now
the stars glide in mid-course, now all the fields are still, and
cattle and the various birds, which haunt clear pools and rough
shrubby pastures far and wide, were sleeping beneath the silent
night. But not Phoenicia's unhappy daughter . . .

In the whitening dawn from her watchtower Dido looks down on
the empty harbor: not an oar left behind, and the Trojan fleet standing out to sea. After an outburst of wild rage she addresses to the
rising sun a solemn prayer for vengeance:—"Sun, whose fires illuminate

all the works of earth . . . ," "Sol, qui terrarum flammis opera omnia lustras . . ." (607). If Aeneas is destined to reach the Italian shore, if fate and Jove so ordain, yet she prays that he may be harassed by a fierce people and look upon his own dead; prays that he too may fall, before his day, and lie unburied on the sand. And finally, she prays that her hatred may pursue his race forever:

> "exoriare aliquis nostris ex ossibus ultor
> qui face Dardanios ferroque sequare colonos,
> nunc, olim, quocumque dabunt se tempore uires.
> litora litoribus contraria, fluctibus undas
> imprecor, arma armis; pugnent ipsique nepotesque."
>
> (4.625–29)

"Arise from my bones, unknown avenger, and attack the Dardanian settlers with fire and sword, now, in the future, whenever strength is given. Shore against shore, wave against wave (this is my prayer), sword against sword; let them fight, themselves and their descendants."

The last line of Dido's prayer is one of the most daring and expressive in Latin poetry: the extended line,[64] the unending hatred . . . Dido echoes—but with a profound historical resonance—Ariadne's curse on Theseus at the close of her lament:[65]

> "sed quali solam Theseus me mente reliquit,
> tali mente, deae, funestet seque suosque."
>
> (Catull. 64.200–201)

"With the mind Theseus had when he abandoned me, with that mind, goddesses, may he bring the pollution of death upon himself and his own."

Dido's death has often been called tragic, in the vague unliterary sense of the term. It is, however, tragic in the strictest sense, for it conforms to a pattern discernible in Greek, and especially Sophoclean, tragedy.[66]

First, the heroine, emotionally overwrought, rushes into her chamber and falls upon the marriage bed. Since she is out of sight, her behavior must be reported to the audience, although Dido, like Ajax, dies "onstage."

Soph. *Oedipus Tyrannus* 1241–43 (the messenger speaking):

ὅπως γὰρ ὀργῇ χρωμένη παρῆλϑ᾽ ἔσω
ϑυρῶνος, ἵετ᾽ εὐϑὺς ἐς τὰ νυμφικὰ
λέχη . . .

When in her frenzy she had passed into the vestibule, she rushed
straight toward her marriage bed . . .

Soph. *Trachiniae* 912–13 (the nurse speaking):

ἐξαίφνης σφ᾽ ὁρῶ
τὸν Ἡράκλειον θάλαμον εἰσορμωμένην.

Suddenly I saw her rushing into the chamber of Heracles.

And 915–18:

ὁρῶ δὲ τὴν γυναῖκα δεμνίοις
τοῖς Ἡρακλείοις στρωτὰ βάλλουσαν φάρη.
ὅπως δ᾽ ἐτέλεσε τοῦτ᾽, ἐπενθοροῦσ᾽ ἄνω
καθέζετ᾽ ἐν μέσοισιν εὐνατηρίοις . . .

I saw the woman flinging coverlets on Heracles' bed. That done,
she leaped up and settled herself in the middle of the bed . . .

Eur. *Alcestis* 175 (the handmaid speaking):

κἄπειτα θάλαμον ἐσπεσοῦσα καὶ λέχος . . .

Then rushing into her chamber she fell on her bed . . .

Alcestis is not properly a suicide, but since she has agreed to her own
death, Euripides describes her as if she were.

A. 4.645–47:

interiora domus inrumpit limina et altos
conscendit furibunda rogos ensemque recludit
Dardanium, non hos quaesitum munus in usus.

She rushes into the inner court and in her frenzy climbs the
high pyre and unsheathes the Dardanian sword, a gift not
sought for this purpose.

The marriage bed has been piled on top of the pyre, and on the bed
Dido has placed an effigy of Aeneas, pieces of his clothing, and the
sword left hanging in the chamber, "exuuias ensemque relictum"
(4.507), the relics of love.

Second, the heroine weeps and utters her last words.

Soph. *OT* 1249–50:

γοᾶτο δ' εὐνάς, ἔνθα δύστηνος διπλοῦς
ἐξ ἀνδρὸς ἄνδρα καὶ τέκν' ἐκ τέκνων τέκοι.

She bewailed the marriage bed, on which, poor woman, she had borne a double brood, husband by husband and children by child.

Soph. *Trach.* 919–20:

καὶ δακρύων ῥήξασα θερμὰ νάματα
ἔλεξεν, "ὦ λέχη τε καὶ νυμφεῖ' ἐμα' ..."

Bursting into streams of hot tears, she spoke: "O my marriage bed and chamber ..."

Eur. *Alc.* 176–79:

ἐνταῦθα δὴ 'δάκρυσε καὶ λέγει τάδε·
"Ὦ λέκτρον, ἔνθα παρθένει' ἔλυσ' ἐγὼ
κορεύματ' ἐκ τοῦδ' ἀνδρός, οὗ θνῆσκω πάρος
χαῖρ'."[67]

There indeed she wept, and spoke: "O marriage bed, on which I yielded up my maidenhood to the man in whose stead I die, farewell."

A. 4.648–51:

hic, postquam Iliacas uestis notumque cubile
conspexit, paulum lacrimis et mente morata
incubuitque toro[68] dixitque nouissima uerba:
"dulces exuuiae ..."

Then, after she had looked at the Trojan garments and the bed she knew so well, pausing a little, weeping, she lay down upon it and spoke her last words: "Sweet relics ..."

Third, after speaking, the heroine kisses the bed.

Eur. *Alc.* 183:

κυνεῖ δὲ προσπίτνουσα ...

She falls on the bed and kisses it ...

A. 4.659:

dixit, et os impressa toro ...

She spoke, and having kissed the bed ...

Medea also kisses her bed as she is about to leave her chamber for the last time, κύσσε δ' ἐόν τε λέχος (Ap. Rhod. 4.26).[69]

Last, the manner of the heroine's death is described.

Soph. *OT* 1263–64:

οὐ δὴ κρεμαστὴν τὴν γυναῖκ᾽ εἰσείδομεν,
πλεκταῖς ἐώραις ἐμπεπλεγμένην.[70]

There we saw the woman hanging, caught up and swinging in the woven ropes.

Soph. *Trach.* 929–31:

κἀν ᾧ τὸ κεῖσε δεῦρό τ᾽ ἐξορμώμεθα,
ὁρῶμεν αὐτὴν ἀμφιπλῆγι φασγάνῳ
πλευρὰν ὑφ᾽ ἧπαρ καὶ φρένας πεπληγμένην.

In the time it took to hurry there and back again, we discovered that she had driven a double-edged sword through her side to the heart.

A. 4.659–65:[71]

dixit, et os impressa toro "moriemur inultae,
sed moriamur" ait. "sic, sic iuuat ire sub umbras.
hauriat hunc oculis ignem crudelis ab alto
Dardanus, et nostrae secum ferat omina mortis."
dixerat, atque illam media inter talia ferro
conlapsam aspiciunt comites, ensemque cruore
spumantem sparsasque manus.

She spoke, and, having kissed the bed, "I die unavenged," she cried, "but let me die. Thus—thus will I go down to darkness. May the cruel Dardanian gaze from the sea at this fire and take with him the omen of my death." While she was still speaking her attendants saw her fallen on the sword, the blade foaming with blood, blood spattered on her hands.

Dido's death is presented from the spectators' point of view, and after the fact, as in tragedy: her attendants see her, not falling but fallen on the sword.[72]

Like Ajax, Dido kills herself with the sword of an enemy, for as such she now regards Aeneas.

i, soror, atque hostem supplex adfare superbum.

(4.424)

Go then, sister, and appeal to my haughty foe.

In her first happiness she had called him "husband" (*coniunx*), then,
since nothing else remained of that earlier name, "guest" (*hospes*:
4.323–24); but now it is "foe" (*hostis*). As Ajax plants his sword in
the hostile earth of Troy, he remembers that it had been Hector's
sword:

δῶρον μὲν ἀνδρὸς Ἕκτορος ξένων ἐμοὶ
μάλιστα μισηθέντος, ἐχθίστου θ᾽ ὁρᾶν.

(*Ajax* 817–18)

The gift of Hector, of all foemen-friends the most hated and
hateful to my sight.

Dido falls on the Dardanian sword, "a gift not sought for this purpose"; hence, in speaking of Aeneas for the last time, she calls him,
exceptionally, "the Dardanian."[73]

The tragic heroine's death naturally affects those near and dear to
her, as Dido's death affects Anna. But Dido is a queen, descended
of royal kings, not merely a beloved sister; her death convulses the
nation—as if, with her death, her city and people were dying too.

it clamor ad alta
atria: concussam bacchatur Fama per urbem.
lamentis gemituque et femineo ululatu
tecta fremunt, resonat magnis plangoribus aether,[74]
non aliter quam si immissis ruat hostibus omnis
Karthago aut antiqua Tyros, flammaeque furentes
culmina perque hominum uoluantur perque deorum.

(4.665–71)

A cry rises in the high chamber and Rumor runs wild through
the stricken city. Houses are loud with lamentation, with moan-
ing and women wailing; the heavens echo the mighty sound—
as if, the enemy let suddenly in, all Carthage were falling or
ancient Tyre, and raging flames were rolling over the rooftops
of men and gods.

So also with Dido's last speech; it resembles that of a tragic heroine
in its pathos, but not in its length, its grave pride,[75] or in density of
reference. (Dido's speech may be compared, however unequally, with

that of Ajax; like Ajax, she falls on the sword as she finishes speaking.)

"dulces exuuiae, dum fata deusque sinebat,
accipite hanc animam meque his exsoluite curis.
uixi et quem dederat cursum Fortuna peregi,
et nunc magna mei sub terras ibit imago.
urbem praeclaram statui, mea moenia uidi,
ulta uirum poenas inimico a fratre recepi,
felix, heu nimium felix, si litora tantum
numquam Dardaniae tetigissent nostra carinae."

(4.651–58)

"Sweet relics, while fate and god permitted, receive my spirit and free me from this suffering. I have lived my life and finished the course Fortune gave me, and now my shade shall go in majesty beneath the earth. I have founded a glorious city, I have seen my walls, I have avenged my husband, punishing his false brother—happy, O too happy, if only the Dardanian ships had never touched my shore."

In effect Dido pronounces her own epitaph, an epitaph of two lines (655–56) which recalls, in its starkness and simplicity, the *elogia* or sepulchral inscriptions of Roman worthies, men such as Appius Claudius Caecus, censor and twice consul.[76]

complura oppida de Samnitibus cepit.
Sabinorum et Tuscorum exercitum fudit.
pacem fieri cum Pyrrho rege prohibuit.
in censura uiam Appiam strauit et aquam in urbem adduxit.
aedem Bellonae fecit.

He seized many towns from the Samnites.
He routed the army of the Sabines and Etruscans.
He forbade making peace with King Pyrrhus.
He paved the Appian Way as censor and brought water into
    the city.
He built the temple of Bellona.

Virgil mitigates the severity of Dido's *elogium*, and thus accommodates it to the style of her speech (and to his own style), by casting it in the form of a tricolon of which each colon is discrete and ends with an active verb:[77]

"urbem praeclaram statui, mea moenia uidi,
ulta uirum poenas inimico a fratre recepi."

The plaintive, lovely lines which follow, closing her speech, are full of echoes, presences:

"felix, heu nimium felix, si litora tantum
numquam Dardaniae tetigissent nostra carinae."

Immediately we are aware of Ariadne:

"Iuppiter omnipotens, utinam ne tempore primo
Cnosia Cecropiae tetigissent litora puppes."

(Catull. 64.171–72)

"Almighty Jupiter, would that the Cecropian ships had never touched the shore of Cnossus."

And, through Catullus, of Medea's nurse in Ennius:[78]

"Vtinam ne in nemore Pelio securibus
caesa accidisset abiegna ad terram trabes ..."

(*Medea exul* 246–47 V.² = 208–9 J.)

"Would that in Pelion's forest the fir-wood timber had not been hewn and fallen to earth ..."

That Ariadne, and after her Dido, speaks for herself is owing to Apollonius. For in Apollonius it is Medea, not, as in the tragedies of Euripides and Ennius, her nurse, who wishes that Jason had never come:

κύσσε δ' ἑόν τε λέχος καὶ δικλίδας ἀμφοτέρωθεν
σταθμούς, καὶ τοίχων ἐπαφήσατο· χερσί τε μακρὸν
τμηξαμένη πλόκαμον, θαλάμῳ μνημήια μητρὶ
κάλλιπε παρθενίης, ἀδινῇ δ' ὀλοφύρατο φωνῇ·
    "Τόνδε τοι ἀντ' ἐμέθεν ταναὸν πλόκον εἰμὶ λιποῦσα,
μῆτερ ἐμή· χαίροις δὲ καὶ ἄνδιχα πολλὸν ἰούσῃ·
χαίροις, Χαλκιόπη καὶ πᾶς δόμος. αἴθε σε πόντος,
ξεῖνε, διέρραισεν πρὶν Κολχίδα γαῖαν ἱκέσθαι."

(*Arg.* 4.26–33)

She kissed her bed and the posts on either side of the folding-door and stroked the walls; she tore out a long lock of hair and left it in the chamber as a memorial of her virginity, for her mother. Then, weeping piteously: "I go, Mother, leaving this

long tress in my stead; be happy, even though I am going far
away; be happy, Chalciope, and all my house. Would that the
sea had dashed you to pieces, stranger, before you reached the
land of the Colchians."

Medea's speech ends, as does Dido's, with the pathetic wish that her
lover had never come.[79]

As Virgil imitates the *elogium* by modifying its antique simplicity,
so he imitates Catullus here by modifying his neoteric complexity.

> "Iuppiter omnipotens, utinam ne tempore primo
> Cnosia Cecropiae tetigissent litora puppes . . ."
>
> (Catull. 64.171–72)

Line 172 is one of those "which they call golden, or two Substantives
and two Adjectives, with a Verb betwixt them to keep the peace"[80]—
a neoteric preciosity which Virgil tends to avoid in the *Aeneid*.[81]
Similarly, in the moving iteration "felix, heu nimium felix," he avoids
the neoteric interjection *a*,[82] even though *heu* somewhat strains the
idiom.[83] So intricately, so beautifully composed are these lines, in
which we hear, for the last time, the accents of the forsaken Ariadne:

> "felix, heu nimium felix, si litora tantum
> numquam Dardaniae tetigissent nostra carinae."

V

ARCADIA REVIEWED

> The perception comes quickly . . . of the singular and
> beautiful but almost crushing mission that has been laid,
> as an effect of time, upon this limited territory, which
> has arisen to the occasion, from the first, so consistently
> and bravely.
>
> Henry James, *The American Scene*

Turnus raises the red flag of battle over the Laurentian citadel, trum-
pets blare, and the peaceful countryside is thrown into disorder. We
have arrived at last—through various hazards, through so many per-
ils, "per uarios casus, per tot discrimina rerum" (1.204)—in Latium.
The sons of Dardanus will come into their kingdom, the Sibyl had
prophesied to Aeneas, and wish they had not come: "War, I see a
grim war and the Tiber foaming with blood," "bella, horrida bella, /
et Thybrim multo spumantem sanguine cerno" (6.86–87).

So begins Book 8. Book 7 ended with the gathering of the Italian
tribes, and in particular with two brilliant, doomed figures, Turnus
and the virgin huntress Camilla. Camilla's hair is bound up in a
golden clasp and she carries a shepherd's myrtle staff, fitted with a
spearhead, "et pastoralem praefixa cuspide myrtum" (817)[1]—the last
line of the Book.

Observing all this, Aeneas is deeply troubled—"tossed on a great
sea of trouble," "magno curarum fluctuat aestu" (19). His mind veers
swiftly this way and that—

> sicut aquae tremulum labris ubi lumen aenis
> sole repercussum aut radiantis imagine lunae
> omnia peruolitat late loca, iamque sub auras
> erigitur summique ferit laquearia tecti.
> nox erat et terras animalia fessa per omnis
> alituum pecudumque genus sopor altus habebat . . .
>
> (8.22–27)

As when, in a brazen basin, the water's tremulous light, reflected by the sun or the moon's radiance, flies everywhere about a room and now shoots upward and strikes the paneled ceiling high above. It was night, and all the world over, weary creatures, bird and beast alike, were sound asleep . . .

Virgil's simile is modeled on a simile in Apollonius, although for his language he draws also on a passage in Lucretius:

> quod simul ac primum sub diu splendor aquai
> ponitur, extemplo caelo stellante serena
> sidera respondent in aqua radiantia mundi.[2]

(4.211–13)

When water is placed in the open under a starry sky, immediately the bright constellations of the firmament glitter in the splendor of the water.

Apollonius' simile describes the turmoil of passion in the heart of the young and inexperienced Medea.

> Νὺξ μὲν ἔπειτ' ἐπὶ γαῖαν ἄγεν κνέφας, οἱ δ' ἐνὶ πόντῳ
> ναυτίλοι εἰς Ἑλίκην τε καὶ ἀστέρας Ὠρίωνος
> ἔδρακον ἐκ νηῶν, ὕπνοιο δὲ καί τις ὁδίτης
> ἤδη καὶ πυλαωρὸς ἐέλδετο, καί τινα παίδων
> μητέρα τεθνεώτων ἀδινὸν περὶ κῶμ' ἐκάλυπτεν,
> οὐδὲ κυνῶν ὑλακὴ ἔτ' ἀνὰ πτόλιν, οὐ θρόος ἦεν
> ἠχήεις, σιγὴ δὲ μελαινομένην ἔχεν ὄρφνην·
> ἀλλὰ μάλ' οὐ Μήδειαν ἐπὶ γλυκερὸς λάβεν ὕπνος.
> πολλὰ γὰρ Αἰσονίδαο πόθῳ μελεδήματ' ἔγειρεν
> δειδυῖαν ταύρων κρατερὸν μένος, οἷσιν ἔμελλεν
> φθεῖσθαι ἀεικελίῃ μοίρῃ κατὰ νειὸν Ἄρηος.
> πυκνὰ δέ οἱ κραδίη στηθέων ἔντοσθεν ἔθυιεν,
> ἠελίου ὥς τίς τε δόμοις ἐνιπάλλεται αἴγλη,
> ὕδατος ἐξανιοῦσα τὸ δὴ νέον ἠὲ λέβητι
> ἠέ που ἐν γαυλῷ[3] κέχυται, ἡ δ' ἔνθα καὶ ἔνθα
> ὠκείῃ στροφάλιγγι τινάσσεται ἀίσσουσα—
> ὣς δὲ καὶ ἐν στήθεσσι κέαρ ἐλελίζετο κούρης.

(3.744–60)

Then night spread darkness over the earth; at sea, sailors looked from their ships to the Bear or the stars of Orion; now the wayfarer and the gatekeeper longed for sleep; and deep sleep enveloped the mother whose children were dead; not a dog barked in the city, there was no sound of voices; only silence and the deepening night. But to Medea sweet sleep did not come, for, since she was in love with Jason, many anxious thoughts kept her awake. She dreaded the bulls, beneath whose brutal fury he must die shamefully in the field of Ares. Thick and fast throbbed the heart in her breast—as, inside a house, a sunbeam dances when reflected by water that has just been poured into a basin or a pail; agitated by the swirling water, it darts about everywhere: so did the girl's heart tremble in her breast.

Virgil had already imitated this passage, omitting the simile, in Book 4.[4] Dido, emotionally exhausted but unable to sleep, experiences a sudden resurgence of passionate anger.

Nox erat et placidum carpebant fessa soporem
corpora per terras, siluaeque et saeua quierant
aequora, cum medio uoluuntur sidera lapsu,
cum tacet omnis ager, pecudes pictaeque uolucres,
quaeque lacus late liquidos quaeque aspera dumis
rura tenent, somno positae sub nocte silenti.
at non infelix animi Phoenissa, neque umquam
soluitur in somnos oculisue aut pectore noctem
accipit: ingeminant curae rursusque resurgens
saeuit amor magnoque irarum fluctuat aestu.

(4.522–32)

It was night, and all the world over, weary creatures enjoyed peaceful slumber; the woods and the wild seas were quiet; now the stars glide in mid-course, now all the fields are still, and the cattle and the various birds, which haunt clear pools and rough shrubby pastures far and wide, were sleeping beneath the silent night. But not Phoenicia's unhappy daughter; never does she relax or draw the night into her eyes or breast: her pain redoubles, her wild passion comes surging back, and she is tossed on a great sea of anger.

Whether Virgil has succeeded in adapting Apollonius' exquisitely homely—and quintessentially Hellenistic—simile to his troubled hero ("Laomedontius heros," 18) is a question. Opinions vary, ranging from the critical to the absurdly favorable.[5] But however interesting such opinions may be (and every reader will have his own), it is more interesting, and more illuminating, to follow the imaginative process[6] by which Virgil came to employ Apollonius' simile here.

Apollonius alludes to a celebrated scene in the *Iliad*, the opening of Book 10.[7] The situation of the Greeks is desperate: they have been beaten back to their ships by Hector; the embassy to Achilles has failed; and the Trojans lie encamped in full view on the plain, waiting until dawn to renew the attack.

Ἄλλοι μὲν παρὰ νηυσὶν ἀριστῆες Παναχαιῶν
εὗδον παννύχιοι, μαλακῷ δεδμημένοι ὕπνῳ·
ἀλλ' οὐκ Ἀτρεΐδην Ἀγαμέμνονα, ποιμένα λαῶν,
ὕπνος ἔχε γλυκερὸς πολλὰ φρεσὶν ὁρμαίνοντα.
ὡς δ' ὅτ' ἂν ἀστράπτῃ πόσις Ἥρης ἠϋκόμοιο,
τεύχων ἢ πολὺν ὄμβρον ἀθέσφατον ἠὲ χάλαζαν
ἢ νιφετόν, ὅτε πέρ τε χιὼν ἐπάλυνεν ἀρούρας,
ἠέ ποθι πτολέμοιο μέγα στόμα πευκεδανοῖο,
ὣς πυκίν' ἐν στήθεσσιν ἀναστενάχιζ' Ἀγαμέμνων
νειόθεν ἐκ κραδίης, τρομέοντο δέ οἱ φρένες ἐντός.
ἤτοι ὅτ' ἐς πεδίον τὸ Τρωϊκὸν ἀθρήσειε,
θαύμαζεν πυρὰ πολλά, τὰ καίετο Ἰλιόθι πρό.

(10.1–12)

The other princes of the Achaeans lay beside their ships all night long, overcome with soft sleep; but to Atreus' son Agamemnon, shepherd of the people, sweet sleep did not come, so many things he was debating in his mind. As when the lord of fair-haired Hera flashes lightning and causes a vast storm of rain or hail, or a blizzard that strews the plowlands with snow—or a great and cruel battle:[8] so thick and fast, from the bottom of his heart, rose Agamemnon's groans, and his spirit trembled within him. Whenever he looked out upon the Trojan plain, he marveled at the watch fires, so many of them, burning before Ilium.

Apollonius sentimentalizes Homer, after the Hellenistic fashion, as Virgil recognized; for instead of adapting Homer's simile here, or constructing another, he adapts the simile of Apollonius—and thus recalls, while imitating Apollonius, the passage in Homer to which Apollonius alludes.

Locating a poet's sources is not, however, equivalent to criticism. Such research cannot, that is to say, explain—insofar as the mystery can be explained—why poetry is good or bad (it is possible to imitate a great poet assiduously, and yet be Silius). But given the character

of ancient poetry, of Latin poetry especially, and our relative igno-
rance, such research is essential, a necessary condition of criticism;
for the poet expected in his reader a literary culture not unlike his
own, and without it, or an approximation of it, we may miss some
part of what he intended, or even fail to understand him.

Deeply troubled by the prospect of war, Aeneas lies down by the
riverbank (the night is chill) and at last falls asleep. As he lies sleeping, there appears, rising among his own poplars, the river-god, old
Tiberinus, to assure him that he has reached the promised land.

> "O sate gente deum, Troianam ex hostibus urbem
> qui reuehis nobis aeternaque Pergama seruas,
> exspectate solo Laurenti aruisque Latinis . . ."
>
> (8.36–38)
>
> "O sprung of the race of the gods, who bring Troy back to us
> from her enemies and save Pergamum forever, O long-awaited
> on Laurentian soil and in the fields of Latium . . ."

And so that Aeneas will not suppose his vision merely a dream, he
will find, on awakening, a prodigious confirmation: a huge white
sow, lying beneath the holm-oaks by the riverbank, with a newborn
litter of thirty, as white as herself[9]—a sign that when thirty years
have elapsed Ascanius will found the famed white city, Alba. Meanwhile, Aeneas is to seek help from the Arcadians and their king,
Evander, who now occupy Pallanteum and wage war constantly with
the Latins. The river-god engages to conduct Aeneas upstream to
Pallanteum—to conduct the father of the Roman people to the future
site of Rome by the historic river—and, in conclusion, identifies himself: I am, he declares, "sky-blue Tiber, the river dearest to heaven,"
"caeruleus Thybris, caelo gratissimus amnis" (64).[10]

Aeneas awakens, turns toward the rising sun, takes water from the
river in his cupped hands, and prays, calling now on the nymphs
and the river-god by name. (Earlier, a stranger come into a strange
land, he had prayed "to the genius of the place, to Earth, eldest of
the gods, and to the nymphs and the river as yet unknown," "gen-
iumque loci primamque deorum / Tellurem nymphasque et adhuc ig-
nota precatur / flumina" [7.136–38].[11])

> "Nymphae, Laurentes Nymphae, genus amnibus unde est,
> tuque, o Thybri tuo genitor cum flumine sancto,
> accipite Aenean et tandem arcete periclis."
>
> (8.71–73)

"Nymphs, Laurentian Nymphs, whence rivers have their birth, and thou, O father Tiber, with thy sacred stream, receive Aeneas and keep him at last from peril."

"Nymphae, Laurentes Nymphae": a Latin place-name is incorporated in an elegant Hellenistic phrase. The reader will hardly fail to hear a distant echo of Pasiphae's lovely, sad speech, "claudite, Nymphae, / Dictaeae Nymphae" (*E.* 6.55–66), in Virgil's miniature of an epyllion.[12] Here, as in line 43, the modern is gracefully joined with the antique: "tuque, o Thybri tuo genitor cum flumine sancto" being an imitation of Ennius *Ann.* 54 V.[2]: "teque, pater Tiberine, tuo cum flumine sancto."[13] And the rest of Aeneas' prayer bears a strong resemblance to that of Horatius at the bridge asking father Tiber to receive him propitiously: "Tiberine pater, te sancte precor, haec arma et hunc militem propitio flumine accipias" (Livy 2.10.11).[14]

Such reminiscences of Ennius, of his archaic language, impart an appropriate gravity to the scene; the Trojans are new arrivals, present to imagination as we read, yet belonging (we are reminded) to a remote and idealized past.

There is another poet involved here too: Homer.[15] The Phaeacians deposit Odysseus, fast asleep, on the beach of Phorcys' harbor and sail away. On awakening, he fails to recognize his own country, after so many years, and thinks he has been marooned. Athena, disguised as a comely young shepherd, soon appears, disperses the mist she has poured around him, and eventually succeeds in convincing him that he has reached Ithaca. He sees Ithaca and rejoices, the long-suffering Odysseus; he kisses the earth, then raises his hands in prayer to the nymphs.

"νύμφαι, νηϊάδες, κοῦραι Διός, οὔ ποτ' ἐγώ γε
ὄψεσθ' ὔμμ' ἐφάμην . . ."
        (*Od.* 13.356–57)

"Nymphs, naiads, daughters of Zeus, never had I thought to see you again . . ."

A more extensive passage in the *Odyssey*, Telemachus' visit to Pylos, enabled Virgil to imagine Aeneas' arrival at Pallanteum.[16]

Although Pallanteum, primitive Rome, is romanticized to some extent, it is not "la pastorale Arcadia," the ideal, harmonious landscape Virgil discovered as a young poet (though for that matter pastoral Arcadia is mainly the invention of Sannazaro and Sir Philip Sidney); it is, rather, the harsh Arcadia of reality: a small, isolated commu-

nity—a few scattered houses with a wall and a citadel, as the Trojans
first see it from the river—exposed on every side to its enemies.

The Trojans arrive at high noon.[17] That day, as it happened, Evander was sacrificing to Hercules and the other gods[18] in a grove outside
the town. With him were his son, Pallas, all the young princes, and
the frugal senators, offering incense, while warm blood smoked on
the altar—a tranquil scene of sylvan piety. Suddenly, terrified, they
see the tall ships gliding through the dark wood, the feathered oar-
blades making no noise. They rise from the tables, but Pallas—the
reckless young prince[19]—forbids them to interrupt the meal; seizing
a spear, he rushes to meet the intruders[20] and calls out to them from
the riverbank.

> "iuuenes, quae causa subegit
> ignotas temptare uias? quo tenditis?" inquit.
> "qui genus? unde domo? pacemne huc fertis an arma?"
>
> (8.112–14)

"Warriors, what has driven you to explore unknown ways?
Where are you bound? Who are your people? Where is your
home? Do you bring us peace or war?"

In contrast with this excited, brusque questioning is Aeneas' grave
and measured response.

> tum pater Aeneas puppi sic fatur ab alta
> paciferaeque manu ramum praetendit oliuae:
> "Troiugenas ac tela uides inimica Latinis,
> quos illi bello profugos egere superbo.
> Euandrum petimus."
>
> (8.115–19)

Then father Aeneas speaks from the high stern, holding in his
outstretched hand the pacific olive branch: "You see Trojan
men-at-arms hostile to the Latins, exiles whom they have har-
ried with war and outrage. We seek Evander."

Such direct questioning is Homeric; but in Homer it is ordinarily
courteous and deferential, and takes place only after the stranger has
been welcomed and finished eating. Thus Telemachus notices Mentes
(Athena in disguise) standing in the doorway of the courtyard; angry
and embarrassed that a stranger should be kept waiting, he grasps
her hand and takes her spear.

"Χαῖρε, ξεῖνε, παρ᾽ ἄμμι φιλήσεαι· αὐτὰρ ἔπειτα
δείπνου πασσάμενος μυθήσεαι ὅττεό σε χρή."

(*Od.* 1.123–24)

"Greetings, stranger, you shall be welcome here; and when you
have eaten, you can tell us what you want."

He leads her into the great hall and places her spear on the rack.

αὐτὴν δ᾽ ἐς θρόνον εἷσεν ἄγων, ὑπὸ λῖτα πετάσσας,
καλὸν δαιδάλεον· ὑπὸ δὲ θρῆνυς ποσὶν ἦεν.

(1.130–31)

Spreading a coverlet, he seated her on a richly carved chair,
with a footstool beneath.

Only when they have shared a private meal does Telemachus question her.

"τίς πόθεν εἰς ἀνδρῶν; πόθι τοι πόλις ἠδὲ τοκῆες;
ὁπποίης τ᾽ ἐπὶ νηὸς ἀφίκεο· πῶς δέ σε ναῦται
ἤγαγον εἰς Ἰθάκην; τίνες ἔμμεναι εὐχετόωντο;"

(1.170–72)

"Who are you and where are you from? Where is your city
and who are your parents? On what kind of ship did you come?
How did the sailors bring you to Ithaca? Who did they say they
were?"

When Telemachus and Mentor (again, Athena in disguise) arrive
at Pylos, they find the populace sacrificing to Poseidon on the seashore, for they have no fear of an attack. Everyone comes to greet
them, Nestor's son Peisistratus in the lead.

ἀμφοτέρων ἕλε χεῖρα καὶ ἵδρυσεν παρὰ δαιτὶ
κώεσιν ἐν μαλακοῖσιν, ἐπὶ ψαμάθοις ἁλίῃσι,
πάρ τε κασιγνήτῳ Θρασυμήδεϊ καὶ πατέρι ᾧ·
δῶκε δ᾽ ἄρα σπλάγχνων μοίρας . . .

(3.37–40)

He grasped their hands and seated them on soft lambskins on
the sand by his brother Thrasymedes and his father;[21] then gave
them pieces of the sacrificial entrails . . .

Now is the time, says Nestor, since they have enjoyed a meal, to ask
our guests who they are.

"ὦ ξεῖνοι, τίνες ἐστέ; πόθεν πλεῖθ᾽ ὑγρὰ κέλευθα;
ἤ τι κατὰ πρῆξιν ἢ μαψιδίως ἀλάλησθε
οἷά τε ληϊστῆρες ὑπεὶρ ἅλα, τοί τ᾽ ἀλόωνται
ψυχὰς παρθέμενοι, κακὸν ἀλλοδαποῖσι φέροντες;"

(3.71–74)

"Who are you, strangers? Where are you sailing from on the highways of the deep? Are you on some business? or wandering aimlessly over the sea like pirates, who risk their lives bringing evil to others?"

There is such a moment in Book 8. Evander orders the food and drink replaced on the tables, then himself seats the Trojans on a grassy bank.

haec ubi dicta, dapes iubet et sublata reponi
pocula gramineoque uiros locat ipse sedili,
praecipuumque toro et uillosi pelle leonis
accipit Aenean solioque inuitat acerno.
tum lecti iuuenes certatim araeque sacerdos
uiscera tosta ferunt taurorum, onerantque canistris
dona laboratae Cereris, Bacchumque ministrant.[22]
uescitur Aeneas simul et Troiana iuuentus
perpetui tergo bouis et lustralibus extis.

(8.175–83)

Aeneas he welcomes especially, bidding him occupy a throne of maple wood cushioned with a lion's shaggy pelt. Then, vying with one another, chosen young men and the priest of the altar bring portions of roasted beef, pile the baskets high with bread, and serve the wine. Aeneas and his Trojan warriors feast on a whole chine of beef and the sacrificial entrails.

At this point, in a secure, well-ordered society like that of Pylos, Aeneas would be asked to identify himself and state his business. But he has already done so, of necessity, and in a ceremonious exchange with Evander claimed a distant kinship.[23] Even in the Arcadian wilderness Homeric etiquette prevails.

Instead of the conversation that would ordinarily follow, Evander, anticipating his guest's curiosity, tells the story of Hercules and Cacus, a violent local incident of which he had been an eyewitness. He begins with an emphatic apology; we have not, he insists, yielded to superstition, nor have we forgotten the old gods.

"saeuis, hospes Troiane, periclis
seruati facimus meritosque nouamus honores."

(8.188–89)

"Delivered from a cruel danger, Trojan guest, we perform anew
from year to year these due rites."

The story as told by Livy (1.7.3–13), whose version was certainly
known to Virgil,[24] is essentially a simple one. When Hercules was
returning from Spain with the cattle of Geryon, he stopped overnight
by the Tiber, in a peaceful, grassy place, to refresh the cattle and
himself. And there, full of food and sodden with wine, he fell asleep.
A local shepherd named Cacus, a bold, violent fellow,[25] was much
taken with the beauty of the cattle and determined to steal some of
them. And so that Hercules would not be able to follow the tracks
to his cave, he turned the bulls around, first choosing out the hand-
somest, and dragged them in by their tails. On rising at first light
and noticing that some of the cattle were gone, Hercules proceeded
to the nearest cave, to see if the tracks led there; but the tracks all
seemed to lead out of the cave. Perplexed and troubled, he began to
drive the herd away from this unfriendly place. Some of the cows,
missing the bulls, were lowing, and there came an answering bellow
from the cave. As Hercules hurried toward the cave, Cacus tried to
stop him by force, calling on the other shepherds for help; but Hercules struck him with his club and he died. At that time Evander,
an exile from the Peloponnesus, was ruling there, not so much by
compulsion as by personal ascendancy, being revered by the ignorant
country people for his knowledge of writing, and even more because
of his mother, the prophetic nymph Carmenta, whom they believed
divine. Evander, roused by the turbulence of the shepherds, who were
angrily accusing the stranger of murder, listened to their story; then
perceiving in the stranger's appearance and demeanor something
more than human, asked him who he was; on hearing his name, with
that of his father and country, he saluted him: "Jove-born Hercules,
hail!"[26] My mother, he continued, prophesied that you would be
added to the number of the gods, and that an altar, the greatest in
all the world, would be dedicated to you here. Thereupon an altar,
the Ara Maxima, was built and dedicated, and a cult established, to
commemorate the event. This, Livy remarks in conclusion, was the
one foreign cult adopted by Romulus, who already favored immor-
tality won by valor, to which his own destiny was leading him, "haec
tum sacra Romulus una ex omnibus peregrina suscepit, iam tum im-

mortalitatis uirtute partae, ad quam eum sua fata ducebant, fautor"
(1.7.15).²⁷

The Cacus story became popular in the reign of Augustus.²⁸ But
why should Virgil tell such a story? And why at such length, and in
such vivid detail?

It has long been recognized that Virgil turns Cacus into a monster,
half man, half brute ("semihominis," 194; "semiferi," 267), an em-
bodiment of violence and disorder; more recently, that Mezentius has
also become, like Cacus, a grisly monster of violence.²⁹ In Livy 1.2.3
Mezentius is simply a flourishing Etruscan king, secure in his realm
of Caere yet suspicious of the Trojans and their increasing power,
who accepts Turnus and the Rutulians as allies: "inde Turnus Ru-
tulique diffisi rebus ad florentes opes Etruscorum Mezentiumque
regem eorum confugiunt, qui Caere, opulento³⁰ tum oppido, imperi-
tans."

Here is Evander's description of Cacus:

> "semperque recenti
> *caede* tepebat humus, foribusque adfixa *superbis*
> ora uirum tristi pendebant pallida *tabo.*
> huic monstro Volcanus erat pater . . .
>
> . . . .
>
> at furis Caci mens *effera* . . ."
>
> (8.195–98, 205)

"The ground was always warm with fresh butchery; men's
heads were fastened to the haughty doorposts and hung there
with faces horribly pale and putrefying. To this monster Vulcan
was father . . . But the brutal mind of the thief Cacus . . ."

And here is his description of Mezentius:

> "hanc multos florentem annos rex deinde *superbo*
> imperio et saeuis tenuit Mezentius armis.
> quid memorem infandas *caedes*, quid facta tyranni
> *effera?* . . .
> mortua quin etiam iungebat corpora uiuis
> componens manibusque manus atque oribus ora,
> tormenti genus, et sanie *taboque* fluentis
> complexu in misero longa sic morte necabat."
>
> (8.481–88)

"This city flourished for many years, until Mezentius became
king; his rule was haughty and cruel. Why tell of the tyrant's

dreadful butcheries? of his brutality? . . . He would even bind
the living to the dead, adjusting hand to hand and face to face
(a kind of torture!), and thus, in a hideous embrace, dripping
with putrefied gore, slowly put them to death."

Nowhere else in the *Aeneid*, nowhere else in Virgil, are these words—
caede, superbis, tabo, effera : *superbo, caedes, effera, tabo*—found
together. Virgil obviously intended to create an impression of un-
mitigated savagery and horror;[31] less obviously, to suggest or imply
a relation between Hercules and Aeneas:[32] as Hercules kills the monster Cacus, Aeneas kills the monster (though strangely redeemed in
his death) Mezentius.[33] But such suggestions are involved in the poetry, and cannot be abstracted—not even where, as on Aeneas'
shield, they are expressed more distinctly—and proposed as explicit
equations, such as Cacus = Turnus,[34] without violence to the poem.

Evander finishes his story and then invites the young men to join
him in offering a libation to Hercules.[35] It is now evening; a male
choir sings a hymn to Hercules, and everyone returns to the town.
The aged king, walking slowly, keeps Aeneas by him, to alleviate his
fatigue with conversation. He tells the newcomer, in response to his
eager questions, of the legendary past of Latium, of woods inhabited
by fauns and nymphs; of men sprung from the trunks of trees, a race
without laws, without culture; of the coming of Saturn, an exile from
Olympus, and that golden springtime so soon faded and vanished;
of the truculent giant Thybris who gave his name to the river; and
of himself, exiled from his country, a fate-driven wanderer; then,
moving slowly along, he points out the principal monuments of Pallanteum.

> talibus inter se dictis ad tecta subibant
> pauperis Euandri, passimque armenta uidebant
> Romanoque foro et lautis[36] mugire Carinis.
> ut uentum ad sedes, "haec" inquit "limina victor
> Alcides subiit, haec illum regia cepit.
> aude, hospes, contemnere opes et te quoque dignum
> finge deo, rebusque ueni non asper egenis."
> dixit, et angusti subter fastigia tecti
> ingentem Aenean duxit stratisque locauit
> effultum foliis et pelle Libystidis ursae:
> nox ruit et fuscis tellurem amplectitur alis.

(8.359–69)

Conversing thus they approached Evander's modest house, and here and there saw cattle, lowing, in the Roman Forum and the luxurious Carinae district. On arriving, Evander said: "The victor Hercules stooped to enter this door, this palace had room for him. Dare, my guest, to despise riches, make yourself worthy of a god, and visit our poverty with compassion." With these words, he led great Aeneas beneath the sloping roof of his small house and showed him to a bed of heaped-up leaves covered with the skin of a Libyan bear. Night rushes on and folds the earth in dark wings.

The hour for leave-taking has now come. Aeneas revisits his ships, chooses his best men, and sends the others downstream with messages for Ascanius. The Arcadian horsemen are ready, Pallas commanding. Rumor flies about the little town. Mothers, in fear, redouble their prayers, and now the spectre of war looms larger. Evander clings to the hand of his departing son, weeping uncontrollably, and speaks.[37]

"o mihi praeteritos referat si Iuppiter annos,
qualis eram cum primam aciem Praeneste sub ipsa
straui scutorumque incendi uictor aceruos
et regem hac Erulum dextra sub Tartara misi,
nascenti cui tris animas Feronia mater—
horrendum dictu—dederat, terna arma mouenda
(ter leto sternendus erat, cui tunc tamen omnis
abstulit haec animas dextra et totidem exuit armis):
non ego nunc dulci amplexu diuellerer usquam,
nate, tuo, neque finitimo Mezentius umquam
huic capiti insultans tot ferro saeua dedisset
funera, tam multis uiduasset ciuibus urbem.
at uos, o superi, et diuum tu maxime rector
Iuppiter, Arcadii, quaeso, miserescite regis
et patrias audite preces. si numina uestra
incolumem Pallanta mihi, si fata reseruant,
si uisurus eum uiuo et uenturus in unum,
uitam oro, patior quemuis durare laborem.
sin aliquem infandum casum, Fortuna, minaris,
nunc, nunc o liceat crudelem abrumpere uitam,
dum curae ambiguae, dum spes incerta futuri,
dum te, care puer, mea sola et sera uoluptas,
complexu teneo, grauior neu nuntius auris

uulneret." haec genitor digressu dicta supremo
fundebat; famuli conlapsum in tecta ferebant.

    (8.560–84)

"If only Jupiter would give me back my lost years, make me
the man I was when beneath Praeneste's walls I struck down
the enemy's front rank and burned their piled-up shields in
triumph, and with this right hand dispatched King Erulus to
Hades, to whom his mother, Feronia, had given at birth three
lives—monstrous to relate—three sets of armor (three times I
had to strike him down, and yet this right hand took away all
his lives and stripped him of all his armor): I would never be
torn from your sweet embrace, my son, nor would Mezentius
ever have heaped insults on his neighbor's head and caused so
many cruel deaths, of so many men widowed this city. But O
you gods above, and you, great ruler of the gods, Jupiter, have
pity, I beseech you, on an Arcadian king and hear a father's
prayer. If your will, if fate keeps Pallas safe for me, if I live to
see him again, to meet him again, then I wish for life, can
endure any hardship. But if Fortune threatens the unspeakable,
then now, O now let me break off this painful life, while fears
are vague and hope uncertain of the future, while I embrace
and hold you, my dear boy, my late and only pleasure, and let
no terrible message wound my ears." All this the father poured
forth at their final parting; he collapsed, and his servants carried
him to the house.

Evander's speech, a lament for his lost youth—and for all lost
youth—begins appropriately with a twofold reminiscence of Nestor,
on whom the figure of Evander is modeled.

"αἲ γάρ, Ζεῦ τε πάτερ καὶ Ἀθηναίη καὶ Ἄπολλον,
ἡβῶμ᾽ ὡς ὅτ᾽ ἐπ᾽ ὠκυρόῳ Κελάδοντι μάχοντο
ἀγρόμενοι Πύλιοί τε καὶ Ἀρκάδες ἐγχεσίμωροι,
Φειᾶς πὰρ τείχεσσιν, Ἰαρδάνου ἀμφὶ ῥέεθρα."

    (*Il.* 7.132–35)[38]

"O father Zeus, Athena, Apollo, if only I were young, as I was
when the Pylians and Arcadian spearmen gathered and fought
by the swift-flowing Celadon, beneath Pheia's walls, about the
stream of Iardanus."

"εἴθ᾿ ὣς ἡβώοιμι βίη δέ μοι ἔμπεδος εἴη,
ὡς ὁπότ᾿ Ἠλείοισι καὶ ἡμῖν νεῖκος ἐτύχθη
ἀμφὶ βοηλασίη, ὅτ᾿ ἐγὼ κτάνον Ἰτυμονῆα . . ."

(*Il.* 11.670–72)[39]

"If only I were young and strong, as I was when that quarrel
came up between Elis and ourselves over cattle-raiding, when
I killed the brave Itymoneus . . ."[40]

Nestor's prolixity is artfully suggested by the structure of Evander's
necessarily shorter speech, which is divided into two approximately
equal sections: the first consisting of a single rambling—and expressive—period of twelve lines (Virgil's periods are normally of
four lines or fewer and paratactic in structure)[41] and ending with
emphasis on "funera" (571); the second, which is further divided
into two approximately equal sections, ending with final emphasis
on "uulneret."[42]

But Nestor merely regrets the lost prowess of his youth; his speech
has none of the emotional intensity of Evander's, represented phys-
ically by his collapse at the end.[43] This high pathos is Hellenistic,
and here mainly owing to Apollonius—or rather, to Virgil's reading
and assimilation of Apollonius. As Jason prepares to leave his parents
(1.261–306), his mother throws her arms about him, clinging to him,
weeping uncontrollably, like a motherless girl all alone; she wishes
that she were dead and buried, and laments that she, once so admired
among the women of Achaea, will be left behind like a bondwoman
in her empty halls, longing for him. Jason tries to comfort her, but
can say nothing to his father, an old and stricken man, desolate in
his grief. The old are left behind to grieve, while the young heroes
go forth in glory[44]—Jason like Apollo, Pallas like the Morning Star,
whom Venus loves above all other stars, "quem Venus ante alios
astrorum diligit ignis" (590).[45]

Aeneas and the Arcadian cavalry, resplendent in bronze, issue from
the gates of Pallanteum; on the walls anxious mothers stand gazing
after them. They make their way through the thickets; then, with a
shout, form a column and gallop over the dusty plain, "quadripe-
dante putrem sonitu quatit ungula campum" (8.596). Near the cold
stream of Caere there is an immense grove, "est ingens gelidum lucus
prope Caeritis amnem" (597)—Virgil now slows the pace of his narrative—a grove reverenced from time immemorial, shut in on all sides
by dark wooded hills and sacred to Silvanus, god of the fields and

the fold. Not far from here were encamped Tarchon and the Etruscan force. Here Aeneas halts, to rest the horses and his weary men. (The reader may be surprised that Aeneas does not proceed directly to the Etruscan encampment, the ostensible goal of his journey and now so near. Later, in summarizing and resuming the narrative of the journey, Virgil implies that he did: "namque ut ab Euandro castris ingressus Etruscis / regem adit et regi memorat nomenque genusque / quidue petat" [10.148–50]. But had Aeneas done so now, he would have been obliged to approach Tarchon at once and state his business; and that was far from Virgil's immediate purpose.)

In the grove of Silvanus, in the timeless pastoral world, Aeneas is to have, as he had in the world of the dead, a vision of Roman history, to which he will respond, not, as there, with profound sadness, but with mute joy, even though he can understand only dimly what he sees.

Venus descends gleaming through the clouds and finds Aeneas, pensive and alone, in a silent valley by the cold stream. "Here it is," she says, revealing herself and Vulcan's armor, "completed as promised by my husband's art." She urges Aeneas now to challenge Turnus and the Rutulians to battle, then embraces him and sets down before him the armor, glittering, under an oak tree, "arma sub aduersa posuit radiantia quercu" (616).[46] Characteristically, Aeneas remains silent, rejoicing in his mother's gift, in the beauty of the armor. Again and again he looks at it, but cannot be satisfied with looking.[47] Marveling, he takes in his hands the horrific plumed helmet spewing flame,[48] the fateful sword, the huge corselet of bronze, blood-red— "like a dark cloud when it catches fire from the sun's rays and shines far off," "qualis cum caerula nubes / solis inardescit radiis longeque refulget" (622–23)[49]—then the polished greaves of electrum and molten gold, the spear, and (but who could describe it?) the great figured shield.

The reader is, by now, well aware of the reference of this scene: to the Shield of Achilles in Books 18 and 19 of the *Iliad*. At the beginning of Book 19, in the clear morning light, Thetis brings the armor of Hephaestus to Achilles. She finds him lying on the ground, wailing shrilly, with the dead Patroclus in his arms, and his Myrmidons grieving around him. (It would be difficult to imagine Aeneas receiving his armor in similar circumstances—surrounded by Arcadians, in broad daylight.) She clasps him by the hand and speaks briefly—"My child, although we grieve for him, we must let this man lie here"—then sets down before him the elaborate, clashing armor.

The Myrmidons tremble, too frightened even to look; but Achilles takes the armor in his hands—the great figured shield, the corselet brighter than fire, the strong, close-fitting helmet, intricate and beautiful work, with its golden crest, the greaves of pliant tin—and inspects each piece with savage joy. Yet he pays no attention to the scenes on the shield; they mean nothing to him.[50] This armor, he says to his mother (for, unlike Aeneas, Achilles is never silent with emotion)—this is such as might be expected of the gods; no mortal man could have made it. His acknowledgment is almost perfunctory, for he is eager to arm himself and return to the battle; yet he fears that flies will get into Patroclus' wounds and cause his flesh to rot. The concerns of Achilles—for vengeance, for his dead friend—are entirely personal.

The scenes on the shield are described, before Achilles sees it, in 18.483–608. Homer presents not the completed shield but Hephaestus at work on the shield, enlivening its blank surface with scene after vivid scene.[51] Since the shield is a work of the imagination, a poet's artifact, the relative position of the scenes on it is immaterial.[52] Only the River of Ocean is located, flowing around the rim and encompassing all the scenes, as it encompassed, for the ancients, all human life.

> On it he fashioned the earth and the sky and the sea, the untiring sun and the full moon, and all the constellations the sky holds. . . .
> On it he made two cities of mortal men, beautiful cities. In the first there were marriages and banquets; they were conducting the brides from their chambers through the streets with blazing torches; loud and clear rose the epithalamium. And young men were whirling in the dance. . . . The people were assembled in the marketplace, a quarrel was going on; two men were arguing over the blood-price of a man dead. . . . Around the other city lay two armies, their armor gleaming. They were undecided whether to sack it or to divide all the wealth of the choice city and share it with the inhabitants. But they were not yet ready to yield, and armed in secret for an ambush. Their wives and little children stood watch on the wall with the old men; they sallied forth. And leading them were Ares and Pallas Athena, both of gold, wearing garments of gold, beautiful and tall in their armor, being gods, and conspicuous from afar; the people were smaller. When they reached the place that seemed

good for an ambush, by the river where all the herds came to drink, they sat down and waited, clad in glittering bronze. At a distance lay two scouts, waiting until they should see the sheep and the shambling cattle. Presently they came into view, and with them two herdsmen playing on their panpipes. . . .

On it he placed a broad rich field, a soft fallow, triple-plowed. Many plowmen were driving their teams to and fro in it, wheeling them about. As often as they reached the boundary of the field after turning, a man would approach and put a bowl of honey-sweet wine in their hands, and they would turn again to the furrows, eager to reach the boundary of the deep fallow. And the field grew black behind them, looking as if it had been plowed, even though it was of gold. This was the marvel of the work.

On it he placed the demesne of a king, where day-laborers were reaping with sharp sickles. One after another the handfuls of grain fell to earth along the swath, while the sheaf-binders were tying others with twisted straw. . . .

On it he placed a beautiful golden vineyard, heavily laden with clusters. The vines were supported throughout on silver poles, the grapes were black. Around it he ran a ditch of dark-blue enamel, and around that a fence of tin; there was only one path leading to the vineyard, along which the carriers passed when gathering the vintage. Lighthearted girls and boys carried the honey-sweet fruit in wicker baskets; in their midst a youth played charmingly on the ringing strings of a lyre, accompanying himself as he sang the beautiful Linus-song in a fine clear voice; while the others, stamping and leaping together in the dance, followed with song and shout.

On it he placed a herd of straight-horned cattle. The cows were fashioned of gold and tin, and hurried lowing from the barnyard to pasture by the swift river, by the quivering reeds. Four golden herdsmen strode beside them, and nine nimble dogs followed after. But among the cows in front two terrible lions had caught hold of a bull, who was bellowing mightily as they dragged him away. . . .

On it he devised—the glorious lame god—a dancing-place like that which Daedalus made in wide Cnossus once for Ariadne of the fair hair. There young men and highly prized maidens were dancing, with hands on one another's wrists. The maidens wore robes of fine linen, the young men well-woven tunics that glistened faintly with olive oil. . . .

On it he placed, around the rim of the well-made shield, the
great and powerful River of Ocean.

The Shield of Aeneas is modeled on the Shield of Achilles; but
the relation is not so simple or immediate as commentators imply.
Other poets intervene, Hellenistic poets, with certain refinements
of technique.[53]

On the Shield of Achilles there are eight scenes, varying greatly in
length: 7 lines, 51,[54] 9, 11, 12, 14, 3, 16; Homer was not concerned
with symmetry. But his Hellenistic imitators were—an unobtrusive
symmetry: scenes tend to be shorter and equal, or approximately
equal, in length. Thus on Jason's mantle in Apollonius 1.730–67 (the
hero arms himself, as it were, for the battle of love)[55] there are seven
scenes: 5, 7, 5, 5, 7, 4, 5. Similarly, on the goatherd's drinking-cup
in Theocritus 1.32–54 there are three scenes: 7, 6, 10; and three on
Europa's flower-basket in Moschus *Europa* 44–61: 6, 5, 7. On the
Shield of Aeneas there are seven scenes of early Roman history (630–
70): 5, 7, 4, 6, 11 (the siege of the Capitol, somewhat longer for
emphasis, as will be explained below), 4 –, 4 + —or 41 lines in all,
balanced by a single scene of 39 lines (675–713), the Battle of Actium.[56] The scenes which Aeneas sees in the portico of Juno's temple
may also be compared (1.466–93): 3, 5, 5, 4, 5, 2, 4.[57]

In the *Scutum*, scenes are regularly introduced, as in Homer, [58] but
with a form of the verb "to be," with no verb, or with a verb in the
passive;[59] so also in Apollonius and Moschus, with some variation.[60]
The shield of Heracles is identified as the work and gift of Hephaestus
(123, 244, 297, 313), Jason's mantle as the work and gift of Athena
(1.721–22, 768)—like Europa's flower-basket, beautiful things for
the reader to admire.[61] You would be dazzled, Apollonius tells his
reader, and gaze at the mantle expecting to hear the ram speak to
Phrixus (1.725–26, 765–67).

Virgil avoids the regularity of the old epic style, and for this too
he had Hellenistic precedent, in Theocritus[62] and possibly others.[63]
But at the same time, to recall his Homeric prototype, he intersperses
a few active verbs with Vulcan as subject, such as "fecerat ignipotens" (628), "the Lord of Fire had fashioned."[64]

illic res Italas Romanorumque triumphos
haud uatum ignarus uenturique inscius aeui
fecerat ignipotens, illic genus omne futurae
stirpis ab Ascanio pugnataque in ordine bella.

(8.626–29)

There the Lord of Fire had fashioned—no stranger he to prophecy nor ignorant of time to come—the tale of Italy and Roman triumphs, there the whole line of kings from Ascanius onward and the long succession of hard-fought wars.

Yet only a few scenes are described:[65] the she-wolf suckling the twins in Mars's green cavern; the rape of the Sabine women, war between Romulus' people and old Tatius, the peace treaty; Mettus (false Alban!) torn asunder by chariots driven suddenly apart, and Tullus dragging the torn flesh through the woodland—"the brambles were sprinkled and dripping with a bloody dew";[66] Porsenna besieging the city—"you could see him looking angry and threatening"[67]—with Horatius at the bridge and Cloelia swimming to freedom; the siege of the Capitol by the Gauls—"under cover of darkness, favored by dense night, they had gained the summit; their hair golden, their clothing golden; they gleam in striped cloaks, their milk-white necks are entwined with gold"—in 390 B.C.; exultant Salii dancing, naked Luperci, the shields that fell from heaven, chaste matrons making their solemn progress through the city in cushioned carriages; Catiline cowering in Hades, Cato legislating in Elysium; and, the grand finale of Roman history, the Battle of Actium—"you could see . . . the water a blaze of gold"—and the triple triumph of Augustus.

Of many scenes possible, as may be supposed, these few are described; scenes noticed by Aeneas as he inspects the shield[68]—as in 1.456–93, when, confronted with a series of murals depicting the Trojan War ("Iliacas ex ordine pugnas," 456), he noticed only a few scenes which engaged him emotionally.[69] Here the fiction is necessarily less perfect: since Aeneas is unable to comprehend the full significance of what he sees, all he can feel, finally, is a vague sense of wonder and joy, "miratur rerumque ignarus imagine gaudet" (730).

The fiction of Aeneas as spectator, bewilderedly studying the various scenes on the shield, allows Virgil to present, subtly and without embarrassment, the Augustan conception of Roman history. Attention is concentrated almost equally on early Rome, that era of pristine virtue extending from the infancy of Romulus to the sack of the city by the Gauls, the first great crisis of the Republic;[70] and on the Battle of Actium, the second great crisis, the culmination, in the view of Virgil and Livy,[71] of Roman history. Virgil wishes to associate Augustus with Romulus, as he does in 6.777–95, and the year 31 with the year 390, when the very identity of the *nomen Romanum* was endangered by the Gauls, as it was again, according to Augustan propaganda, in 31 by Cleopatra and the besotted Antony.[72] Aeneas simply overlooks the period from 390 to 31—an extensive inadvertence for which Virgil has been blamed[73]—save for one exemplary scene: Catiline and Cato, the worst and best of the old Republic, with the worst attracting more attention.

Throughout these scenes of early Roman history the figure of Romulus is kept before the reader, with an arresting patronymic,[74] and especially, in the scene of the Gallic invasion, with a reference to the *casa Romuli*, the straw-thatched hut of Romulus, preserved by the Romans ever afterward with meticulous reverence.[75]

On being appointed dictator, Camillus raised an army and defeated the Gauls. For this great service to the state, Livy says, he was saluted as Romulus, Father of the Country and Second Founder of the City, "Romulus ac parens patriae conditorque alter urbis haud uanis laudibus appellabatur" (5.49.7). Whether true or not, the tradition that Camillus was so honored would have had a contemporary reference for the first readers of Livy and Virgil; for Augustus was regarded as Father and Founder, and some of his counselors had advised him to take the name Romulus, "quasi et ipsum conditorem urbis" (Suetonius *Augustus* 7.2).[76]

Virgil further associates the Gallic invasion and the Battle of Actium by means of two phrases, "in summo" (652) and "in medio" (675), and by a careful arrangement of words denoting the color of the metalwork. While reference to the medial position ("in medio," ἐν μέσσῳ) is a feature of post-Homeric ecphrases,[77] reference to the highest position ("in summo") is unique. Virgil's purpose, it would seem, was not so much to locate the Gallic invasion on the shield's surface as to relate it to the Battle of Actium. In his use of color-words Homer is, on the whole, sparing (*Il.* 18.548, 549, 562, 563, 564, 565, 574, 577); the poet of the *Scutum* lavish. Apollonius uses color-words of Jason's mantle (1.728, 729) but not in describing the scenes on it. Virgil confines color-words to the scene of the Gallic invasion (655, 659, 661) and to the introduction of the Actium scene (672, 673, 677), thus highlighting the two.[78]

Virgil is also at pains to associate Augustus with Aeneas. As in the ecphrasis of the Trojan War Aeneas saw himself fighting in the forefront (1.488), he sees here, in the Porsenna scene, his descendants hurling themselves on the sword for freedom, "Aeneadae in ferrum pro libertate ruebant" (648).

hinc Augustus agens Italos in proelia Caesar
cum patribus populoque, Penatibus et magnis dis,
stans celsa in puppi, geminas cui tempora flammas
laeta uomunt patriumque aperitur uertice sidus.

(8.678–81)

On one side is Augustus Caesar standing on the high stern and
leading the Italians into battle, with the senate and people and
the great household gods: his joyful brows spew twin flames,
and over his head dawns his father's star.

The impressive, somewhat obscure phrase "Penatibus et magnis
dis"—all the more impressive, perhaps, for being somewhat obscure—is found only once elsewhere in the poem, in 3.12, when
Aeneas, weeping, sets sail "with his companions and son and the
great household gods," "cum sociis natoque Penatibus et magnis
dis," leaving behind the desolate shore and the plains where Troy
had been.

"Standing on the high stern"—as Aeneas stands when, catching
sight of the Trojans' beleaguered encampment, he raises his blazing
shield to signal his approach with the Etruscan fleet: "stans celsa in
puppi,[79] clipeum cum deinde sinistra / extulit ardentem" (10.261–
62).

Most remarkable, however, is Virgil's metaphorical use of *uomo*,
of which there are three instances:[80] here, of the radiant forehead of
Augustus; in 620, of the blazing helmet Aeneas receives from his
mother; and in Book 10, when he is about to land and spread havoc
among the enemy, the top of his helmet ablaze, fire streaming down
from its crest, his golden shield-boss spewing enormous flames, "ardet apex capiti cristisque a uertice flamma / funditur et uastos umbo
uomit aureus ignis" (270–71). It would be a negligent reader who
failed to recall Augustus at Actium.

Finally, marveling, ignorant of the reality yet rejoicing in the appearance, Aeneas shoulders the great shield, taking upon himself the
fame and the fate of his descendants, "miratur rerumque ignarus
imagine gaudet / attollens umero famamque et fata nepotum"[81]
(730–31).

VI

THE DEATH OF TURNUS

Troius Aeneas, pietate insignis et armis,
ad genitorem imas Erebi descendit ad
umbras.

Aeneid 6.403–4

L' "alessandrinismo" di Virgilio esiste, anche
nell' *Eneide*, ma guai a farne una chiave che
apre tutte le porte.

Sebastiano Timpanaro

Much has been made, and rightly so, of Virgil's humanity, of his
sympathy for suffering and loss. Aeneas abandons Dido, he kills Turnus—or rather, he must abandon Dido, must kill Turnus, for so the
logic of Virgil's fiction requires; still, the reader experiences a certain
disquiet, and a corresponding dissatisfaction with Aeneas. Glamor
accrues to the lost cause, and especially, as we know from our own
history, to the cause bravely, hopelessly lost.

In Book 8 Virgil presents the Battle of Actium with what may seem,
to the modern reader, excessive brilliance—and yet not without a
moment of profound compassion as the Nile, the great river personified and grieving, welcomes the vanquished to his sky-blue bosom
and sheltering stream:

> contra autem magno maerentem corpore Nilum
> pandentemque sinus et tota ueste uocantem
> caeruleum in gremium latebrosaque flumina uictos.[1]
>
> (8.711–13)

Yet Virgil would not have had the battle end otherwise.

This settled and mature awareness of suffering, of final, irretrievable loss, not excluding (the reader senses) even Rome itself, "Rome

and kingdoms that shall perish," "res Romanae perituraque regna" (G. 2.498)—such an awareness cannot, however, diminish the monumental fact: "res Romanae."² Turnus must die—and so perish all who would do such things:

"ὣς ἀπόλοιτο καὶ ἄλλος ὅτις τοιαῦτά γε ῥέζοι."
        (*Od.* 1.47)³

This line was quoted by Scipio Aemilianus when news of the death of his turbulent kinsman Tiberius Gracchus reached him during the siege of Numantia (133 B.C.).⁴ On a famous earlier occasion (146), as he watched Carthage burning with his friend and mentor Polybius at his side, Scipio had also quoted Homer; thinking of the great empires that had fallen, of Ilium once so proud, of the Assyrians, the Medes, the Persians, and of the glorious empire of the Macedonians (which Scipio himself had helped to bring down, for as a very young man he took part in the battle of Pydna), he wept and quoted two lines from Hector's farewell to Andromache:

"ἔσσεται ἦμαρ ὅτ᾽ ἄν ποτ᾽ ὀλώλῃ Ἴλιος ἱρὴ
καὶ Πρίαμος καὶ λαὸς ἐϋμμελίω Πριάμοιο."
        (*Il.* 6.448–49)

"There will come a day when sacred Ilium shall perish,
and Priam, and the people of Priam of the strong ash spear."

On being asked by Polybius what he meant, Scipio, in whose nature a mystical prescience⁵ was so strangely joined with extreme brutality,⁶ replied that he feared the same fate would one day befall his own country.⁷

We first hear of Turnus, early in Book 7, as the foremost among Lavinia's suitors, a young prince of exceptional beauty, "ante alios pulcherrimus omnis" (7.55).⁸ And we meet him in person, so to speak, later in the Book when the Fury Allecto, whom Juno has called up from the Underworld to cause mischief in Latium, visits him in the night at Ardea, "*audacis* Rutuli ad muros" (7.409). Again, at the beginning of Book 9, when Juno sends Iris, the rainbow-goddess, to tell him of Aeneas' absence, Turnus is so characterized, "Irim de caelo misit Saturnia Iuno / *audacem* ad Turnum" (9.2–3); a characterization subsequently confirmed, "at non *audaci* Turno" (9.126).

Why is Turnus introduced with so special an emphasis? The adjective *audax* is generally pejorative, denoting a bold or reckless disregard of danger, and is applied in this sense to Pallas when he for-

bids the Arcadians to interrupt their sacrificial meal and rushes off
alone to confront the armed strangers.[9] But the sleeping Turnus has
not, so far as the reader is aware, been guilty of any ill-considered
or violent action. It is the monstrous apparition of Allecto, infuriated
by his mockery, that goads him to recklessness and violence.[10]

By Cicero's time, and no doubt partly owing to Cicero, *audax* had
acquired a political connotation:[11] the *audaces* were those hostile to
the *boni*, the good, respectable citizens; those who would subvert the
established order by violence—"euersores rei publicae," as Cicero
terms them;[12] men like Catiline, Clodius, Antony, great Caesar himself. That Virgil was aware of the political connotation of *audax*—
and how could he fail to be?—is indicated by a singular fact: the
occurrence of *euersor*, a word apparently invented by Cicero,[13] in *A.*
12.545: "Priami regnorum euersor Achilles," "Achilles the subverter
of Priam's kingdom." The Sibyl had warned Aeneas that another
Achilles was waiting for him in Latium, "alius Latio iam partus
Achilles" (6.89); and Turnus, in replying to the taunts of Pandarus
before dispatching him, identifies himself with Achilles, "hic etiam
inuentum Priamo narrabis Achillem" (9.742), "You shall tell Priam
that here too you have found an Achilles."[14]

To an impartial observer, however, it might appear that the Trojan
invaders, not Turnus and his followers, were the *audaces*; that Turnus stood for the established order in Italy. Such indeed was Juno's
view, passionately urged against Venus.

"indignum est Italos Troiam circumdare flammis
nascentem et patria Turnum consistere terra,
cui Pilumnus auus, cui diua Venilia mater."

(10.74–76)

"Shameful (you say) for Italians to surround the infant Troy
with flames, for Turnus to take a stand on his native soil—
Turnus whose grandfather was Pilumnus, whose mother the
goddess Venilia."

But it is Turnus, moved by personal resentment and incited to violence by his nightmare, who first takes up arms and desecrates the
peace ("polluta pace," 7.467); Turnus who orders his captains to
march on King Latinus, to protect Italy, to thrust the foe from their
shores, "tutari Italiam, detrudere finibus hostem" (7.469); Turnus
who fills the Rutulians with reckless courage, "Rutulos animis au-
dacibus implet" (7.475). In any case, the Trojans were destined to
become Romans and inherit the future; to them the promise had

been given: empire without end, "imperium sine fine" (1.279)—and the old order, after a doomed struggle, could only yield.

Virgil recognizes the native claim, the claim of birth and place, and regrets—no one more poignantly—the passing of an older Italy.

> quin et Marruuia uenit de gente sacerdos
> fronde super galeam et felici comptus oliua
> Archippi regis missu, fortissimus Vmbro,
> uipereo generi et grauiter spirantibus hydris
> spargere qui somnos cantuque manuque solebat,
> mulcebatque iras et morsus arte leuabat.
> sed non Dardaniae medicari cuspidis ictum
> eualuit neque eum iuuere in uulnera cantus
> somniferi et Marsis quaesitae montibus herbae.
> te nemus Angitiae, uitrea te Fucinus unda,
> te liquidi fleuere lacus.
>
>   (7.750–60)

And from the Marruvian people, sent by King Archippus, there came a warrior priest,[15] brave Umbro, his helmet wreathed with fruitful olive leaves. By charm and touch he would sprinkle sleep upon serpents and noisome watersnakes; he soothed their rage and, with his skill, cured their bites. Yet he was not able to heal the blow of a Dardanian spear, nor did drowsy charms and herbs gathered on the Marsian hills avail against his wound.

> For you Angitia's grove,
> For you Fucinus with his crystal wave,
> The bright lakes wept for you.

We first encounter Turnus on the battlefield early in Book 9, mounted on a Thracian piebald and wearing a golden helmet with a red plume;[16] a brilliant figure as, well in advance of his main force, he reconnoiters the Trojans' walled encampment. He hurls a javelin into the air as a prelude and challenge to battle; then, since the Trojans, acting on Aeneas' orders, make no reply, rides around the walls in a wild rage,[17] searching everywhere for an entrance.

> ac ueluti pleno lupus insidiatus ouili
> cum fremit ad caulas uentos perpessus et imbris
> nocte super media; tuti sub matribus agni

balatum exercent, ille asper et improbus ira
saeuit in absentis; collecta fatigat edendi
ex longo rabies et siccae sanguine fauces:
haud aliter Rutulo muros et castra tuenti
ignescunt irae, duris dolor ossibus ardet.

(9.59–66)

As a wolf prowling around a crowded sheepfold howls beside
the pens, enduring wind and rain, in the middle of the night;
safe beneath their mothers, the lambs keep on bleating, while
he, exasperated and furious, rages against the animals within;
a long-accumulated, fierce hunger, his jaws thirsting for blood,
torment him: so Turnus, as he surveys the walls and camp,
kindles with anger; grief and pain burn in his hard bones.

It was long ago noticed[18] that in this simile Virgil is imitating Apollonius, with some reference to Homer and to his own earlier poetry.

ἠύτε τις θὴρ
ἄγριος, ὅν ῥά τε γῆρυς ἀπόπροθεν ἵκετο μήλων,
λιμῷ δ᾽ αἰθόμενος μετανίσεται, οὐδ᾽ ἐπέκυρσε
ποίμνῃσιν—πρὸ γὰρ αὐτοὶ ἐνὶ σταθμοῖσι νομῆες
ἔλσαν—ὁ δὲ στενάχων βρέμει ἄσπετον, ὄφρα κάμῃσιν·
ὡς τότ᾽ ἄρ᾽ Εἰλατίδης μεγάλ᾽ ἔστενεν, ἀμφὶ δὲ χῶρον
φοίτα κεκληγώς.

(Arg. 1.1243–49)

Like a wild beast whom the bleating of sheep has reached from
afar; burning with hunger, he follows but does not overtake
the flocks, for the shepherds have already penned them in the
fold; he groans and roars mightily until he is spent: so then the
son of Eilatus groaned loudly and wandered shouting around
the spot.

Yet the novelty of Virgil's imitation seems not to have been appreciated. In Homer it is not the wolf but the lion who attacks and ravages a sheepfold or is beaten off—or, in Apollonius, simply frustrated; and the single warrior attacking is compared to this magnificent beast, never to a wolf.[19] Apollonius' "wild beast" must be a lion, as Virgil no doubt recognized,[20] and added to his imitation of Apollonius from a simile in the *Odyssey* in which the hungry and naked Odysseus, as he is about to show himself to Nausicaa and

her handmaids, is compared to a storm-battered lion.[21] Virgil may
have felt that Apollonius' apparent lack of specificity permitted some
latitude; in any case, it was only natural for a poet of the Italian
countryside to think of a wolf in this context.

Later in Book 9, in a twofold simile, Turnus is again compared to
a wolf—to an eagle soaring aloft with a hare or a swan in his talons,
or to a wolf who has snatched a lamb from the fold, a lamb sought
with much bleating by its mother, "quaesitum aut matri multis balatibus agnum / Martius a stabulis rapuit lupus" (9.565–66). Here
Virgil imitates and modifies, again with reference to his own earlier
poetry,[22] a simile of Homer in which Hector is compared to an eagle,
swooping earthward through the dark clouds to snatch a tender lamb
or a timorous hare, ὅς τ᾿ εἶσιν πεδίονδε διὰ νεφέων ἐρεβεννῶν /
ἁρπάξων ἢ ἄρν᾿ ἀμαλὴν ἢ πτῶκα λαγωόν (*Il.* 22.309–10). Only
one other warrior in the *Aeneid* is compared to a wolf: the mean
and cowardly Arruns as he hurries away from the battlefield after
killing Camilla; and again Virgil imports a wolf into his imitation of
Homer.[23]

Once begun, the war drags on and the warriors perish: Pallas, Mezentius, Camilla. . . . Finally, the Latins and Rutulians are defeated
in the field, and Turnus, responding to public expectation, agrees to
meet Aeneas in single combat—not discouraged or humbled, however, but violent and implacable, lion-mettled.

> Poenorum qualis in aruis
> saucius ille graui uenantum uulnere pectus
> tum demum mouet arma leo, gaudetque comantis
> excutiens ceruice toros fixumque latronis
> impauidus frangit telum et fremit ore cruento:
> haud secus accenso gliscit[24] uiolentia Turno.
>
> (12.4–9)

As on the plains of Africa, gravely wounded in the breast by
hunters, a lion at last joins battle, exulting, shaking the muscles
along his shaggy neck; fearlessly he snaps the foeman's spear
lodged in his flesh, roaring with blood-stained mouth: so Turnus, on being aroused, grows more violent.

This simile, powerful in itself and emphatically placed,[25] has a certain
cumulative force as being the fifth in a series of such lion-similes.[26]

Violence, *uiolentia*, is a quality attributed to Turnus, and to Turnus alone, in the *Aeneid*. (This extraordinary violence, like the cruelty of Cacus and Mezentius, must be Virgil's innovation; in the traditional story, as told by Livy 1.2.1, Turnus is simply a native prince who resents losing his bride to a stranger and takes up arms against Aeneas and Latinus.) In recommending himself as an ally, Aeneas warns the Etruscan king Tarchon of Turnus' violent nature, "uiolentaque pectora Turni" (10.151). Elsewhere in Virgil the adjective *uiolentus* is applied to the east wind (G. 2.107), to the Eridanus, mightiest of rivers (G. 4.372–73), and to the irresistible south wind (A. 6.355–56)—to natural forces, that is, beyond human control; and to such forces Turnus is compared in Book 12, to the fierce north wind (365–69) and to an avalanche (684–90). Turnus is accused of violence by Drances, a rich and unprincipled politician, no warrior himself yet envious of Turnus' glory, who urges Latinus to make peace with Aeneas. All know what the time demands, he says, but fear to speak. Let him grant us freedom of speech, "det libertatem fandi" (11.346), and abate his arrogance, the man responsible for the fall of so many illustrious princes, for the grief of a whole city. To the many gifts you will send, Drances continues, add one, only one, the hand of your daughter in marriage—and let no man's violence prevent you, "nec te ullius uiolentia uincat" (11.354). At this, the violent nature of Turnus flares up, "talibus exarsit dictis uiolentia Turni" (11.376), and he makes a long and vehement reply.[27] Similarly, with barely concealed impatience[28] he rejects the reasoned, compassionate appeal of Latinus.

> haudquaquam dictis uiolentia Turni
> flectitur; exsuperat magis aegrescitque medendo.
>
> (12.45–46)

In no way is the violence of Turnus altered by the king's words; it increases and grows worse with the attempt at healing.

Virgil was thinking of a passage in Lucretius:[29]

> ergo animus siue aegrescit, mortalia signa
> mittit, uti docui, seu flectitur a medicina.
>
> (3.521–22)

Therefore if the mind grows worse or if it is altered by medicine, it shows, as I have proved, signs of mortality.

Turnus suffers, Virgil seems to imply, from a latent disposition to violence, a sickness of the soul.

Violentia is a strong word, stronger than its English derivative, in part because of a felt connection (etymologically true) with *uis*, brute force—as in Lucretius 3.296–98: "quo genere in primis uis est uiolenta leonum, / pectora qui fremitu rumpunt plerumque gementes / nec capere irarum fluctus in pectore possunt," "first in this category is the force and violence of lions, who so often burst their breasts with groaning and roaring, and cannot contain their surges of rage."[30] Again, as with *audax*, Cicero helps us to understand the force of *uiolentia*. *Violentia* (*uiolentus*) is the term Cicero applies to Antony, one of the *audaces*, the enemy of all good men and true: "uiolentus et furens" (*Philippics* 2.28.68), "violent and frenzied" (preceded by the exclamation "o audaciam maximam!"); "at ille homo uehemens et uiolentus, qui hanc consuetudinem libere dicendi excluderet" (*Phil.* 5.7.19), "but that vehement and violent man, who would do away with our custom of speaking freely"; "noui hominis furorem, noui effrenatam uiolentiam" (*Phil.* 12.11.26), "I know the man's frenzy, I know his unbridled violence."

We have, by now, endured much on sea and land with Aeneas, the driven wanderer, self-doubting, conscious of his destiny—his famous *pietas*—yet rarely happy about it; a man of sensibility, we feel, not unlike ourselves. But now, in these latter books, he seems changed; he seems to have become an efficient Homeric killer. We hardly recognize, in the fields of Latium, the man we knew, or thought we knew. Whatever dismay we feel must be owing in part to the chronology of the *Iliad* and *Odyssey*—the chronology of the fiction, that is, of Troy and its aftermath; a chronology inverted, in effect, in the *Aeneid*. We have not observed Aeneas in battle before, in hand-to-hand combat, and have forgotten the man he was, a warrior prince, the equal of Hector[31] and second only to Achilles[32]—Trojan Aeneas, "Troius Aeneas."

As he sets foot again on the Latian shore, Aeneas charges the rustic squadrons opposing him and kills in quick succession Theron, Lichas, Cisseus, Gyas, Pharus, and two brothers, Maeon and Alcanor—a traditional Homeric *aristeia*, reserved to the chief warriors.[33] This display of personal valor and his first words on the battlefield, to his faithful Achates, confirm that Aeneas is unchanged from what he was.

"suggere tela mihi. non ullum dextera frustra
torserit in Rutulos, steterunt quae in corpore Graium
Iliacis campis."

    (10.333–35)

"Hand me my spears. Of all that lodged in Greek flesh on the
plains of Ilium, not one shall my right hand hurl in vain against
the Rutulians."

The atrocities of which Aeneas is guilty are uncharacteristic but
not unintelligible; these savage acts follow upon his receiving the
news of Pallas' death.[34] Maddened by grief, by a sense of failure and
guilt, and thirsting for vengeance, like Achilles when he learns of
Patroclus' death, Aeneas cuts a bloody swath through the enemy
lines, taking alive eight young Italians to be sacrificed later at Pallas'
funeral. With a grim little speech he rejects the huge ransom—a buried wealth of chased silver, masses of worked and unworked gold—
which the suppliant Magus offers in exchange for his life.

"argenti atque auri memoras quae multa talenta
gnatis parce tuis. belli commercia Turnus
sustulit ista prior iam tum Pallante perempto."

    (10.531–33)

"The many talents of silver and gold you speak of, save them
for your sons. Turnus put an end to such trafficking in war
when he killed Pallas."

And in his encounter with Tarquitus, in the death of a vain and
foolish young warrior, Aeneas shows himself even more ruthless than
Achilles; altogether lacking is the awareness of a common humanity
which causes Achilles to see, in the death of Lycaon, whom he will
not spare, his own inexorable fate.[35] While Tarquitus is still pleading
for his life Aeneas strikes off his head, pushes the warm trunk away,
and, in Homeric fashion, taunts his dead foe, as does Achilles—but
Achilles has not beheaded Lycaon, an especially brutal detail, as it
seems here, imported from *Il.* 10.455–57, where Diomedes beheads
the craven Dolon.

And yet, while recognizing the berserk Homeric warrior, we should
be careful not to make Aeneas more ruthless than Virgil intended.
Aeneas fights grimly, for the most part against his will—never, like
Turnus, for the pure animal joy of fighting—and wishes there was a

better way. Thus, when the Latin ambassadors come to him request-
ing a truce, he responds:

"pacem me exanimis et Martis sorte peremptis
oratis? equidem et uiuis concedere uellem."
(11.110–11)

"Do you ask peace for the dead, for those who have perished
by Mars' lottery? Willingly would I grant it to the living too."

Only once is Aeneas described as killing indiscriminately (12.497:
"nullo discrimine"), but then he was provoked beyond endurance by
bad faith and treachery. In the ensuing carnage he is paired with
Turnus in a double *aristeia*, a Virgilian tour de force.[36] Aeneas kills
the Rutulian Sucro, Turnus the brothers Amycus and Diores, then
cuts off their heads and hangs them dripping with blood from his
chariot—a gratuitous act of savagery, without parallel in Homer.[37]
The reader will be reminded of a scene earlier in the poem, for which
there is a Homeric parallel of sorts,[38] when the Rutulians exhibit the
heads of Nisus and Euryalus on uplifted spears to the horrified
Trojans.

> turribus altis
> stant maesti; simul *ora uirum praefixa* mouebant
> nota nimis miseris *atroque fluentia tabo.*
> (9.470–72)

They stand sadly on the high towers, and were moved to pity
by the sight of the all too familiar heads, pierced and streaming
with black gore.

The studied reference to his description of the cave of Cacus[39] indicates what Virgil means his reader to feel here.

> semperque recenti
> caede *tepebat* humus, foribusque *adfixa* superbis
> *ora uirum* tristi pendebant pallida *tabo.*
> (8.195–97)[40]

Unlike Turnus, unlike Homer's warriors—Hector, Patroclus, Achilles, Agamemnon, Ajax, Menelaus, Odysseus, Diomedes, Sarpedon,
Aeneas himself[41]—Virgil's Aeneas is never compared to a lion, and
only twice to an animal of any kind, to a hunting dog (12.753) and,
with Turnus, to a bull (12.716). Turnus, by contrast, is compared
to a wolf (9.59), to an eagle or a wolf (9.564–65), to a tiger (9.730),

to a lion (9.792), to a lion (10.454), to a stallion (11.493), to a lion
(12.6), to a bull (12.103), and, with Aeneas, to a bull (12.716).[42] In
Homer one warrior may be stronger than another, or faster, or perhaps braver in battle; but he will not be—hence the general appli-
cation of lion-similes—essentially different in character.[43] In Virgil,
on the other hand, lion-similes are few and are employed to distin-
guish or characterize certain warriors: the blood-hot young Euryalus,
Turnus seeking out Pallas in the battle, Mezentius in all his ferocity,
the increasing violence of Turnus as he prepares to meet Aeneas.[44]

When Aeneas and Turnus do finally meet, in a furious duel—like
two bulls in the vast Sila or on Taburnus' summit (12.716)—Turnus,
with a surge of confidence, darts forward, puts all his strength into
his upraised sword, and strikes; but the mortal blade shatters, as
fragile as ice, against the Vulcanian armor, and Turnus takes to his
heels with Aeneas in pursuit—like a terrified deer pursued by a hunting dog, a keen Umbrian.[45] Unable to overtake Turnus, because of
a mysterious arrow wound received while he had been trying to prevent a new outbreak of hostilities (12.318–23), Aeneas hurls his
spear at him, missing. The spear lodges instead in the root of a wild
olive tree sacred to Faunus, and Faunus, being angry with the Trojans
(who had rashly cut down his tree) and favoring the native son, will
not release it. Meanwhile his sister, the nymph Juturna, resuming the
shape of Metiscus, supplies Turnus with another sword. Indignant
that so much should be allowed to the presumptuous nymph, "audaci
nymphae" (786),[46] Venus tears the spear loose, and once again Turnus and Aeneas confront each other on something like equal footing.

Jupiter now decides to intervene, and dispatches one of the twin
Furies—grisly creatures, daughters of Night, who wait beside his
throne—to drive Juturna from the battlefield and demoralize Turnus.

> postquam acies uidet Iliacas atque agmina Turni,
> alitis in paruae subitam collecta figuram,
> quae quondam in bustis aut culminibus desertis
> nocte sedens serum canit importuna per umbras—
> hanc uersa in faciem Turni se pestis ob ora
> fertque refertque sonans clipeumque euerberat alis.
> illi membra nouus soluit formidine torpor,
> arrectaeque horrore comae et uox faucibus haesit.
>
> (12.861–68)

On seeing the Trojan lines and Turnus' columns she shrinks,
all at once, to the form of a small bird that sometimes sits on

tombs or lonely rooftops and clamors late into the night, in-
sistently, among the shadows—so transformed, she flies at Turnus' face again and again, noisily, beating his shield with her
wings. Fear, a strange torpor, unnerved him; his hair bristled
with horror, the words stuck in his throat.

Juturna recognizes the monstrous visitation—the beating wings, the
sound of death—and despairs;[47] bitterly reproaching Jupiter for her
lost virginity and for his terrible gift of eternal life ("Now might I
accompany my poor brother into darkness"), she flees from the battlefield.

The duel is all but over. Turnus picks up a huge boundary-stone
to hurl at Aeneas, but hardly knows himself running or moving or
lifting or throwing the huge stone.

> sed neque currentem se nec cognoscit euntem
> tollentemue manu saxumue immane mouentem.
>
>   (12.903–4)

The repeated participles, of which one ("euntem") adds nothing to
the obvious sense, seem to suggest repeated, ineffectual effort.

Finally, Turnus lies wounded at Aeneas' feet and, in a brief, moving speech, pleads for his life. Sword upraised, Aeneas hesitates and
begins to relent, when he sees, gleaming on Turnus' shoulder, the
sword-belt of Pallas . . .

The *aristeia* and death of Pallas are appropriately placed within the
larger *aristeia*—the only "interrupted" *aristeia* in the poem[48]—of
Aeneas, to whom Evander had entrusted him.

> "hunc tibi praeterea, spes et solacia nostri,
> Pallanta adiungam; sub te tolerare magistro
> militiam et graue Martis opus, tua cernere facta
> adsuescat, primis et te miretur ab annis."
>
>   (8.514–17)

> "I will give you, besides, my Pallas, my hope and comfort; with
> you for a teacher let him learn to endure military service and
> the stern work of Mars, observe your deeds, and admire you
> from his earliest years."

The Homeric *aristeia* is a highly conventional form of narrative.[49]
It begins with an arming scene (omitted only in the *aristeia* of
Diomedes, *Il.* 5.1–8) in which the warrior's gear is described piece

by piece: greaves, corselet, sword, shield, helmet, spear(s)—always the same six pieces and, whether simply or elaborately described, in the same order.[50] Virgil imitates the *aristeia* as he imitates Homer elsewhere, with the allusiveness of Apollonius; his aim was to produce, in these latter books, the effect of an *aristeia* without reproducing its Homeric form. Thus no *aristeia* in Virgil begins with an arming scene, and his three arming-scenes[51] are, if referred to their Homeric model, artfully varied and incomplete. Turnus and Aeneas both arm themselves on the evening before their duel; but the arming of Turnus is described in almost Homeric detail, while that of Aeneas is merely indicated; he is clad in the armor of Vulcan, "maternis saeuus in armis" (12.107). Later, however, when he has been miraculously cured of his arrow wound by his mother's occult intervention, the arming, or rather the rearming, of Aeneas is described in comparable detail. It would have been artless to place the two arming scenes together (Virgil was anticipating his double *aristeia*), and the arming of Aeneas is the more dramatic for being deferred.

Although the *aristeia* of Pallas does not begin with an arming scene, there is an allusion to the absence of such a scene in Book 8, where the departure from Pallanteum is described:[52]

> ipse agmine Pallas
> it medio chlamyde et pictis conspectus in armis,
> qualis ubi Oceani perfusus Lucifer unda,
> quem Venus ante alios astrorum diligit ignis,
> extulit os sacrum caelo tenebrasque resoluit.
>
> (8.587–91)

Pallas himself passes in mid-column, conspicuous with cloak and blazoned armor, as, rising bathed in the Ocean wave, the Morning Star, whom Venus loves above all other fiery stars, shows his holy face in the sky and melts the darkness away.

No doubt, as was long ago noticed, Virgil had in mind here the *aristeia* of Diomedes, the only major *aristeia* that does not begin with an arming scene.[53]

> δαῖέ οἱ ἐκ κόρυθός τε καὶ ἀσπίδος ἀκάματον πῦρ,
> ἀστέρ᾽ ὀπωρινῷ ἐναλίγκιον, ὅς τε μάλιστα
> λαμπρὸν παμφαίνῃσι λελουμένος Ὠκεανοῖο.
>
> (*Il.* 5.4–6)

Athena caused the fire to blaze unrelentingly from his helmet and shield, like the star of late summer who rises bathed in Ocean and shines brightest of all.

But Virgil was thinking also of Apollonius, of how he had imitated this simile,[54] transforming it so as to express Medea's astonishment and joy at the appearance of Jason, rising before her—a moment of epiphany—like Sirius, the beautiful but ominous star.

αὐτὰρ ὅ γ᾽ οὐ μετὰ δηρὸν ἐελδομένῃ ἐφαάνθη
ὑψόσ᾽ ἀναθρῴσκων ἅ τε Σείριος Ὠκεανοῖο,
ὃς δ᾽ ἤτοι καλὸς μὲν ἀρίζηλός τ᾽ ἐσιδέσθαι
ἀντέλλει, μήλοισι δ᾽ ἐν ἄσπετον ἧκεν ὀιζύν·
ὣς ἄρα τῇ καλὸς μὲν ἐπήλυθεν εἰσοράασθαι
Αἰσονίδης, κάματον δὲ δυσίμερον ὦρσε φαανθείς.

(*Arg.* 3.956–61)

But soon he appeared to her longing eyes, striding high, like Sirius when he rises from Ocean, beautiful and clear to sight, but bringing immense hardship to the flocks: so Aeson's son appeared, beautiful to see, but bringing to her the misery of an ill-starred love.

The erotic character of Virgil's imitation of Homer must be owing (it seems inexplicable otherwise)[55] to Apollonius.[56]

Pallas is an affectingly virginal figure—the young warrior cut down before his time, in his first battle; on whose sword-belt is portrayed a scene of domestic horror, the wedding night of the Danaids, their young husbands murdered (10.497–98); and who, in death, is compared, with a reminiscence of Catullus' epithalamium (62.43), to a flower plucked by a girl, a soft violet or drooping hyacinth:

qualem uirgineo demessum pollice florem
seu mollis uiolae seu languentis hyacinthi.

(11.68–69)

Turnus does not encounter Pallas accidentally; he seeks him out, ordering his own men to stand back:

"tempus desistere pugnae;
solus ego in Pallanta feror, soli mihi Pallas
debetur; cuperem ipse parens spectator[57] adesset."

(10.441–43)

"Withdraw now from the battle; I go alone against Pallas, to
me alone is Pallas due; I wish his father were here in person
to watch."

As Pallas approaches the experienced and stronger warrior, his Arcadians have a premonition of disaster. Turnus leaps down from his
chariot—like a lion who sees a bull far below him in the plain[58]—
and advances. Recognizing that he is overmatched, Pallas prays to
the now-deified Hercules, who had once enjoyed Evander's hospitality and whose feastday the Arcadians had been celebrating a few
days before. Hercules groans and weeps, for he cannot help—as a
sympathetic Jupiter explains to him:

> "stat sua cuique dies, breue et inreparabile tempus
> omnibus est uitae; sed famam extendere factis,
> hoc uirtutis opus. Troiae sub moenibus altis
> tot gnati cecidere deum, quin occidit una
> Sarpedon, mea progenies; etiam sua Turnum
> fata uocant metasque dati peruenit ad aeui."
> sic ait, atque oculos Rutulorum reicit aruis.
>
>   (10.467–73)

"Each man has his appointed day; for all the span of life is
brief and irretrievable. But to prolong fame by great deeds, this
is the task of valor. So many sons of the gods fell beneath Troy's
high walls; even Sarpedon, my blood, died there. And now his
fate calls Turnus; he has reached the limit of his given time."
So he speaks, and turns his eyes away from the Rutulian plain.

Pallas, brave young Pallas, dies a hard and bloody death—a Homeric death, elaborately described to heighten the pathos of it.[59] Not
a death like that of Mimas, who had been born on the same night
as Paris—a minor, "elegiac" death, momentarily affecting.[60]

> Paris urbe paterna
> occubat, ignarum Laurens habet ora Mimanta.
>
>   (10.705–6)

Paris sleeps in the city of his fathers;
Mimas lies, a stranger, on the Rutulian shore.

Or like the death of Antores, Hercules' comrade, a man sent from
Argos who had attached himself to Evander and settled in Italy.

sternitur infelix alieno uulnere, caelumque
aspicit et dulcis moriens reminiscitur Argos.
> (10.781–82)

Unlucky man, felled by a blow meant for another; he looks up
at the sky and, dying, remembers the sweet life of Argos.

Turnus hurls his spear.

> at clipeum, tot ferri terga, tot aeris,
> quem pellis totiens obeat circumdata tauri,
> uibranti cuspis medium transuerberat ictu
> loricaeque moras et pectus perforat ingens.
> ille rapit calidum frustra de uulnere telum:
> una eademque uia sanguis animusque sequuntur.
> corruit in uulnus (sonitum super arma dedere)
> et terram hostilem moriens petit ore cruento.
> > (10.482–89)

With a shuddering impact the spear breaks through the shield—
through the many plates of iron, of brass, the many bullhides
wrapped around it—and pierces the stubborn mail and his
mighty breast. In vain he tears the warm weapon from the
wound: blood and life follow the same way. He falls upon the
wound (his armor clangs above him) and with his blood-stained
mouth he bites the hostile earth.

Bracing his left foot against the dead body, Turnus strips off the
richly ornamented sword-belt—the prized possession of a young warrior—with its scene of fratricidal violence,[61] which Clonus, the son
of Eurytus, had engraved in gold.[62]

Finally, Turnus lies wounded at Aeneas' feet and, in a brief, moving
speech, pleads for his life. Sword upraised, Aeneas hesitates and begins to relent, when he sees, gleaming on Turnus' shoulder, the
sword-belt of Pallas, the boy Pallas, "Pallantis pueri" (12.943).[63]
Maddened by the sight, by this reminder of his savage grief, and
terrible in his wrath, Aeneas cries out:

> "tune hinc spoliis indute meorum
> eripiare mihi? Pallas te hoc uulnere, Pallas
> immolat et poenam scelerato ex sanguine sumit."

hoc dicens ferrum aduerso sub pectore condit
feruidus; ast illi soluuntur frigore membra
uitaque cum gemitu fugit indignata sub umbras.[64]

    (12.947–52)

"Would you, clad in the spoils of my own, escape from me?
Pallas sacrifices you with this blow, Pallas, and exacts vengeance from your guilty blood." While still speaking, aflame with
anger, Aeneas buries the sword in Turnus' breast. His body goes
slack in the chill of death, and with a moan his spirit flees
unwillingly to the shades below.

Turnus appeals to Aeneas' characteristic virtue, his *pietas*, his reverence for the intimacy and sacredness of the relationship between
father and son:

        "miseri te si qua parentis
tangere cura potest, oro (fuit et tibi talis
Anchises genitor) Dauni miserere senectae . . ."

    (12.932–34)

"If any feeling for a father's grief can touch you, I beg you (you
too had such a father in Anchises), have pity on Daunus in his
old age. . . ."

This from the man who had wished that Evander might be present
to witness his son's death.[65] Touched in his inmost being, Aeneas
hesitates . . . an extraordinary moment of humanity; for the epic warrior never hesitates. He kills almost mechanically, showing no mercy,
exulting in his success—as Turnus kills the young and inexperienced
Pallas, as even Aeneas, in rage and frustration, can kill.[66]

Once before Aeneas had hesitated, or had attempted, rather, to
dissuade a youthful opponent. In 10.769–832, when Aeneas and Mezentius meet in a mortal duel, Aeneas wounds Mezentius in the groin
and would have killed him, disabled and withdrawing as he was, had
Lausus not intervened—"so that the father, protected by his son's
shield, might escape," "dum genitor nati[67] parma protectus abiret"
(800). Lausus' comrades cover the withdrawal of Mezentius with a
shower of missiles, while Aeneas rages and waits; Lausus, however,
does not accompany his father to the safety of the riverside, as he
could have done with no discredit to himself: he remains behind on
the field of battle, to challenge Aeneas.

Aeneas tries to fend him off, scolding him, threatening him, "Lau-
sum increpitat Lausoque minatur" (810). (The repetition of Lausus'

name may remind the reader of Turnus' peremptory claim that Pallas is "owed" to him, "solus ego in Pallanta feror, soli mihi Pallas / debetur.")[68] But Lausus is now beyond restraint: the young warrior elated with his first victory—a notable victory; the warrior he killed was the fierce Etruscan Abas, leader of the contingents from Populonia and Ilva (10.170–74, 426–28)—and the young son determined to kill his father's enemy; betrayed, as Aeneas warns him, by his reckless valor and his devotion to his father, "fallit te incautum pietas tua" (812).[69] Under this sustained furious assault[70] Aeneas' anger erupts and he kills Lausus with a single deep sword-thrust. As he looks down at the dying boy's face, a face growing spectrally pale, Aeneas, "Anchises' son," discerns the image of his own love and devotion. This sudden haunting awareness is beautifully implied in the patronymic *Anchisiades*, "ora modis Anchisiades pallentia miris" (822).[71]

But Turnus cannot be spared, however moving his appeal, for there is the pressing emotional debt that Aeneas owes to Evander, a debt of gratitude originally, now become with Pallas' death a sacred obligation,[72] as both Aeneas and Evander recognize. "Go," says Evander, in a scene of extreme pathos, to the Trojans who have returned his son's body, "go, and remember to take this message to your king":[73]

> "quod uitam moror inuisam Pallante perempto
> dextera causa tua est, Turnum gnatoque patrique
> quam debere uides."
>
>   (11.177–79)

"If I abide this hateful life, with Pallas dead, it is because you see that your right hand owes Turnus to son and father."

How then, under what circumstances, is Turnus to be killed, as he must be, by Aeneas? Not as Mezentius is killed, neither asking for nor expecting mercy, indeed wishing to die (10.878–82, 900–908), but under circumstances that will permit the reader to catch a glimpse of the hero's essential humanity and so be disposed to condone an overwhelming passionate impulse. Such, it may be supposed, was the poet's conscious intention. Yet most readers find the violence and abruptness of the last scene disturbing; Aeneas' uncertainty seems to be not so much resolved as terminated. There is no sense of a high moral purpose attained, or of personal triumph; there is only the grim reality—this terrible, final act of *pietas* required of the hero, which the poet, for reasons sufficient to his imagination, will not mitigate, will not explain away.

NOTES ON

ECLOGUE 6.47–60

Line 47. "quae te dementia cepit?": found here and in *E.* 2.69. Virgil had noticed that the query πᾷ τὰς φρένας ἐκπεπότασαι;, which he is imitating, occurs twice in Theocritus (2.19, 11.72). See Chapter IV n. 83.

Line 50. "concubitus": used only of animals by Virgil; see *TLL* s.v. 100.63. The daughters of Proetus imagined that they had been turned into cows; they did not, however, behave like cows. Since 1962 they have been happily reunited in a single euphonious line of Hesiod's *Catalogue* fr. 129.24 M.-W.: Λυσίππην τε καὶ Ἰφι]νόην καὶ Ἰ-φιάνασσαν. Remarkably, their names reappear in this same order centuries later in prose: Apollod. *Bibl.* 2.2.2: Λυσίππη καὶ Ἰφινόη καὶ Ἰφιάνασσα; DServ. on line 48: "Lysippe, Iphinoe, Iphianassa."

Line 51. "leui ... fronte": "humana scilicet" (DServ.), and this is the interpretation generally accepted. But Virgil must be alluding to their baldness, in Hesiod a symptom of their morbidly excited condition (μαχλοσύνη), *Catalogue* fr. 133.4–5 M.-W.: αἱ δέ νυ χαῖται / ἔρρεον ἐκ κεφαλέων, ψίλωτο δὲ καλὰ κάρηνα. Similarly the lovesick Simaetha loses her hair, Theocr. 2.89: ἔρρεον δ᾽ ἐκ κεφαλᾶς πᾶσαι τρίχες.

Line 54. "ruminat": here first in its literal sense. Four earlier instances are preserved by Nonius, all metaphorical, "to turn over in the mind, to ruminate upon": the earliest from Livius Andronicus (p. 166.26 M.), the other three from Varro (pp. 166.25; 480.18, 19). Although the word had not ceased to be used in its literal sense, it was simply too uncouth for literary use; cf. Columella 6.6.1: "bos . . . ruminat," Pliny *NH* 10.200, 11.161. But why so exquisite a coarseness here? Is Virgil again alluding to Calvus' *Io*? Apart from a clever but tasteless elaboration of Virgil's phrase in [Ov.] *Am.* 3.5.17–18: "dum iacet et lente reuocatas ruminat herbas / atque iterum pasto pascitur ante cibo" (the pentameter is quoted by DServ. here), the word occurs nowhere else in poetry.

Line 55. Pasiphae's speech begins after a bucolic diaeresis, pauses, then continues (57: "forsitan . . .") after a bucolic diaeresis.

Line 58. "errabunda . . . uestigia": see Appendix 7.

Line 60. "Gortynia": the topographic reference is (as so often) to a place in a poem: Catull. 64.75: "Gortynia tecta."

THE WHITE TENTS

OF RHESUS

nec procul hinc Rhesi niueis tentoria uelis
agnoscit lacrimans . . .

(A. 1.469–70)

Heyne, *Excursus* XVI (p. 249): "Nunc *tentoria* narrat *niveis velis*: in quibus non tam illud me movet, quod *nivea* tentoria fecit, eo scilicet, ut vel noctu nitore fulgentia late essent Diomedi et Ulyssi speculantibus conspicua; sed quod Troianis temporibus tentoria nondum erant *lintea*." Other commentators are either silent (La Cerda, Williams) or concerned with the anachronism. Conington: " 'Niveis tentoria velis' is an anachronism. The Homeric κλισίαι, as appears from *Il.* 24.448, were huts of planks thatched with grass." Austin: "Canvas tents are un-Homeric (cf. *Il.* 24.448 ff.)." The horses of Rhesus were notoriously whiter than snow; *Il.* 10.437: λευκότεροι χιόνος; Eur. *Rhesus* 304: πώλων . . . χιόνος ἐξαυγεστέρων. The visual aspect of the scene—the implied contrast of light and dark—of which there is no indication in Homer, might have occurred to Virgil independently; he was, after all, writing an ecphrasis and thinking if minimally in such terms: hence, perhaps, tents for horses as being larger, stationary objects. In the *Rhesus*, however, the contrast—white horses gleaming in the night—is explicit:

πέλας δὲ πῶλοι Θρηκίων ἐξ ἁρμάτων
λευκαὶ δέδενται, διαπρεπεῖς ἐν εὐφρόνῃ·
στίλβουσι δ᾽ ὥστε ποταμίου κύκνου πτερόν.

(616–18)

The adjective *niueus* is first attested in Cicero *Progn*. fr. 3.3 Soubiran: "saxaque *cana* salis *niueo* spumata liquore" (the new adjective is introduced in company with the old); then in Catullus (see D. O. Ross, Jr., *Style and Tradition in Catullus* [Cambridge, Mass., 1969] 61–62). And Catullus applies it to the horses of Rhesus, 58b.4: "non Rhesi niueae citaeque bigae"; cf. "nec procul hinc Rhesi niueis."

APPENDIX 3

BLACK MEMNON

Eoasque acies et nigri Memnonis arma.

(A. 1.489)

In classical Greek poetry and art Memnon, king of the Ethiopians, is not an African (in art, that is, his features are not negroid); see Vian on Quint. Smyrn. 2.101: Μέμνων κυανέοισι μετ' Αἰθιόπεσσιν ἀνάσσων; J. Vercoutter, J. Leclant, F. M. Snowden, Jr., J. Desanges, *The Image of the Black in Western Art*, I: *From the Pharaohs to the Fall of the Roman Empire* (Cambridge, Mass., 1976) 144; J. Boardman, *Athenian Red-Figured Vases: The Archaic Period* (Oxford, 1975) plates 48.1, 292. In the Hellenistic period, however, Memnon was assimilated to his subjects; see R. Holland in Roscher (1894–97) s.v. 2669, adding Callim. *Aet.* fr. 110.52 Pf.: Μέμνονος Αἰθίοπος, whence Catull. 66.52: "Memnonis Aethiopis," and now *Suppl. Hell.* 984.2: Μέμνονος Αἰθιοπῆος (an anonymous epigram probably of "the Alexandrian heyday," P. Parsons, "Callimachus: Victoria Berenices," *ZPE* 24 [1977] 12); see also R. Drews, "Aethiopian Memnon: African or Asiatic?" *RhM* 112 (1969) 191–92. The first reference in Latin is by Laevius, who called him *nocticolor* (Aul. Gell. 19.7.6). Memnon's color becomes an occasion of wit in Ov. *Am.* 1.13.31–32: "inuida, quo properas? quod erat tibi filius ater, / materni fuerat pectoris ille color."

APPENDIX 4

HOW OLD IS DIDO?

Here is a recent guess: "Dido must be middle-aged and serious, with a civic career parallel to Aeneas', while Medea is young and spoiled"; W. W. Briggs, Jr., "Virgil and the Hellenistic Epic," *Aufstieg und Niedergang der röm. Welt* 31.2 (Berlin, 1981) 961. Williams, in attempting to explain "optima Dido" (see above, p. 45), says that "it refers to the respect and gratitude which Aeneas feels towards Dido for her queenly qualities and gracious reception of the Trojans." When commentators speak of Dido's queenly qualities, her benevolence, dignity, and so on, she insensibly becomes older, a mature and experienced woman, widow Dido—"Didon, qui a déjà aimé, qui est une femme héroïque" (Cartault I 300). But she was married for the first time (*A.* 1.345–46) and only briefly to Sychaeus (there are no children) and is newly arrived in North Africa. In this as in other respects the Roman poet imagines Dido as a Roman, and the daughter of a dynastic Roman family would ordinarily be married for the first time when she was fourteen or fifteen: thus Augustus' daughter Julia, born in 39 B.C., was married to M. Marcellus in 25 (I owe this observation to Sir Ronald Syme); cf. Ov. *Met.* 11.302 (Chione): "mille procos habuit bis septem nubilis annis." Similarly, Apollonius imagines Arete, not as she is in the *Odyssey* with grown children, but as a young queen and wife still childless; a woman not much older than herself to whom Medea can appeal:

"ἀλλ' ἐλέαιρε,
πότνα, τεόν τε πόσιν μειλίσσεο· σοὶ δ' ὀπάσειαν

ἀθάνατοι βίοτόν τε τελεσφόρον ἀγλαΐην τε
καὶ παῖδας καὶ κῦδος ἀπορθήτοιο πόληος."
    (*Arg.* 4.1025–28)

See Vian ad loc. (p. 184). Imagine Dido as a very young woman, not much older than Medea or Ariadne: the pathos of her story is increased, and the reminiscences of Catullus' Ariadne seem more appropriate.

IOPAS

cithara crinitus Iopas
personat aurata . . .

　　(*A.* 1.740–41)

"*Crinitus Iopas*: aut puerum intellege, aut imitabatur Apollinis formam, cuius fuerat etiam artis imitator" (Servius); see also La Cerda. *Crinitus*, a very rare word, is found only once before Virgil, in Ennius, who probably invented it:

intendit crinitus Apollo
arcum auratum . . .

　　(*Scen.* 31 V.² = 28 J.)

The phrase *arcum intendere* is equally rare (see *TLL* s.v. *intendere* 2113.20); it is found only once before Virgil, in the same fragment of Ennius, and only once in Virgil:

Actius haec cernens arcum intendebat Apollo
desuper . . .

　　(*A.* 8.704–5)

Aetheria tum forte plaga crinitus Apollo
desuper . . .

　　(*A.* 9.638–39)

... docuit quem maximus Atlas.

(A. 1.741)

For the tradition that Atlas, the mountain personified in *A.* 4.246–51, had been a teacher or even the inventor of astronomy see Pease on *A.* 4.247. Commentators, not recognizing the character of this statement, have failed to relate it to the long series of references in poetry to divine instruction. Austin compares ("the detail is in Virgil's manner") *A.* 5.704–5: "tum senior Nautes, unum Tritonia Pallas / quem docuit multaque insignem reddidit arte," where Heyne remarks, without giving examples: "ut saepe apud Homerum a diis artes edocti inducuntur." Conington and Williams have nothing to the point in either place. In the following list passages already cited by Pfeiffer on Callim. fr. 701 are marked with an asterisk.

Homer *Il.* 5.51–52: δίδαξε γὰρ Ἄρτεμις αὐτὴ / βάλλειν ἄγρια πάντα

23.307–8: Ζεύς τε Ποσειδάων τε, καὶ ἱπποσύνας ἐδίδαξαν / παντοίας

Od. 6.233–34: ὃν Ἥφαιστος δέδαεν καὶ Παλλὰς Ἀθήνη / τέχνην παντοίην

*8.448: ὃν ποτέ μιν δέδαε φρεσὶ πότνια Κίρκη

8.480–81: οὔνεκ' ἄρα σφέας / οἴμας Μοῦσ' ἐδίδαξε

8.488: ἢ σέ γε Μοῦσ' ἐδίδαξε, Διὸς πάις, ἢ σέ γ' Ἀπόλλων

17.518–19: ὅς τε θεῶν ἒξ / ἀείδῃ δεδαὼς ἔπε' ἱμερόεντα βροτοῖσι

*20.72: ἔργα δ' Ἀθηναίη δέδαε κλυτὰ ἐργάζεσθαι

*Theocritus 24.129: Κάστωρ Ἱππαλίδας δέδαεν

Callim. *Aet.* fr. 67.1–3 Pf.: αὐτὸς Ἔρως ἐδίδαξεν Ἀκόντιον ... / τέχνην

*fr. 701 Pf.: δέδαεν δὲ λαχαινέμεν ἔργα σιδήρου

Apollonius *Arg.* 1.65–66: Μόψος Τιταρήσιος, ὃν περὶ πάντων / Λητοΐδης ἐδίδαξε θεοπροπίας οἰωνῶν

1.144–45: Λητοΐδης, αὐτὸς δὲ θεοπροπίας ἐδίδαξεν / οἰωνούς τ' ἀλέγειν ἠδ' ἔμπυρα σήματ' ἰδέσθαι

1.723–24: Παλλάς ... / ... καὶ κανόνεσσι δάε ζυγὰ μετρήσασθαι

2.257–58: Λητοῦς υἱός, ὅ με πρόφρων ἐδίδαξε / μαντοσύνας

2.512: Μοῦσαι, ἀκεστορίην τε θεοπροπίας τ᾽ ἐδίδαξαν

3.529–30: τὴν ῾Εκάτη περίαλλα θεὰ δάε τεχνήσασθαι / φάρμαχ᾽

4.989: Τιτῆνας δ᾽ ἔδαε στάχυν ὄμπνιον ἀμήσασθαι

Quint. Smyrn. 12.83: εἵνεκα τεκτοσύνης, δέδαεν δέ μιν ἔργον Ἀθήνη

In *A.* 5.391–92 Acestes rebukes the elderly Sicilian boxer Entellus for not accepting Dares' challenge: "ubi nunc nobis deus ille, magister / nequiquam memoratus, Eryx?" Eryx, the son of Aphrodite and Poseidon (or Butes), had been in the habit of challenging all comers to a boxing match—until he was killed by Hercules (Apollod. *Bibl.* 2.5.10, in a wrestling match) and buried on the mountain that bears his name; see F. A. Voigt in Roscher s.v. The notion that Eryx had been a divine instructor in the art of boxing seems to be Virgil's invention, on the analogy of Atlas.

APPENDIX 6

SUDDEN DEPARTURE FROM
CARTHAGE

The Trojans must leave Carthage—but how? This was the dramatic problem for Virgil, which he solved with reference to Apollonius and Homer. Roused from sleep by the terrifying apparition of Mercury, Aeneas orders his men to get the ships under way, then snatches his sword from its sheath in a flashing arc and cuts the cable:

> uaginaque eripit ensem
> fulmineum strictoque ferit retinacula ferro.
>
> (A. 4.579–80)

Virgil is imitating Apollonius. As Jason and Medea prepare to escape from Colchis, Jason draws his sword from its sheath and cuts the cable:

> ὁ δὲ ξίφος ἐκ κολεοῖο
> σπασσάμενος πρυμναῖα νεὸς ἀπὸ πείσματ᾽ ἔκοψεν.
>
> (Arg. 4.207–8)

Apollonius (as Virgil no doubt recognized) is imitating Homer. To save himself and his shipmates from the murderous Laestrygonians, Odysseus draws his sword and cuts the cable:

> "τόφρα δ᾽ ἐγὼ ξίφος ὀξὺ ἐρυσσάμενος παρὰ μηροῦ
> τῷ ἀπὸ πείσματ᾽ ἔκοψα νεὸς κυανοπρῴροιο."
>
> (Od. 10.126–27)

Pease and Livrea, while citing Homer, and Pease Apollonius as well, fail to cite the passage which connects, as it were, these two passages, probably because it occurs in a very different context. Automedon cuts loose the trace horse wounded by Sarpedon:

σπασσάμενος τανύηκες ἄορ παχέος παρὰ μηροῦ,
ἀΐξας ἀπέκοψε παρήορον . . .

      (*Il.* 16.473–74)

The participle *fulgens* is commonly applied to weapons (*TLL* s.v. 1513.29; *A.* 10.475: "uaginaque caua fulgentem deripit ensem"), and *fulgeo* is used of lightning (*TLL* s.v. 1508.71). Here "fulmineum" was suggested (such moments in poetry can hardly be explained) by the rhythm and emphasis of σπασσάμενος in Apollonius, and just possibly ("the notion combines brightness and speed," Pease) by ἀΐξας; cf. *Arg.* 3.1265–66: φαίης κεν ζοφεροῖο κατ᾽ αἰθέρος ἀΐσσουσαν / χειμερίην στεροπήν. Unlike Odysseus and his ship- mates (δείσαντες ὄλεθρον, 130), neither Jason nor Aeneas acts in the fear of imminent death: the cutting of the cable is symbolic; see Vian on *Arg.* 4.205 (p. 154), Arend 138: "Entscheidender als alle Bewahrung des physischen Lebens ist, dass Aeneas sein Ziel bewahrt. Das Durchhauen des Taues wird zum Symbol." (In *A.* 3.666–67, however, like Odysseus, Aeneas and his men cut the cable as they flee for their lives.)

The general confusion of departure is conveyed in a single line:

idem *omnis simul* ardor habet, rapiuntque ruuntque.

(*A.* 4.581)

This line is modeled, as Knauer notices, on a line in the *Odyssey* describing the frantic effort of Odysseus' shipmates to escape from the Laestrygonians—which shows, incidentally, that Virgil had Ho- mer as well as Apollonius in mind here:

οἱ δ᾽ ἅμα πάντες ἀνέρριψαν, δείσαντες ὄλεθρον.
(*Od.* 10.130)

Neither "rapiunt" nor ἀνέρριψαν has an object. Stanford: "One would expect an object with ἀνέρριψαν (cp. 7,328); hence ancient critics suggested ἅλα for ἅμα." The use of *rapio* without an object, real or implied (*G.* 3.68), is unparalleled in Virgil; cf. *A.* 2.374–75: "alii rapiunt incensa feruntque / Pergama"; 9.516: "molem uoluunt- que ruuntque." By imitating Homer so precisely—so philologically— Virgil places himself in the tradition of the Alexandrian poet-scholar.

A NOTE ON *AENEID* 6.30

As C. Weber, "Gallus' Grynium and Virgil's Cumae," *Mediterraneus* 1 (1978) 46–51, has shown, *A.* 6.14–33 constitutes "one of the most uncompromisingly neoteric passages in the entire *Aeneid.*" To his brief but compelling argument I add the following observations.

hic crudelis amor tauri suppostaque furto
Pasiphae mixtumque genus prolesque biformis
Minotaurus inest, Veneris monimenta nefandae,
hic labor ille domus et inextricabilis error;
magnum reginae sed enim miseratus amorem
Daedalus ipse dolos tecti ambagesque resoluit,
caeca regens filo uestigia.

    (*A.* 6.24–30)

Line 30 is an imitation of Catullus:

inde pedem sospes multa cum laude reflexit
errabunda regens tenui uestigia filo . . .

    (64.112–13)

Like Conington—like Germanus, Ursinus, and La Cerda—Austin cites Catullus; Norden, curiously, does not. Both, however, comment on the emotional effect of the bucolic diaeresis, without recognizing its source. Norden: "Das durch die starke Interpunktion nach der bukolischen Diaerese isolierte Komma *tu quoque magnam* leitet den nun folgenden wehmütigen Gedanken stimmungsvoll ein." Austin: "The dramatic break after *uestigia* ('bucolic diaeresis') marks an

emotional pause before the pathetic apostrophe (which vividly suggests the viewers' sad imaginings)." Here, as so often elsewhere, Virgil's imitation is twofold: he imitates both Catullus and his own earlier imitation of Catullus in *E.* 6, in Pasiphae's pathetic speech:

>   "claudite, Nymphae,
> Dictaeae Nymphae, nemorum iam claudite saltus,
> si qua forte ferant oculis sese obuia nostris
> errabunda bouis uestigia . . ."
>
>   (55–58)

Only here and in *A.* 6.30 is *uestigia* placed before the bucolic diaeresis. In 27 of the 32 other instances *uestigia* is placed so as to
coincide with the end of the fifth foot, and in 5 with the end of the
fourth foot but without a pause: *G.* 2.402, 3.171; *A.* 3.244, 7.689,
11.290. While retaining the bucolic diaeresis in *A.* 6.30, Virgil rejected *errabundus* as being unfit for epic use. This adjective has a
very short history in poetry: Lucr. 4.692, Catull. 64.113, and *E.* 6.58.
In general, poets avoid such adjectives when formed on verbs of the
first conjugation. Cf. M. Zicàri, "Moribunda ab Sede Pisauri," *Studia
Oliveriana* 3 (1955) 63–64 = *Scritti Catulliani* (Urbino, 1978) 193–
94: "L' aggettivo [*moribundus*] appartiene all' esiguo manipolo di
deverbali in *i/ebundus* accolti dalla poesia, mentre il solo Lucrezio
usò *versabundus* (6, 438; 6, 582), ed *errabundus* non si trova in poeti
dopo Verg. *ecl.* 6, 58. Questa limitazione, oltre che negli epici e in
Ovidio, si osserva anche in Cicerone, che peraltro non influisce sui
prosatori posteriori, nei quali o il tipo manca del tutto, o spesseg-
giano proprio le forme in *abundus*." For a list of such adjectives see
P. Langlois, "Les formations en '–bundus,' " *REL* 39 (1961) 128–
34, and E. Pianezzola, *Gli aggettivi verbali in –bundus* (Florence,
1965) 239–40.

APPENDIX 8

THE SHIELD OF TURNUS

Turnus bears on his shield a strange device: the Argive princess Io turned into a cow:

> at leuem clipeum sublatis cornibus Io
> auro insignibat, iam saetis obsita, iam bos,
> argumentum ingens, et custos uirginis Argus,
> caelataque amnem fundens pater Inachus urna.
>
> (A. 7.789–92)

Almost certainly Virgil was thinking of the ecphrasis in Moschus' *Europa* where the metamorphosis of Io is described:

> ἐν μὲν ἔην χρυσοῖο τετυγμένη Ἰναχὶς Ἰώ
> εἰσέτι πόρτις ἐοῦσα, φυὴν δ᾽ οὐκ εἶχε γυναίην.
>
> (44–45)

Bühler on 45: "Dass Vergil die Stelle des M. vor Augen hatte, ist zwar nicht sicher, aber doch wahrscheinlich." It seems not to have occurred to commentators that Virgil may also be imitating Calvus' *Io* here. Wherever possible Virgil prefers to imitate two Greek poets, or a Greek and a Latin poet (not excluding himself), simultaneously, as in *E.* 6.47: "a, uirgo infelix, quae te dementia cepit?" where he imitates Calvus and Theocritus (and himself) simultaneously; see above, p. 12. There are, in addition, at least two particular reasons for suspecting the presence of Calvus here: (1) the cadence of line 790 seems un-Virgilian: "iam saetis obsita, iam bos"; and (2) the form "bos." (1) Compare *E.* 5.83, 6.9, 7.35, 9.48; *G.* 1.314, 370,

2.103, 3.133, 358, 428, 474, 484, 4.6, 71, 84; *A.* 1.77, 181, 603, 2.163, 3.151, 5.372, 624, 713, 6.466, 7.310, 643, 9.491, 10.9, 11.3, 164, 12.48, 231, 360, 526, 565. (2) The feminine singular "bos" is unique in Virgil, and he might easily have avoided it (as he substituted "bucula" for "bos" in his imitation of Varro of Atax, *G.* 1.375); cf. *G.* 3.153: "Inachiae Iuno pestem meditata iuuencae"; Moschus *Eur.* 51: πόρτιος ᾿Ιναχίης; Ovid *Met.* 1.610–11: "inque nitentem / Inachidos uultus mutauerat ille iuuencam"; *Fasti* 3.658: "Inachiam ... bouem." In telling the story of Io's metamorphosis Ovid too uses the feminine singular, *Met.* 1.612: "(bos quoque formosa est)," then, in 632–34, imitates the same line of the *Io* that Virgil had imitated; see Chapter II n. 15.

THE EXCLUSIVENESS OF

HERCULES

When the Trojans arrive at Pallanteum they find Evander sacrificing
to Hercules and the gods:

> honorem
> Amphitryoniadae magno diuisque ferebat . . .
> (*A.* 8.102–3)

The problem here has been noticed but not solved. Williams: "Plutarch (*Quaest. Rom.* 90) cites Varro as saying that no other god is
mentioned during a sacrifice to Hercules." Eden: "It is strange that
any other gods should be involved in the sacrifice to Hercules." Fordyce simply ignores the problem: "a general invocation is added to
the particular as in iii.19 f. 'sacra Dionaeae matri diuisque ferebam /
auspicibus coeptorum operum' "; cf. Wissowa, *Religion und Kultus*
(Munich, 1912²) 274–75: "im Gegensatze zu der beim römischen
Opfer üblichen *generalis invocatio* . . . durfte hier keines anderen
Gottes Name genannt werden (Varro bei Plut. Qu. Rom. 90)." Conington was the first to cite *A.* 3.19, and the similarity is obvious, but
"Dionaeae matri diuisque" seems to be modeled on "Amphitryo-
niadae magno diuisque"; in any case the cult of Venus was not ex-
clusive (Wissowa 61). Virgil wishes his reader to recall the Homeric
formula Διί τ᾽ ἄλλοισίν τε θεοῖσι (*Il.* 6.475; *Od.* 4.472, 8.432; also
Il. 6.259, 13.818: Διὶ πατρὶ καὶ ἄλλοις ἀθανάτοισι; 20.194: Ζεὺς
. . . καὶ θεοὶ ἄλλοι; *Od.* 14.53: Ζεύς . . . καὶ ἀθάνατοι θεοὶ
ἄλλοι); a formula restricted to Zeus, with a single exception which
Virgil—and Apollonius before him—had noticed. The arrival of the

Trojans at Pallanteum recalls the arrival of Telemachus and Mentor
(Athena) at Pylos; see above, p. 68. When the feast is over and it is
time for sleep Athena proposes a libation to Poseidon and the other
gods, *Od.* 3.333: Ποσειδάωνι καὶ ἄλλοισ᾽ ἀθανάτοισι. Similarly,
when Jason comes to Iolcus to share in the feast he finds Pelias sacrificing to his father Poseidon and the other gods, *Arg.* 1.13–14:
πατρὶ Ποσειδάωνι καὶ ἄλλοις / ῥέζε θεοῖς. The reference to Poseidon instead of to Zeus in this formula is unique in Apollonius as
it is in Homer. (Apollonius does not imitate the standing formula Διί
τ᾽ ἄλλοισίν τε θεοῖσι; cf. *A.* 3.222–23: "diuos ipsumque uocamus /
. . . Iouem.") Like Hercules, Poseidon was not ordinarily associated
with other deities; see E. Wüst, "Poseidon," *RE* 43 (1953) 461–62.
That Virgil was thinking of *Od.* 3.333 (and Apollonius?) is further
indicated by the fact that at Pallanteum, when he has finished telling
the story of Cacus and the feast is nearly over, Evander proposes a
libation to Hercules:

> "quare agite, o iuuenes, tantarum in munere laudum
> cingite fronde comas et pocula porgite dextris,
> communemque uocate *deum* et date uina uolentes."
> dixerat, Herculea bicolor cum populus umbra
> uelauitque comas foliisque innexa pependit,
> et sacer impleuit dextram scyphus. ocius omnes
> in mensam laeti libant *diuosque* precantur.
>
> (*A.* 8.273–79)

THE KINSHIP OF EVANDER
AND DARDANUS

Appealing to Evander for support against their common enemy, Aeneas tells him that they are descended from a common ancestor:

> "Dardanus, Iliacae primus pater urbis et auctor,
> Electra, ut Grai perhibent, Atlantide cretus,
> aduehitur Teucros; Electram maximus Atlas
> edidit, aetherios umero qui sustinet orbis.
> uobis Mercurius pater est, quem candida Maia
> Cyllenae gelido conceptum uertice fudit;
> at Maiam, auditis si quicquam credimus, Atlas,
> idem Atlas generat caeli qui sidera tollit.
> sic genus amborum scindit se sanguine ab uno."
>
> (A. 8.134–42)

This short, highly stylized genealogy begins, as Knauer notices, with a reference to *Il.* 20.215: Δάρδανον αὖ πρῶτον τέκετο νεφεληγερέτα Ζεύς, the beginning of the long genealogy which Aeneas there relates to Achilles. Commentators offer no other parallels. Virgil's model is a similar genealogy in Apollonius, presented under similar circumstances. Seeking to persuade Aeetes to let the Argonauts have the Golden Fleece, his grandson Argus, the son of Chalciope and Phrixus, tells him that Jason and Phrixus are descended from a common ancestor:

> Τόνδε μέν, οἷό περ οὕνεκ᾽ ἀφ᾽ Ἑλλάδος ὤλλοι ἄγερθεν,
> κλείουσ᾽ Αἴσονος υἱὸν Ἰήσονα Κρηθεΐδαο·

εἰ δ' αὐτοῦ Κρηθῆος ἐτήτυμόν ἐστι γενέθλης,
οὕτω κεν γνωτὸς πατρώιος ἄμμι πέλοιτο·
ἄμφω γὰρ Κρηθεὺς 'Αθάμας τ' ἔσαν Αἰόλου υἷες,
Φρίξος δ' αὖτ' 'Αθάμαντος ἔην πάις Αἰολίδαο.

(*Arg.* 3.356–61)

A diagram will make the similarity of the two genealogies evident:

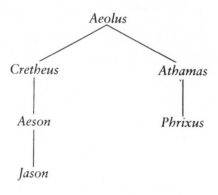

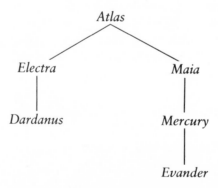

Evander stands in the same relation to Dardanus as Jason does to
Phrixus: he is a first cousin once removed.

MULCIBER

hic Nomadum genus et discinctos Mulciber Afros,
hic Lelegas Carasque sagittiferosque Gelonos
finxerat.

(*A.* 8.724–26)

There must be a reason other than metrical convenience why Virgil employs this old and obscure title of Vulcan here and nowhere else. Quite simply, it is this, that Mulciber is twice identified in earlier poetry as the maker of Achilles' armor:

Mulciber, credo, arma fecit quae habuit Stratippocles:
trauolauerunt ad hostis. EP. Tum ille prognatus Theti
sine perdat: alia apportabunt ei Nerei filiae.

(Plautus *Epid.* 34–36)

See E. Fraenkel, *Elementi plautini in Plauto* (Florence, 1960) 80–81.

heu Mulciber!
arma ignauo inuicta es fabricatus manu.

(Accius *Philocteta* 558–59 R.[3])

Line 559 is metrically defective; see Ribbeck ad loc.

ABBREVIATIONS

Abbreviations for journals generally follow *L'Année Philologique*. In the notes, editors of major editions are often cited by last name only. Other frequently cited works give the author's last name, as shown below, with two exceptions:

CHCL II	=	*The Cambridge History of Classical Literature*, II *Latin Literature*, ed. E. J. Kenney, W. V. Clausen (Cambridge, England, 1982)
Suppl. Hell.	=	*Supplementum Hellenisticum*, ed. H. Lloyd-Jones, P. Parsons (Berlin, 1983)

COMMENTARIES ON THE *AENEID*

Austin	R. G. Austin, *P. Vergili Maronis Aeneidos Liber Primus* (Oxford, 1971); . . . *Liber Secundus* (Oxford, 1964); . . . *Liber Quartus* (Oxford, 1955)
Conington	J. Conington, *P. Vergili Maronis Opera* (London, 1872–75²); *Aeneid* 6–12 with H. Nettleship
Eden	P. T. Eden, *A Commentary on Virgil, Aeneid VIII* (Leiden, 1975)
Fordyce	C. J. Fordyce, *P. Vergili Maronis Aeneidos Libri VII–VIII* (Oxford, 1977)
Gransden	K. W. Gransden, *Virgil, Aeneid Book VIII* (Cambridge, England, 1976)
Heyne	C. G. Heyne, *P. Virgilii Maronis Opera* . . . , ed. G. P. E. Wagner (Leipzig, 1830–33⁴)

La Cerda	J. L. de la Cerda, *P. Virgili Maronis Priores Sex Libri Aeneidos* . . . (Cologne, 1612); . . . *Posteriores Sex Libri* . . . (Cologne, 1617)
Norden	E. Norden, *P. Vergilius Maro Aeneis Buch VI* (Leipzig, 1916²)
Pease	A. S. Pease, *P. Vergili Maronis Aeneidos Liber Quartus* (Cambridge, Mass., 1935)
Williams	R. D. Williams, *The Aeneid of Virgil* (London, 1972–73)

OTHER WORKS

Arend	W. Arend, *Die typischen Szenen bei Homer*, Problemata 7 (Berlin, 1933)
Cartault	A. Cartault, *L'Art de Virgile dans L'Enéide*, 2 vols. (Paris, 1926)
Conrardy	C. Conrardy, *De Vergilio Apollonii Imitatore* (Freiburg, 1904)
Fränkel	H. Fränkel, *Noten zu den Argonautika des Apollonios* (Munich, 1968)
Heinze	R. Heinze, *Virgils epische Technik* (Stuttgart, 1915³)
Henry	J. Henry, *Aeneidea* (London, 1873–92)
Highet	G. Highet, *The Speeches in Vergil's Aeneid* (Princeton, 1972)
Klingner	F. Klingner, *Virgil* (Zurich, 1967)
Knauer	G. N. Knauer, *Die Aeneis und Homer*, Hypomnemata 7 (Gottingen, 1964): "Aeneis-Homer," pp. 371–432; "Homer-Aeneis," pp. 432–527
Livrea	E. Livrea, *Apollonii Rhodii Argonauticon Liber Quartus* (Florence, 1973)
Pfeiffer, Pf.	R. Pfeiffer, *Callimachus*, 2 vols. (Oxford, 1949–53)
Roscher	W. H. Roscher, *Ausfürliches Lexikon der griechischen und römischen Mythologie* (Leipzig, 1884–1937)
Rütten	F. Rütten, *De Vergilii Studiis Apollonianis* (Munster, 1912)
Ursinus	F. Ursinus, *Virgilius Collatione Scriptorum Graecorum Illustratus* (Antwerp, 1568)
Vian	F. Vian, *Apollonios de Rhodes, Argonautiques I–IV* (Paris, 1976–81)
	F. Vian, *Quintus de Smyrne, La Suite d'Homère*, 3 vols. (Paris, 1963–69)

NOTES

I. A NEW POET'S EDUCATION

1. Probably during the reign of Tiberius: see E. Fraenkel, "The Culex," *JRS* 42 (1952) 8 = *Kl. Beitr.* II (Rome, 1964) 194–95; J. Richmond, "Recent Work on the *Appendix Vergiliana* (1950–1975)," *Aufstieg und Niedergang der röm. Welt* 31.2 (Berlin, 1981) 1125–27. This view remained unquestioned from antiquity until recently; see *CHCL* II 317–19.

2. Since 1927, when the text of Callimachus' *Aetia* fr. 1 Pf. was published by A. S. Hunt in *The Oxyrhynchus Papyri* 17 (London, 1927) 45–55.

3. And as some modern scholiasts still think, following Servius and Donatus, *Vita* 19: "mox cum res Romanas incohasset, offensus materia ad Bucolica transiit." The ancient scholiasts may be excused, for they knew nothing of Callimachean poetics, which had long since been forgotten—a good example of how a mistaken inference from the text may be transformed into a scholiastic "fact."

4. See P. Parsons, "Callimachus: Victoria Berenices," *ZPE* 25 (1977) 49–50; *CHCL* II 181–82. The asperity of Callimachus' tone must be owing in part to the fact that he was speaking for a minority; most poets were busily celebrating kings and battles; see K. Ziegler, *Das hellenistische Epos* (Leipzig, 1934, 1966²), and now H. Lloyd-Jones, "A Hellenistic Miscellany," *SIFC* 77 (1984) 58.

5. See *CHCL* II 183; Pfeiffer on fr. 696 and fr. 2a.16–19 (II Addenda). Thus in *E.* 6.64–65 Gallus quits the valley (Aganippe-Permessus) for the heights (Hippocrene); he rises, as it were, from a lower level of poetry to a higher, from love-elegy and Lycoris to aetiology and the Grynean Grove.

6. A metrical convenience; the usual form is λεπτός; see Pfeiffer ad loc.

7. *G.* 3.36. See Clausen, "*Cynthius*," *AJP* 97 (1976) 245–47; also "*Cynthius*: An Addendum," 98 (1977) 362.

8. *Vita Donati*, a congeries of fact and fiction based mainly on Suetonius but given its final shape by Aelius Donatus, the celebrated grammarian, in the fourth century. In later life at any rate Virgil enjoyed equestrian status; see L. R. Taylor, "Republican and Augustan Writers Enrolled in the Equestrian Centuries," *TAPA* 99 (1968) 483–84.

9. Williams, p. x: "of peasant stock."

10. *CIL* 5¹, p. 406: "Mantua quamquam saepe nominatur apud antiquos propter P. Vergilium Maronem poetam oriundum ex Andibus vico Mantuanorum, tamen ipsa exiguam apud posteros sui memoriam reliquit. . . . Territorium Mantuanorum exiguum sine dubio, ut ipsum oppidum parvum fuit." Cf. Martial 14.195: "Tantum magna suo debet Verona Catullo, / quantum parua suo Mantua Vergilio."

11. See R. Syme, *The Roman Revolution* (Oxford, 1939) 79, 251 n. 3. The notion that Virgil's father accompanied him to school (like Horace's father?) rests on the improbable assumption that Virgil is the author of *Catalepton* 8.

12. See F. H. Sandbach, "*Lucreti Poemata* and the Poet's Death," *CR* 54 (1940) 72–74.

13. See A. D. Booth, "Virgile: Ses Années Scolaires," in *Mélanges Etienne Gareau* (Ottawa, 1982) 150.

14. As was the case with Horace, whose father was better off than has been generally recognized; see E. Fraenkel, *Horace* (Oxford, 1957) 2–3, 4–5, 13.

15. See Booth, "Virgile."

16. See Fraenkel, *Horace* 7.

17. *De gramm.* 16.3: "primusque Vergilium et alios poetas nouos praelegere coepisse."

18. See *CHCL* II 178–80; Clausen, "Cicero and the New Poetry," *HSCP* 90 (1986) 159–70.

19. Cf. the new epigram of Gallus, 6–7: "tandem fecerunt carmina Musae / quae possem domina deicere digna mea." Lines 8–9 contain two names: Viscus, a contemporary critic, and Valerius Cato, an older poet and critic. See R. D. Anderson, P. J. Parsons, R. G. M. Nisbet, "Elegiacs by Gallus from Qaṣr Ibrîm," *JRS* 69 (1979) 140, 144, 145, 147.

20. See T. P. Wiseman, *Cinna the Poet* (Leicester, 1974) 56–57.

21. Does Virgil imply that Cinna was also his teacher? Cf. Georgius Choeroboscus, *Grammatici Graeci* IV.1 (Leipzig, 1889) 333.10–11: Φιλητᾶς ὁ διδάσκαλος Θεοκρίτου—clearly an inference from this passage, which Choeroboscus does not, however, cite. I owe this reference to R. A. Kaster.

22. See A. S. Hollis, "L. Varius Rufus, *De Morte* (frs. 1–4 Morel)," *CQ* n.s. 27 (1977) 187–90; also chapter VI n. 18.

23. Calvus appears to have died at about the same time as Catullus or

not much later; see G. W. Bowersock, "Historical Problems in Late Republican and Augustan Classicism," *Fondation Hardt, Entretiens* 25 (Geneva, 1979) 60–61.

24. Macrob. *Sat.* 5.17.18: "uersus [*G.* 1.437] est Parthenii, quo grammatico in Graecis Vergilius usus est."

25. See Clausen, "Ariadne's Leave-taking: Catullus 64.116–20," *ICS* 2 (1977) 219–23.

26. R. Helm, *Hieronymus' Zusätze in Eusebius' Chronik, Philologus*, Suppl. 21.2 (1929) 40: "qui postea XXXV annum agens Graecas litteras cum summo studio didicit."

27. Virgil paid Varro the extraordinary compliment of "stealing" one of his lines, *G.* 1.377: "aut arguta lacus circumuolitauit hirundo"; see T. E. V. Pearce, "The Enclosing Word Order in the Latin Hexameter," *CQ* n.s. 16 (1966) 301–3; also G. Williams, *Tradition and Originality in Roman Poetry* (Oxford, 1968) 255–59. If the *Argonautae* or much of it had survived, almost certainly we should find imitations of it in Virgil, especially in *A.* 4; see Seneca the Elder *Contr.* 7.1.27.

28. This account of Parthenius and Callimachus reproduces, with additions and modifications, that in *CHCL* II 182–86 and Clausen, "Callimachus and Latin Poetry," *GRBS* 5 (1964) 188–91.

29. See R. Pfeiffer, *History of Classical Scholarship* (Oxford, 1968) 88–89.

30. *Suda* s.v. Παρϑένιος. On the influx of such learned Greeks into Rome see G. W. Bowersock, *Augustus and the Greek World* (Oxford, 1966) 122–39.

31. Wilamowitz conjectures that Propertius had someone like Parthenius to help him, *Hellenistische Dichtung* I (Berlin, 1924) 230 n. 2.

32. A Callimachean of the generation after Callimachus; for his importance see *CHCL* II 186–87.

33. For a brief history of the term *epyllion* in its modern sense see G. W. Most, "On the Arrangement of Catullus' Carmina Maiora," *Philologus* 125 (1981) 111 n. 9. There is no reason to avoid the term because it is, like other useful terms (e.g., *recusatio*), modern.

34. For an analysis see *CHCL* II 184–85.

35. Ibid. 200–201.

36. See ibid. 184–85. The Satrachus or Setrachos appears only three times in Greek poetry: Lycophron 448; Nonnus *Dionys.* 13.459, with an allusion to Myrrha (Zmyrna); and Parthenius, *Suppl. Hell.* 641—a difficult river for a young Latin poet to find without a knowledgeable guide. For a similar if more extravagant conceit cf. Tasso, *Loda il Signor Luigi Camoens, il Quale ha scritto in lingua Spagnola de' Viaggi del Vasco*: "Ed or quella [penna] del colto e buon Luigi / tant' oltra stende il glorioso volo, / ch' i tuoi spalmati legni andar men lunge."

37. This seems to be the implication of *cauus*; cf. Lucan 2.421–23: "dex-

teriora petens montis decliuia Thybrim / unda facit Rutubamque cauum. delabitur inde / Vulturnusque celer"; also Livy 5.37.7: "flumen Allia, Crustuminis montibus praealto defluens alueo . . . Tiberino amni miscetur."

38. On the significance of this image see Pfeiffer, *History of Classical Scholarship* 125–126.

39. This curious little book, which can never have been intended for general circulation, survives by some chance in a single ninth-century MS, and was first published in 1531 by Janus Cornarius, a physician of Zwiccau, as an antidote to the lovesickness then prevalent, in his opinion, among the youth of Germany.

40. For an analysis see *CHCL* II 186.

41. Noted by Fränkel on 1.1067. Parthenius tells the story of Cleite in Περὶ ἐρωτ. παθ. 28, without, however, mentioning that she, like Byblis, was transformed into a fountain.

42. Cf. τὴν δὲ καὶ αὐταί / . . . ἀλσηίδες ὠδύραντο: ταὶ δ᾿ ἐπ᾿ ἐκείνῃ / Μιλησίδες ἐρρήξαντο. ἀλσηίδες is found only in Apollonius (here and 4.1151: αἱ δ᾿ ἔσαν ἐκ πεδίων ἀλσηίδες). Μιλησίδες only in Parthenius.

43. σαρωνίς and βεύδεα are found only in Callimachus: σαρωνίς, *Hymn* 1.22, *Suppl. Hell.* 276.10; βεύδεα, *Aet.* fr. 7.11, where see Pfeiffer. In addition, κλαῖεν ἀηδονίδων θαμινώτερον is a reminiscence of Callim. *Hymn* 5.94–95: μάτηρ μὲν γοερᾶν οἶτον ἀηδονίδων / ἆγε βαρὺ κλαίοισα; the form ἀηδονίδων not being found elsewhere. (This negative information is derived from the *Thesaurus Linguae Graecae* database currently available at Harvard.) See A. W. Bulloch, *Callimachus: The Fifth Hymn* (Cambridge, 1985) ad loc.

44. Hence Rohde's conjecture, *Der griechische Roman* (Leipzig, 1914²) 101 n. 1, that some words had dropped out after ἐνεθήκατο; Rohde quotes the defense by W. Schmid against Hercher. But the fact of Parthenius' imitation of Apollonius proves that Rohde was wrong. See Clausen, *GRBS* 5 (1964) 190 n. 8.

45. See Pfeiffer, *History of Classical Scholarship* 126–33.

46. Fr. 612 Pf.; see Norden on *A.* 6.14.

47. See Pfeiffer on fr. 282.

48. See, e.g., the notes of F. Williams, *Callimachus, Hymn to Apollo* (Oxford, 1978), on lines 108–12; quoted above, p. 7.

49. See H. Herter, "Kallimachos," *RE*, Suppl. 13 (1973) 247–51 (247: "Homer, in dessen Bahnen K. sich bewegt, um doch unhomerisch zu sein").

50. Fr. 67.11–13 Pf.; not very useful, and nothing further is known of this spring on Naxos.

51. See *OCD²* s.v. "Satyrs and Silenoi." See *CHCL* II 317–18.

52. It seems impossible to determine what connection (if any) obtains between Virgil's sixth *Eclogue* and the fragment of an anonymous pastoral poem in D. L. Page, *Select Literary Papyri* III (Cambridge, Mass., 1950) no. 123.

53. Quoted on p. 30.

54. For notes on these lines see Appendix 1.

55. Fr. 9 M. Twice later in this *Eclogue* Virgil uses the adjective *amarus*, as if he were thinking of "herbis pasceris amaris" but chooses not to imitate it directly: "amarae / corticis" (62–63); "apio . . . amaro" (68). Cf. Ovid's exuberant but precise imitation, *Met.* 1.632–34: "frondibus arboreis et *amara pascitur herba* / proque toro terrae non semper gramen habenti / incubat *infelix.*" See below, chapter II n. 15.

56. Virgil's first patron may have been Pollio. If so, Horace, writing in about 35 B.C., seems to indicate a changed allegiance, *Serm.* 1.10.81: "Plotius et Varius, Maecenas Vergiliusque," and, at a discreet distance, 85: "Pollio, te, Messalla."

57. *Vita Donati* 31–32; Augustus writing even during the grim and arduous Spanish campaign (26–24 B.C.) to inquire about the progress of the *Aeneid.*

58. The Hylas story is hardly attested before the Hellenistic period, when it becomes suddenly popular: Theocritus 13, Apollonius *Arg.* 1.1207–73; see Gow, *Theocritus* II (Cambridge, 1952) 231. Virgil alludes to it in *E.* 6.43–44, where it serves to introduce (45 "et fortunatam . . .") the Pasiphae story, similar in type but unhackneyed. Delos is the subject of Callimachus' fourth *Hymn*, and Parthenius wrote a *Delos* (*Suppl. Hell.* 620–22).

59. *Varia* 18 V.²: "uolito uiuos per ora uirum." Along with this reminiscence of Ennius there are several of Callimachus. *Line 2:* "pastor ab Amphryso": Apollo, who tended animals for Admetus king of Pherae. Callimachus alone of Greek writers sets the scene by the Amphrysus, *Hymn* 2.47–49, where see F. Williams, *Callimachus, Hymn to Apollo. Line 11:* "Aonio . . . uertice": a Callimachean adjective, before Virgil only in Catull. 61.27–30: "perge linquere Thespiae / rupis Aonios specus, / nympha quos super irrigat / frigerans Aganippe." Virgil has two other such allusions to Helicon, both involving Gallus: *E.* 6.65: "Aonas in montis" (Pfeiffer on fr. 572: "Nominis Ἀόνων etc. nullum certum exemplum ante Call."; see also Ardizzoni on Ap. Rhod. 3.1178); and *E.* 10.12: "Aonie Aganippe" (Pfeiffer on fr. 696: "De Aganippe autem nihil nobis notum ante Call."; see also Addenda et Corrigenda on fr. 2a.20–5, 25). *Line 36:* "Cynthius": a uniquely Callimachean epithet previously used by Virgil in his rejection of epic, *E.* 6.3; see Clausen, *AJP* 97 (1976) 245–47. *Line 37:* "Inuidia": Callimachean Βασκανίη; see Clausen, ibid. 245 n. 2.

60. For a discussion of various opinions see L. P. Wilkinson, *The Georgics of Virgil* (Cambridge, 1969), Appendix III; for his own, pp. 166–72. See now R. F. Thomas, "Callimachus, the *Victoria Berenices*, and Roman Poetry," *CQ* n.s. 33 (1983) 92–101.

61. Macrob. *Sat.* 1.24.11: "de Aenea quidem meo, si mehercule iam dignum auribus haberem tuis, libenter mitterem, sed tanta incohata res est ut paene uitio mentis tantum opus ingressus mihi uidear."

62. Cf. Heinze 263: "das Werk muss die Eigenschaften eines 'zusammen-hängenden' langen Gedichts homerischer Art und eines Kranzes von Einzel-gedichten kallimacheischer Art in such vereinigen"; also 370.

63. "A prolonged literary allusion to Homer"—so I described it, some years ago, in "An Interpretation of the *Aeneid*," *HSCP* 68 (1964) 139 = *Virgil: A Collection of Critical Essays*, ed. S. Commager (Englewood Cliffs, N.J., 1966) 75. And so it is, but with an essential qualification, which I was then incapable of making. I refer to the Hellenistic character of the poem, less evident than in the *Eclogues* and *Georgics* but hardly less pervasive.

II. TWO SIMILES AND A WEDDING

1. "She went away," ἀπέβη—over the sea to Athens, to the house of Erechtheus, her principal cult-place. The usual reaction to an epiphany is speechless amazement (θάμβος) or fear; see N. J. Richardson, *The Homeric Hymn to Demeter* (Oxford, 1974) on 188–90.3.

2. 1.456: "Iliacas ex ordine pugnas"; cf. 8.629: "pugnataque in ordine bella." See p. 79.

3. See H. Williamson, "Virgil, *Aen.* 1.460," *CR* 33 (1919) 30; E. J. Kenney, "Two Footnotes," *CR* n.s. 14 (1964) 13.

4. See pp. 77–82.

5. The only major ecphrasis in Apollonius, no doubt by design.

6. Heinze 399: "da ist wirklich der Eindruck erzielt, dass uns nicht sowohl Bildwerke beschrieben als die wechselnden Empfindungen des Aeneas erzählt werden." See further R. D. Williams, "The Pictures on Dido's Temple," *CQ* n.s. 10 (1960) 148–51 (150: "the pictures . . . coloured and interpreted by his emotions"); Austin ad loc.

7. 1.465: "multa gemens, largoque umectat flumine uultum." The adjective *largus* is not elsewhere in Virgil applied to a river, but Lucretius 1.1031 has "largis . . . fluminis undis." Cf. *A.* 2.271: "largosque effundere fletus" (not attested before Virgil but thought by Vahlen, on *Ann.* 6, to be a reminiscence of Ennius); 6.699: "largo fletu simul ora rigabat" (7.738: "quae rigat aequora Sarnus"). The metaphorical *flumen* of tears is apparently Virgil's, imitated only by Claudian *De rapt. Pros.* 3.128. But Lucretius uses *flumen* of blood: "calidum de pectore flumen" (2.354), whence Virgil *A.* 9.414; cf. 9.813–14: "piceum . . . flumen." Cf. also Statius *Theb.* 4.590–91: "Pelops et . . . / Oenomaus largis umectant imbribus ora." The phrase "largis imbribus," in a nonmetaphorical sense, first occurs in Lucr. 1.282; "imbre," in a metaphorical sense, first in Catull. 68.56, where the preceding line prepares for the metaphor: "maesta neque assiduo tabescere lumina fletu / cessarent tristique imbre madere genae"; cf. Asclepiades 12.3 Gow-Page (= *A.P.* 5.145): κάτομβρα γὰρ ὄμματ᾽ ἐρώντων, cited by Luck on Ov. *Tr.* 1.3.18: "imbre per indignas usque cadente genas."

1.485: "tum uero ingentem gemitum dat pectore ab imo." The phrase "ingentem gemitum" is found elsewhere in Virgil only in *A.* 3.555: "gemitum ingentem pelagi" (in connection with Mt. Aetna); and 11.37–38: "ingentem gemitum tunsis ad sidera tollunt / pectoribus, maestoque immugit regia luctu" (of the Trojan women beating their breasts and wailing over the body of Pallas). Cf. 3.674: "curuisque immugiit Aetna cauernis"; *immugio* is not found before Virgil nor elsewhere in Virgil.

Excessive emotion, excessive language?

8. "Cristatus Achilles"; cf. Milton, *Paradise Lost* 4.988–89 (Satan): "and on his crest / Sat Horror plumed"; *Il.* 16.138 (Patroclus puts on Achilles' armor): δεινὸν δὲ λόφος καθύπερθεν ἔνευεν. Servius: "*cristatus Achilles secundum Homerum, qui dicit in Achillis cristis terribile quiddam fuisse.*" Conington: "The crest of Achilles is described *Il.* 19.380 and again 22.314 foll., just as he is going to give Hector his death-wound, so that we are doubtless intended to be reminded of its terrors." Nor is the chariot an inert detail; it will recur shortly.

The figure of Achilles dominates these scenes: "Achillem" (458), "Achilles" (468), "Achilli" (475), "Achilles"(484). The intended effect? The man of sensibility contemplates the man of violence.

9. See Appendix 2.

10. 473–74: "Xanthumque bibissent. / parte alia fugiens amissis Troilus armis." Something may be owing here to Homer's description of Lycaon fleeing from Achilles by the Xanthus, *Il.* 21.50–52: γυμνόν, ἄτερ κόρυθός τε καὶ ἀσπίδος, οὐδ' ἔχεν ἔγχος, / ἀλλὰ τὰ μέν ῥ' ἀπὸ πάντα χαμαὶ βάλε· τεῖρε γὰρ ἱδρὼς / φεύγοντ' ἐκ ποταμοῦ. Troilus has flung away his helmet and shield but kept his spear, to use as a goad. So R. D. Williams, *CQ* n.s. 10 (1960) 145–46, citing *A.* 9.609–10: "uersaque iuuencum / terga fatigamus hasta." Cf. *A.* 10.586–87: "Lucagus ut pronus pendens in uerbera telo / admonuit biiugos"; *Il.* 10.500–501 (Odysseus drives off the horses of Rhesus, striking them with his bow): τόξῳ ἐπιπλήσσων, ἐπεὶ οὐ μάστιγα φαεινὴν / ποικίλου ἐκ δίφροιο νοήσατο χερσὶν ἑλέσθαι; Quint. Smyrn. 9.155–56 (Melanthius replaces a dead charioteer): ἵπποισι δ' ἐκέκλετο μακρὰ τινάσσων / εὔληρ', οὐδ' ἔχε μάστιν, ἔλαυνε δὲ δούρατι θείνων. Troilus is associated with Lycaon in the tradition, both being young and pathetic victims of Achilles: Apollod. *Bibl.* epit. 3.32: Ἀχιλλεὺς ἐνεδρεύσας Τρωίλον ἐν τῷ τοῦ Θυμβραίου Ἀπόλλωνος ἱερῷ φονεύει, καὶ νυκτὸς ἐλθὼν ἐπὶ τὴν πόλιν Λυκάονα λαμβάνει; Dictys Cretensis 4.9: "capti etiam Lycaon et Troilus Priamidae, quos in medium productos Achilles iugulari iubet."

11. See Appendix 3.

12. An attempt to translate 493: "audetque *uiris* concurrere *uirgo*." Festus p. 314.15 L.: "feminas antiqui . . . uiras appellabant, unde adhuc permanent uirgines et uiragines." Cf. Cic. *De off.* 1.18.61 (quoting an unnamed poet): "uos enim iuuenes animum geritis muliebrem, illa uirgo uiri"; Ov. *Met.*

4.681–82: "nec audet / appellare uirum uirgo" (Henry). Native rhetoric; see Norden on *A.* 6.204.

A comparison with Triphiodorus (who is independent of Virgil; see chapter III n. 27) suggests that, to an extent, the choice and arrangement of these scenes is traditional and not Virgil's own. Triphiodorus: 21–22 Hector, 25–28 Sarpedon, 29–30 Rhesus, 30–32 Memnon, 33–39 Penthesilea (37: θηλείης ὑπὸ χειρὸς ἀπεσκέδασεν νέφος ἀνδρῶν); Virgil: 469–73 Rhesus, 474–78 Troilus, 483–87 Hector, 489 Memnon, 490–93 Penthesilea. See below, chapter III n. 50.

13. Notably Valerius Probus, whose harsh criticism of Virgil—"nihil quicquam tam inprospere Vergilium ex Homero uertisse quam uersus hos amoenissimos, quos de Nausicaa Homerus fecit"—has been preserved by Aulus Gellius 9.9.12–17. Though taken seriously by some, Probus' criticism has merely a historical value as indicating (should we care to generalize) how dull and unimaginative literary instruction must have been in the Roman classroom. Probus seems not to know Apollonius.

14. With the exception of Conrardy 30–31 and especially Rütten 33. Conington, Austin, and Williams neglect Apollonius, as do M. Hügi, *Vergils Aeneis und die hellenistische Dichtung* (Bern, 1952) 50, Klingner 401, and G. Carlson, *Die Verwandlung der homerischen Gleichnisse* (Heidelberg, 1972) 74. Like Heinze 120 n. 1 and Cartault I 166 ("Vergile ne lui a rien emprunté"), R. Rieks asserts that Virgil owes nothing to Apollonius ("Die Gleichnisse Vergils," *Aufstieg und Niedergang der röm. Welt* 31.2 [Berlin, 1981] 1047): "Das Dianagleichnis (1, 498–502) beruht auf ausschliesslicher Ausprägung des homerischen Musters (6, 102–9), während die apollonische Ausprägung des Motivs (*Arg.* 3, 876–85) unbeachtet bleibt"; but see W. W. Briggs, Jr., ibid. 965. See also B. Otis, *Virgil: A Study in Civilized Poetry* (Oxford, 1963) 73–76.

15. See p. 12. Cf. *E.* 8.41: "ut uidi, ut perii, ut me malus abstulit error!" and Ov. *Her.* 12.33: "et uidi et perii nec notis ignibus arsi"; S. Timpanaro, *Contributi di filologia e di storia della lingua latina* (Rome, 1978) 279: "Ovidio avrà voluto far vedere che si ricordava non solo di Virgilio, ma anche del modello di quel verso virgiliano"; that is, Theocr. 2.82: ὥς μοι πυρὶ θυμὸς ἰάφθη. See also Nisbet and Hubbard on Hor. *Carm.* 1.22.23.

16. See Vian on Ap. Rhod. 3.869 (p. 137).

17. 500–501: "illa pharetram / fert umero"; cf. Callim. *Hymn* 3.212–13: ἀμφ᾽ ὤμοισι φαρέτρας / ἰοδόκους ἐφόρησαν.

18. Vian on Ap. Rhod. 3.876 (p. 138). The Parthenius is found once earlier in Apollonius, 2.936–39: it is the gentlest of rivers, in which Artemis bathes after the hunt before ascending to Olympus.

19. "Reedy" is a standing epithet of the Eurotas; Theognis 785: Εὐρώτα δονακοτρόφου; Eur. *IT* 399–400; *Helen* 210–11, 349–50, 492–93; *IA* 179.

20. Cf. *A.* 1.498: "qualis in Eurotae."

21. Attested before Virgil only in Bion *Epit. Adon.* 19: καὶ νύμφαι

κλαίουσιν Ὀρειάδες; still, Ὀρειάδες cannot have been so very uncommon in Hellenistic poetry: see Nonnus, ed. Keydell, Index nominum s.v.

22. As it is in the *E.*, 9.60 (Greek name): "incipit apparere Bianoris. hic ubi densas," and *G.*, 4.339 (Greek name): "Cydippe et flaua Lycorias, altera uirgo." See Norden, p. 432.

23. A rare variant; see Allen and von der Mühll ad loc. For Apollonius as a textual critic of Homer see Pfeiffer, *History of Classical Scholarship* 146–48.

24. Heinze 263: "diese Poesie will in kleinen Abschnitten genossen sein, damit alle ihre Feinheiten zur Geltung kommen; wo jedes Wort vom Dichter erwogen ist, soll auch jedes Wort vom Hörer gewürdigt werden; dazu bedarf es gespanntester Aufmerksamkeit, frischester Empfänglichkeit, konzentriertester Teilnahme."

25. 4.133: "reginam thalamo cunctantem"—"as a bride might" (Austin). Cf. Catull. 61.79: "tardet ingenuus pudor"; 90–91: "sed moraris, abit dies. / ⟨prodeas noua nupta⟩." The hesitation of the bride may be a conventional motif; see P. Fedeli, *Il carme 61 di Catullo, Seges* 16 (Freiburg, 1972) 61. For the usual, undramatic interpretation of "cunctantem" ("the proverbial slowness of ladies in making their toilet") see Pease.

26. Austin has no comment. Pease (on 134 "auro") cites, among other references, Callim. *Hymn* 2.32–34 and 4.260–64, but curiously misses 3.110–12. Cartault misses the point entirely, I 346: "C'est la même conception un peu vulgaire du luxe qu'au banquet du Iᵉʳ livre."

27. So Pease. Compare—and contrast—*A.* 11.774–76.

28. So Williams.

29. Cf. *Hymn* 4.260–64 (the effects of Apollo's birth on Delos). Apollo and Artemis are the only gods Callimachus describes as golden; see F. Williams, *Callimachus, Hymn to Apollo* on 32.

30. Cf. Ap. Rhod. 1.309: Λυκίην εὐρεῖαν ἐπὶ Ξάνθοιο ῥοῇσι. ῥοαί is usually plural and usually poetic in classical Greek (*LSJ* s.v.), *fluenta* always plural and always poetic in classical Latin (rare and chiefly Virgilian: Lucr. 5.949; *G.* 4.369, *A.* 4.143, 6.327, where see Norden, 12.35; Silius 12.548, 14.150). Virgil even reproduces the rhythm: Ξάνθοιο ῥοῇσι: "Xanthique fluenta."

31. "Why Virgil should introduce them into the worship of Apollo is not clear, unless to indicate the distances from which worshippers came to Delos" (Pease). Apollonius 2.674–82 describes the awesome epiphany of Apollo (to the Argonauts on the island of Thynias) as he proceeds from Lycia to the country of the Hyperboreans, whose connection with Delos was immemorial; see Daebritz, "Hyperboreer," *RE* 17 (1914) 264–66. The Agathyrsi, a remote Scythian people, may be taken for the fabled Hyperboreans; so Wilamowitz, "Apollon," *Hermes* 38 (1903) 578 n. 2: "Agathyrsen, d. h. Hyperboreer" (Serv.: "populi sunt Scythiae, colentes Apollinem Hyperboreum"). Wilamowitz supposes Hellenistic erudition here, ibid.: "Diese Feinheiten können nicht wohl von Vergil stammen."

32. Facial radiance is a characteristic of epiphanies; cf. the *Homeric Hymn to Aphrodite* 174–75: κάλλος δὲ παρειάων ἀπέλαμπεν / ἄμβροτον and Richardson, *The Homeric Hymn to Demeter* on 276, who does not, however, cite *A.* 4.150.

33. DServ.: "*pulcherrimus* ex animo Didonis."

34. Cartault I 346: "c'est un couple parfaitement assorti." Cf. "pulcherrima" (1.496), "pulcherrimus" (4.141); "per iuga Cynthi" (1.498), "iugis Cynthi" (4.147); "exercet ... choros" (1.499), "instauratque choros" (4.145); "quam mille secutae /hinc atque hinc glomerantur Oreades" (1.499–500), "mixtique altaria circum / Cretesque Dryopesque fremunt pictique Agathyrsi" (4.145–46); "illa pharetram / fert umero" (1.500–1), "tela sonant umeris" (4.149); "gradiens" (1.501), "graditur" (4.147). See chapter IV n. 36.

35. The converse of the relationship between Catullus and Lesbia, 8.7: "quae tu uolebas nec puella nolebat."

36. See p. 42 ("huic uni ... culpae"), p. 37 ("pedibusque rotarum").

37. Cf., in general, Ap. Rhod. 3.6–110.

38. And will occur only once later, 6.638: "deuenere locos," when Aeneas, led by the Sibyl, comes to the Fields of Light. *Deuenio* is not found in *E.* or *G.*

39. Melancholy and beautiful: Wilamowitz, *Hellenistische Dichtung* II (1924) 226 n. 1: "Wirklich schön, unübersetzbar, auch klangvoll, allerdings mehr hellenistisch als homerisch"; Livrea on 4.1165: "l'improvviso afforamento di una riflessione pessimistica può stupire per la sua originalità." No doubt Virgil recognized a kindred voice in these lines.

40. On Virgil's use of the terms *spelunca* and *antrum* see F. Münzer, *Cacus der Rinderdieb* (Basel, 1911) 33 n. 29; Norden on *A.* 6.10 f.

41. In 4.163 Ascanius (so called in 156) is referred to as "Dardaniusque nepos Veneris." The periphrasis ("so strange to our ears": Austin) was apparently suggested by *Arg.* 4.1134: Διὸς Νυσήιον υἷα in Apollonius' account of the cave of Macris. Livrea cites Ar. *Frogs* 215–16: Νυσήιον / Διὸς Διώνυσον, and mentions *Il.* 6.132–33: μαινομένοιο Διωνύσοιο τιθήνας / σεῦε κατ᾿ ἠγάθεον Νυσήιον (cf. *Arg.* 4.1131: ἄντρῳ ἐν ἠγαθέῳ). But why such a periphrasis here? Because Virgil wanted Venus somehow to be present, with Juno, at her son's wedding. La Cerda, in his *Explicatio*, asks and answers the question: "Sed quare in nominando Ascanio periphrasis ista, *Dardanius nepos Veneris*? quia videlicet in hoc malo deesse Venus nepoti suo non potuit." Rather, "filio suo." This is not a case of transferred epithet, as in *A.* 6.57, "Dardana ... Paridis ... tela," since *Dardanius* cannot be applied to Venus (nor can Νυσήιος to Zeus); cf. *E.* 2.61: "Dardaniusque Paris." In 10.132–33 Ascanius is described as "Veneris iustissima cura, / Dardanius ... puer"; but there after Venus, passionately questioning the ways of Jupiter to the Trojans, has expressed her fears for his personal safety in the beleaguered encampment and for the very survival of the Trojan race,

10.46–47: "liceat dimittere ab armis / incolumen Ascanium, liceat superesse nepotem."

42. See p. 31.

43. Not a verbal imitation, but rather an imitation by position; see Knauer 542 s.v. Strukturelles. Also Heinze 370–71.

44. In Virgil only here and in 7.660 of the bastard Aventinus. *Furtiuus* in an erotic sense belongs to the vocabulary of love poetry (*TLL* s.v. 1644.42) and, with the exception of Silius 2.416 (alluding to this passage), is not found elsewhere in epic.

III. THE WOODEN HORSE

1. A Hellenistic name; see O. Jessen, "Antheus," *RE* 1 (1894) 2376. Cf. C. Saunders, "Trojans and Latins in Vergil's *Aeneid*," *TAPA* 71 (1940) 541 n. 18: "Particularly striking are three successive lines (*Dionys.* 32.186–88) which contain three of Vergil's hero-names (Opheltes, Antheus, Thronios). These names occur in a list of 11 of the god's followers who fell in a battle between Dionysus and Deriades." Cf. Ov. *Met.* 3.605 (Opheltes).

2. 1.572: "uultis et his mecum pariter considere regnis?" Dido's spontaneous generosity may surprise the reader. Virgil was thinking of Ap. Rhod. 1.827–29 (Hypsipyle to Jason): τῶ ὑμεῖς στρωφᾶσϑ᾽ ἐπιδήμιοι. εἰ δέ κεν αὖϑι / ναιετάειν ἐϑέλοις καί τοι ἅδοι, ἦ τ᾽ ἂν ἔπειτα / πατρὸς ἐμεῖο Θόαντος ἔχοις γέρας; noticed by Heyne, Forbiger (after Heyne); also by J. Kvičala, *Vergil-Studien* (Prague, 1878) 147, and Conrardy 26; though not by Rütten nor by commentators (with the exception of Forbiger) since Heyne. Austin: "Dido's warm magnanimity finds clear expression here"; indeed, especially as compared (as Virgil no doubt intended it should be) with Hypsipyle's uncandid and self-serving invitation to Jason (μύϑοισι . . . αἱμυλίοισι, 792). That Virgil was thinking of Hypsipyle's speech is confirmed by 561: "uultum demissa profatur." Dido modestly lowers her eyes as she begins to speak, as does Hypsipyle, 790–91: ἡ δ᾽ ἐγκλιδὸν ὄσσε βαλοῦσα / παρϑενικὰς ἐρύϑηνε παρηίδας, and as Medea does after speaking, 3.1008: ἡ δ᾽ ἐγκλιδὸν ὄσσε βαλοῦσα. Cf. also 3.1022–23 (Jason and Medea): ἄμφω δ᾽ ἄλλοτε μέν τε κατ᾽ οὔδεος ὄμματ᾽ ἔρειδον /αἰδόμενοι. For the motif in general see Richardson, *The Homeric Hymn to Demeter* on 194. The phrase "uultum demissa" is not found elsewhere in Virgil (cf., however, *A.* 3.320, 11.480), and here Heinze considers it a mistake, 138: "Dido ist, kurz gesagt, das Idealbild eines heroischen Weibes, wie es sich Virgil darstellte. So ist sie denn zu charakterisieren vor allem negativ: es ist ferngehalten von ihrer Person alles mädchenhaft Naive, Zaghafte"; n. 2: "Das *voltum demissa* I 561 (nach Hypsipyle ἐγκλιδὸν ὄσσε βαλοῦσα I 790, ebenso Medea III 1008) kann daher als Fehlgriff erscheinen." On the question of Dido's age see Appendix 4.

3. Radiance is a feature of epiphany; see Richardson, *The Homeric Hymn to Demeter* on 188–90.2. Cf. *A.* 1.402 (Venus revealing the goddess to her son): "rosea ceruice refulsit"; also Catull. 68.70–71 (Lesbia's appearance in the house of Allius): "quo mea se molli candida diua pede / intulit et trito fulgentem in limine plantam."

4. Elegant Virgilian rhetoric. The word order represents what the words describe; that is, "flauo . . . auro" encloses "argentum Pariusue lapis."

5. See p. 16.

6. On this curious evanescence see B. Fenik, *Studies in the Odyssey, Hermes* Einzelschr. 30 (1974) 61–63; J. Griffin, *Homer on Life and Death* (Oxford, 1980) 78. Arete does not hesitate to speak out later, 11.335–41. There seems to be a reminiscence of this scene in Ap. Rhod. 4: when Medea supplicates Arete she receives no answer (1011–29), but the Argonauts, to whom she also appeals, try to cheer her up. Only later, in bed with Alcinous, does Arete express her feelings in the matter.

7. See Heinze 122–23. In contemporary erotic poetry *obstupesco* portrays the astonished reaction of a lover: Prop 1.3.28, 2.29.25, 4.4.21 (Tarpeia at first sight of the Sabine king Tatius): "obstipuit regis facie et regalibus armis." See P. E. Knox, "A Note on *Aeneid* 1.613," *CP* 79 (1984) 304–5. "Primo aspectu" is not found elsewhere in Virgil. Stupefaction or amazement is also the common reaction to an epiphany; cf. *A.* 4.279: "at uero Aeneas aspectu obmutuit amens" and Richardson, *The Homeric Hymn to Demeter* on 188–90.3.

8. The Medea, that is, of Apollonius (3.275–98), the Ariadne of Catullus (64.86–93).

9. See Heinze 313.

10. Austin: "Significantly, the child is named first; he is more important than any of the gifts"; important, that is, to Dido, a young and childless widow.

11. Cf. 1.685–88 (Venus to Cupid): "ut, cum te gremio accipiet laetissima Dido / . . . / cum dabit amplexus atque oscula dulcia figet, / occultum inspires ignem fallasque ueneno"; 4.83–85: "illum absens absentem auditque uidetque, / aut gremio Ascanium genitoris imagine capta / detinet." The implication is clear enough, that when Dido embraces and kisses Ascanius she is thinking of Aeneas. See Fränkel on 4.423–34 (p. 491); and on kissing, or rather nonkissing, in epic, J. Wackernagel, *Sprachliche Untersuchungen zu Homer* (Göttingen, 1916) 229.

12. See Pease on Cic. *De nat. deor.* 3.42.

13. In this sense *proluo* is colloquial or vulgar; cf. Hor. *Serm.* 1.5.16: "multa prolutus uappa nauta"; 2.4.26–27: "leni praecordia mulso / prolueris melius"; Persius *Prol.* 1: "Nec fonte labra prolui caballino." Here it is redeemed for epic employment by the encompassing phrase "pleno . . . auro" ("with pleasure swilled the gold": Dryden); cf. Varius Rufus *De morte* fr. 2 M.: "incubet ut Tyriis atque ex solido bibat auro," which Macrobius

Sat. 6.1.40 says Virgil imitated in *G.* 2.506: "ut gemma bibat et Sarrano dormiat ostro." "Gemma" is a novelty (*TLL* s.v. 1756.63), apparently to match the novelty "auro." Henry (quoted approvingly by Williams): "The expression *auro*, in the sense of gold cup or goblet . . . seems sufficiently strange to us, to whom the expression *glass*, in the sense of glass cup or goblet . . . does not, such is the force of habit, seem in the least degree strange." Stimulating, as always; but *glass*, in this sense, is as old as Middle English, whereas *aurum*, in this sense, is a poet's invention and never became part of the common speech.

14. See Appendix 5.

15. Cf. *Od.* 8.367–69: αὐτὰρ Ὀδυσσεὺς / τέρπετ᾽ ἐνὶ φρεσὶν ᾗσιν ἀκούων ἠδὲ καὶ ἄλλοι / Φαίηκες δολιχήρετμοι (Knauer); *Il.* 1.474 (Apollo hearing the paean): ὁ δὲ φρένα τέρπετ᾽ ἀκούων.

16. Ap. Rhod. 1.472–74: ἦ καὶ ἐπισχόμενος πλεῖον δέπας ἀμφοτέρῃσι / πῖνε χαλίκρητον λαρὸν μέθυ, δεύετο δ᾽ οἴνῳ / χείλεα κυάνεαί τε γενειάδες (Ursinus). Cartault I 171: "boit en véritable ivrogne"—rather, a violent gesture consistent with a violent nature. As Heinze 213 n. 2 points out, Virgil's Mezentius owes something to Idas.

17. Both Apollonius and Virgil refer to *Od.* 8.469 ff., the farewell banquet which Alcinous holds for the mysterious stranger. Demodocus, at the stranger's request, sings of the Wooden Horse. At a banquet earlier in the day Demodocus had also sung of the Trojan War, in particular of the quarrel between Odysseus and Achilles (νεῖκος Ὀδυσσῆος καὶ Πηλεΐδεω Ἀχιλῆος, 8.75). What was the quarrel about? According to Aristarchus, it seems, whether Troy was to be taken by force (βίη) or by guile (μῆτις, δόλος). An ancient *zetema*; see G. Nagy, *The Best of the Achaeans* (Baltimore, 1979) 22–25. Here too there is a quarrel (νεῖκος, 492) between two heroes, Idmon, a seer, knower, and Idas, headstrong and violent, which Orpheus sublimates by singing of the "quarrel" in the universe. Cf. also Quint. Smyrn. 12.19–20: τῷ νῦν μή τι βίῃ πειρώμεθα Τρώιον ἄστυ / πέρσεμεν, ἀλλ᾽ εἴ πού τι δόλος καὶ μῆτις ἀνύσσῃ. Neoptolemus, his father's son (Ἀχιλλέος . . . υἱός, 66), resumes the old quarrel with Odysseus.

18. Evident to us but not, we should remember, to readers and critics of late antiquity, who were unacquainted with Hellenistic poetry. They found the song objectionable, as we may infer from Macrob. *Sat.* 7.1.14, and might in any case have guessed. Servius commends Virgil's tact: "bene philosophica introducitur cantilena in conuiuio reginae adhuc castae." We may smile, but is Austin's interpretation—"Iopas' song is no more than a reflection of Augustan intellectual interests"—better? However ineptly, Servius was at least trying to explain the song in dramatic terms.

19. See Appendix 5.

20. For an even more refined and expressive tricolon in the *Aeneid*, cf. 8.230–32:

ter totum feruidus ira

lustrat Auentini montem, ter saxea temptat
limina nequiquam, ter fessus ualle resedit.

A tricolon diminuendo with anaphora, "ter . . . , ter . . . , ter . . . ," as if
calling attention to its structure. Three times Hercules blazes with anger (16
syllables), three times he is frustrated (12), three times weary (8).

21. Austin: "The epithet is not otiose, for it marks the contrast between
the patines of bright gold in the serene heaven and the horror upon earth."

22. Why briefly? Servius: "*et breuiter* praescripsit quia Dido dixerat 'a
prima dic, hospes, origine nobis' "; DServ.: "ergo non ad Didonis uolun-
tatem sed narrantis officium." Modern commentators offer no explanation.
Is there an allusion here to the amplitude and variousness of the tradition?
Cf. Triphiodorus 1–5. Cf. also *A.* 2.361–62: "quis cladem illius noctis, quis
funera fando / explicet . . . ?"; *Od.* 3.113–14 (Nestor speaking): ἄλλα τε
πόλλ᾽ ἐπὶ τοῖς πάθομεν κακά· τίς κεν ἐκεῖνα / πάντα γε μυθήσαιτο
καταθνητῶν ἀνθρώπων;; Triph. 664–65: πᾶσαν δ᾽ οὐκ ἂν ἔγωγε μόθου
χύσιν ἀείσαιμι / κρινάμενος τὰ ἕκαστα καὶ ἄλγεα νυκτὸς ἐκείνης.

23. Book 3 concludes with a formal reference to the audience, "Sic pater
Aeneas intentis omnibus unus" (716), which recalls the opening line of Book
2, "Conticuere omnes intentique ora tenebant."

24. Shakespeare, *Titus Andronicus* 5.3.82.

25. See Heinze 71–72, Austin xiii. Hence Aeneas' passionate asseveration
that he had avoided no danger and deserved to fall at the hands of the Greeks
(2.431–34).

26. 2.608–23. Heyne on 622: "Grande et mirabile phantasma!" Cf.
Triph. 559–69; Heinze 51–52.

27. I believe, with Heinze 81 and Vian, that Quintus and Triphiodorus
are independent of Virgil; see F. Vian, *Recherches sur les Posthomerica de
Quintus de Smyrne* (Paris, 1959) 95–101; M. Campbell, *A Commentary on
Quintus Smyrnaeus Posthomerica XII* (Leiden, 1981) 115–25, 133–37,
147–48. In general, Quintus and Triphiodorus represent the tradition before
Virgil. Therefore, when Virgil differs from them we have, or may have, innovation on his part.

28. Although Quint. Smyrn. 13.300–308 states that he fought valiantly
and fled when there was no longer any hope.

29. Contrast Marlowe, *Dido, Queene of Carthage* 2.1.169–70: "In which
unhappie work was I employed, / These hands did helpe to hale it to the
gates."

30. See Heinze 25.

31. Anticipated, however, by "Tyndaridem" (464) and "Troiiugenas"
(465).

32. Munro's translation, slightly modified; too literal perhaps, but giving
some idea of the high archaic style which Lucretius adopts here under the
influence of Ennius.

33. Cf. Ennius, *Alexander, scen.* 76–77 V.² = 72–73 J.: "nam maximo saltu superabit grauidus armatis equus, / qui suo partu ardua perdat Pergama"; imitated by Virgil, *A.* 6.515–16: "cum fatalis equus saltu super ardua uenit / Pergama et armatum peditem grauis attulit aluo"; see Fraenkel on Aesch. *Ag.* 826. The metaphor of pregnancy is implicit in *Ag.* 825: ἵππου νεοσσός, explicit in Eur. *Tro.* 11: ἐγκύμον᾽ ἵππον τευχέων and Lycophron 342: τὸν ὠδίνοντα μορμωτὸν λόχον; and described, perhaps too casually, by Gow-Page on Antiphilus of Byzantium 35.1–2 (πῶλον / εὐόπλου Δαναῶν ἔγκυον ἡσυχίης) as "a conventional motif." Quintus of Smyrna virtually ignores the metaphor (νηδύα, 12.140, is a single feature among others); Triphiodorus uses it six times: 63, 135, 200, 384, 386–90, 533. Virgil is the only poet who relates it to the Trojans' deluded act.

34. An arresting word, seldom found in poetry and only here in Virgil (*TLL* s.v.). The allusion is to shipbuilding, no doubt a traditional metaphor; cf. Triph. 63–64: γαστέρα κοιλήνας, ὁπόσον νεὸς ἀμφιελίσσης / ὀρθὸν ἐπὶ στάθμην μέγεθος τορνώσατο τέκτων; Epeios would necessarily be a ship's carpenter. Both Servius and DServius refer to Cicero, apparently *Verr.* 2.2.13: "nauem onerariam maximam Messanae esse publice coactis operis aedificatam." On "intexunt" DServ. comments: "naues texi dicuntur; nam ideo ubi naues fiunt textrinum uocatur, ut ipse alibi (*A.* 11.326) 'bis denas Italo texamus robore naues' "; cf. also *A.* 2.112–13: "cum iam hic trabibus contextus acernis / staret equus"; 186: "roboribus textis"; Enn. *Alex.* 65–66 V.² = 43–44 J.: "classis cita / texitur"; *Ann.* 477 V.²: "textrinum nauibus longis"; Catull. 64.10: "pinea coniungens inflexae texta carinae"; Ov. *Her.* 16.112: "texitur et costis panda carina suis." Here too, following on "aedificant" and "intexunt," "costas" may suggest the curved frame-timbers, or ribs, of a ship (not so listed in *TLL* s.v. 1084.81–84: Pers. 6.31: "costa ratis lacerae"; Pliny *NH* 13.62: "nauium costis"). In any case, with "equum" standing before the caesura and "costas" at the end of the next line, a pattern of emphasis, the reader will be reminded of the ribs of a living animal; cf. Lucr. 5.1297: "armatum in equi conscendere costas." For the apparent metaphor from weaving see now O. Skutsch on Enn. *Ann.* 504; for the actual process of ancient shipbuilding, L. Casson, *Ships and Seamanship in the Ancient World* (Princeton, 1971) 203–8.

35. *Recutio* is a new verb, by its novelty calling attention to the reverberation in the following line; and there reinforced by "insonuere," which also seems to be new (the "old" verb being *resono*); at any rate, *insono* is not found before Virgil and the reader of Virgil first finds it here. Cf. *A.* 7.451: "uerberaque insonuit"; the transitive is a novelty, imitated by Claudian 28.625, as is the transitive *resono* in 7.11–12: "lucos ... resonat," imitated by Silius 14.30.

36. Triph. 216: μοῦνος δὲ πληγῇσιν ἑκούσια γυῖα χαραχθείς, like Odysseus, *Od.* 4.244: αὐτόν μιν πληγῇσιν ἀεικελίῃσι δαμάσσας, who disguised himself as an ill-used beggar and entered Troy. For Sinon as a

double of Odysseus see Zwicker, "Sinon," *RE* 2.5 (1927) 249. Triphiodorus
suggests the likeness without mentioning Odysseus (cf. also 291: πολυμήχα-
νος ἥρως); in Quint. Smyrn., however, as in Virgil, Sinon blames Odysseus
for his troubles.

37. In Quintus the same three names are cited in the same order—not,
however, by Sinon but by Ajax, in his angry denunciation of Odysseus
(5.183, 195, 198). See Vian, *Posthomerica* 64 (for "Philoctète, Palamède et
Ajax" read "Achille, Philoctète et Palamède").

38. Heinze 9, 81: "Alles, meine ich, führt darauf, in Tryphiodors Fassung
... eine Wiedergabe der ursprünglichen zu sehen, in Virgils Fassung nicht
originale Erfindung, sondern steigernde Ausgestaltung." Vian, *Posthomerica*
100: "Nous avons cru pouvoir montrer en outre que l'histoire de Sinon, chez
Virg., QS et Tryph., remonte à une source commune dont Tryph. est le
témoin le plus fidèle."

39. Austin on 2.82: "it may well be an idea of Virgil's own to bring it
[the story of Palamedes] into this context"; Macrob. *Sat.* 5.22.12: "in talibus
locis grammatici excusantes imperitiam suam inuentiones has ingenio magis
quam doctrinae Maronis adsignant." Virgil, ignoring Achilles and apparently
Philoctetes, develops the reference to Palamedes, whose judicial murder had
become an *exemplum*; see E. Wüst, "Palamedes," *RE* 36 (1943) 2503. Virgil
seems to have drawn on Euripides' *Philoctetes*; see Heinze 8–9. Or on Accius' *Philocteta*? According to Macrob. *Sat.* 6.1.57, Virgil imitates Accius'
Telephus at the beginning of Sinon's speech. See also the next note.

40. *A.* 2.103–4 (at the end of Sinon's first speech): "iamdudum sumite
poenas: / hoc Ithacus uelit et magno mercentur Atridae"; Triph. 279–80 (at
the end of Sinon's first speech): χάρμα γὰρ Ἀργείοισι γενήσομαι, εἴ κεν
ἐάσσεις / χερσὶν ὕπο Τρώων ἱκέτην καὶ ξεῖνον ὀλέσθαι. Ursinus compares *Il.* 1.255: ἦ κεν γηθήσαι Πρίαμος Πριάμοιό τε παῖδες; so also La
Cerda, Conington, and Heyne with the following line, ἄλλοι τε Τρῶες μέγα
κεν κεχαροίατο θυμῷ. Cf. Soph. *Philoct.* 314–15 (at the end of Philoctetes'
first speech): τοιαῦτ' Ἀτρεῖδαί μ' ἥ τ' Ὀδυσσέως βία, / ὦ παῖ, δεδράκασ'.

The verb *mercari* is rare in classical poetry; apart from one other instance
in Virgil (*A.* 1.367) it is not found elsewhere in epic except, predictably, in
Silius 1.24; nor is it found in Lucretius, Catullus, Tibullus, Ovid, Seneca,
Statius, Martial, or Juvenal. Horace uses it twice (*Serm.* 1.2.86, *Epist.*
2.2.158); Propertius 3 times. But it is found some 23 times in Plautus and
4 times in Terence: obviously a word that might be used by an early dramatic
poet.

41. Whose poem Triphiodorus knew: see Vian, *Posthomerica* 62 n. 5.

42. See also Campbell, *Posthomerica XII* 177–78.

43. Virgil alludes to the torture, 2.64: "certantque inludere capto," as La
Cerda notices. Vian, *Posthomerica* 64: "or, si Virgile, plus humain ou plus
favorable à Ilion, supprime la scène de la torture, il y fait allusion, puisque
Sinon prévoit à plusieurs reprises qu'on va le supplicier (*En.*, II, 64, 72,

103)." Conington has no comment; Austin only "Virgil knows human nature."

44. 12.375–86; Campbell, *Posthomerica XII* 123: "curt and barren of solid detail." Sinon's speech in Triphiodorus consists of 30 lines, in two parts (265–82, 292–303); in Virgil of 106 lines, in three parts (see above, n. 38).

45. 12.389–90: οἳ δ᾽ ἄρ᾽ ἔφαντο / ἔμμεναι ἠπεροπῆα πολύτροπον. Quintus' language is incongruous (cf. *Od.* 1.1, 11.364), for his Sinon hardly resembles Odysseus.

46. Clinical detail; see Campbell, *Posthomerica XII* 135 f.

47. And again, for the last time, 2.258–59: "inclusos *utero* Danaos et *pinea* furtim / laxat *claustra* Sinon." "Pinea . . . claustra" may be a reminiscence of Catull. 64.10: "pinea . . . texta"; see above, n. 34.

48. Mackail (*The Aeneid* [Oxford, 1930]): "A phrase like *lapsus rotarum*, 'slidings of wheels,' was a recognized Grecism, and Virgil in using it was following rather than setting a fashion." Which does not of course explain why he used it. Austin: "lapsus with *rotarum*, a Virgilian invention . . . (cf. G. 1.143 'ferri rigor'); so Soph. *El.* 718 f. [cited by Conington] ὁμοῦ γὰρ ἀμφὶ νῶτα καὶ τροχῶν βάσεις / ἤφριζον. The abstract noun gives a vivid feel of movement, as if the wheels were in motion when they were being fitted." Williams: "*lapsus rotarum* (literally 'the gliding of wheels') is a very ornate phrase, cf. *remigium alarum* (1.301)." Commentators on Soph. *El.* 718, Jebb and now Kells and Kamerbeek, cite no parallels.

49. La Cerda: "Vt digessi, sententia est clara: non ita si dicas, *subiiciunt lapsus pedibus rotarum*. . . . obsecro, qui erunt *pedes rotarum*? vel quae haec phrasis?" On such momentary ambiguity see pp. 24, 42.

50. Andromache's lament, *scen.* 92 V.² = 87 J.: "o pater, o patria, o Priami domus." Compare the epilogue Aeneas pronounces on Priam, 2.554–58, with that of Quint. Smyrn. 13.246–50.

51. See H. Kleinknecht, "Laokoon," *Hermes* 79 (1944) 66 ff., whose article is fundamental to any discussion of this scene. The idea of the monstrous (which lay within the range of contemporary experience) might have occurred to Virgil independently, but there are intimations of it in the tradition: Triph. 247–48: οἱ δ᾽ ὅτε τεχνήεντος ἴδον δέμας αἰόλον ἵππου, / θαύμασαν ἀμφιχυθέντες; 288–89: ἀλλ᾽ ἄγε καὶ σύ μοι εἰπέ, τί τοι τόδε θαῦμα τέτυκται, / ἵππος, ἀμειλίκτοιο φόβου τέρας; Quint. Smyrn. 12.358–59: ἀμφὶ δ᾽ ἄρ᾽ αὐτῷ / θάμβεον ἑσταότες.

52. Kleinknecht, *Hermes* 79 (1944) 74.

53. *Insinuo* is a favorite Lucretian verb (Munro on 1.116); *sinuo*, to describe the huge undulating length of the snakes, "sinuatque immensa uolumine terga" (208), is Virgil's invention, as commentators note. What commentators fail to note, however, is that neither verb occurs elsewhere in the *Aeneid*: a philological fact with a significant literary bearing. Virgil implies a connection between Laocoon's death, the Horse, and the Trojans' irrationality (*furor*). Cf. 2.225–26: "at gemini lapsu delubra ad summa dra-

cones / effugiunt," on which Servius comments: "*labi* proprie serpentum est"; 235–36: "pedibusque rotarum / subiciunt lapsus"; 240: "illa subit mediaeque minans inlabitur urbi"; also *TLL* s.v. *labor* 787.48; Kleinknecht, *Hermes* 79 (1944) 72, 73, 74; B. M. W. Knox, "The Serpent and the Flame," *AJP* 71 (1950) 384–86 = *Virgil, A Collection of Critical Essays*, ed. S. Commager (Englewood Cliffs, N.J., 1966) 128–30.

54. 2.250: "ruit Oceano nox." Commentators routinely cite *Od.* 5.294 (= 9.69): ὀρώρει δ᾽ οὐρανόθεν νύξ, and no doubt Virgil had the Odyssean phrase in mind. But at precisely the same point in the narrative, at the end of the Cassandra episode, to which Virgil for reasons already explained merely alludes, Quint. Smyrn. 12.575 has μάλα γὰρ τάχ᾽ ἐπήιεν ὑστατίη νύξ, Triph. 452–53 δαιμονίη δὲ / Ἴλιον αἰπεινὴν ὀλεσίπτολις ἀμφέβαλεν νύξ.

IV. DIDO AND AENEAS

1. The transition from Book 3 to Book 4 was criticized in antiquity as too abrupt; see Servius on 4.1.

2. See Heinze 119–25; *CHCL* II 189 n. 1.

3. Note also the pronounced alliteration, "*u*ulnus alit *u*enis et *c*aeco *c*arpitur igni. / *multa uiri uir*tus animo *mult*usque," which is reminiscent of the high archaic style of Ennius, "*n*am *n*umquam *e*ra *e*rrans mea domo ecferret pedem, / *a*nimo *a*egro *a*more *sae*uo *s*aucia."

4. Virgil is also indebted to Lucretius, who "quotes" Ennius, 4.1048: "idque petit corpus, mens unde est saucia amore," then elaborates the metaphor, 1049: "namque omnes plerumque cadunt in uulnus." With "caeco ... igni" cf. Lucr. 4.1120: "uulnere caeco"; *caecus* in this sense is Lucretian; see *TLL* s.v. 45.45 (it will be noticed that Cicero *De or.* 2.357 explains "res caecas").

5. Ariadne and Medea had already been associated by Apollonius 3.997–1006; see *CHCL* II 191–92.

6. For an example of equal precision of reference see below, n. 38.

7. See Henry ad loc.

8. Eros with his bow and arrows becomes popular in the Hellenistic period; see A. Furtwängler in Roscher s.v. 1365. Cupid, his Roman counterpart, is out of place in epic; he belongs rather to comedy and elegy; see *TLL* Onomast. C-D s.v. *Cupido* 748.78. Virgil daringly introduced him into the *Aeneid*, 1.657–722; but contrast Virgil's Cupid with the Eros of Apollonius, here as in 3.156–57 equipped with bow and arrows. Although Apollonius constantly uses, or abuses, Homeric language, he did not, like Virgil, aspire to write a Homeric epic.

9. The metaphor appears to be Cicero's, *Post red. ad Quir.* 25: "atque haec cura, Quirites, erit infixa animo meo sempiterna"; *Phil.* 2.64: "infixus

haeret animo dolor": *TLL* s.v. 1421.44. But in Cicero the metaphor is incidental and hardly felt.

10. According to Servius, each word in the line is to be stressed: "singula pronuntianda sunt; ingenti enim dicta sunt libra, quibus confessioni desiderii sui quandam inicit refrenationem." Several Italian scholars felt that "huic uni" should refer to Aeneas (see Pease's note) but were unable to construe the line. For similar cases of ambiguity see above, pp. 24, 37.

11. *Succumbere* in a sexual sense is attested before Virgil: Catull. 111.3: "sed cuiuis quamuis potius succumbere par est"; as is *culpa*: Catull. 68.139: "coniugis in culpa." *Succumbere* occurs only here in Virgil; *culpa* only twice in Book 4, here and in 172. "Culpae" is emphasized by its position and, as Pease notes, by the alliteration "succumbere culpae." (Note also the emphasis on "coniugis" at the beginning of 21.) Cf. Ovid's reading of this line, *Met.* 7.748–50: "et peccasse fatebar / et potuisse datis simili succumbere culpae / me quoque muneribus."

12. ἀνίας is in apposition to τοὺς; see Chantraine, *Grammaire homérique* II (Paris, 1963) 15.

13. The form of her oath is Homeric, e.g. *Il.* 4.182 (= 8.150): τότε μοι χάνοι εὐρεῖα χθών (see Pease's note)—"mais dans l'*Iliade* ce n'est qu'une façon de parler courante, une formule qui a perdu l'énergie de son sens primitif; elle la reprend dans la bouche de Didon" (Cartault I 341). But Dido was not the first woman in literature to voice this sentiment; cf. *Il.* 6.410–11 (Andromache): ἐμοὶ δέ κε κέρδιον εἴη / σεῦ ἀφαμαρτούσῃ χθόνα δύμεναι; Ap. Rhod. 3.798–801 (Medea): ἤ τ᾽ ἂν πολὺ κέρδιον εἴη / τῇδ᾽ αὐτῇ ἐν νυκτὶ λιπεῖν βίον ἐν θαλάμοισι, / πότμῳ ἀνωίστῳ, κάκ᾽ ἐλέγχεα πάντα φυγοῦσαν, / πρὶν τάδε λωβήεντα καὶ οὐκ ὀνομαστὰ τελέσσαι; Quint. Smyrn. 5.537–38 (Tecmessa): ὥς μ᾽ ὄφελον τὸ πάροιθε περὶ τραφερὴ χάνε γαῖα, / πρὶν σέο πότμον ἰδέσθαι ἀμείλιχον.

14. Again, note the repetition "ille . . .; ille," the emphasis on "abstulit," and the alliteration "secum seruetque sepulcro."

15. And only once again by Virgil, *A.* 8.294 (the Hymn to Hercules), where Eden detects "a rhapsodic Greek flavour." See *TLL* Onomast. s.v. *Cretes* 710.49. Κρήσιος is an extremely rare adjective: it occurs once in Euripides (*Hipp.* 372; choral), once in Callimachus (fr. 202.82, where see Pfeiffer), but not in Theocritus or Apollonius.

16. See *TLL* Onomast. s.v. Δικταῖος is first attested in Aratus *Phaen.* 35, then Callim. *Hymn* 1.4, 47:Δικταῖαι Μελίαι, 3.199; *Epigr.* 22.3; Ap. Rhod. 1.509, 1130, 2.434, 4.1640.

17. See above, p. 11.

18. No commentator, not even Pease, has anything to say about "pastor." Virgil's "armentarius Afer," who owned a Cretan quiver (*G.* 3.344–45), might at least be mentioned.

19. *Hymn* 1.45, where see McLennan; *Hymn* 3.197.

20. *Hymn* 3.81: Κυδώνιον . . . τόξον; also fr. 560 Pf. Theocritus prefers the form Κυδωνικός.

21. See Nisbet and Hubbard on Hor. *Carm.* 1.15.17.

22. Whose simile was suggested by a simile in *Il.* 10.360–62. Cf. Fränkel on 4.12–19: "dies ist eines der eindrucksvollsten Gleichnisse der *Argon.*"

23. See Clausen, "Silua Coniecturarum," *AJP* 76 (1955) 51.

24. Pease compares *E.* 1.3: "dulcia linquimus arua." But Meliboeus' reference to his lost fields is bittersweet. The tone here is rather that of *A.* 6.455, when Aeneas meets Dido in the Underworld, "dulcique adfatus amore est."

25. 4.293–94: "temptaturum aditus et quae mollissima fandi / tempora." What Virgil means is clear enough from 4.423 (Dido to Anna): "sola uiri mollis aditus et tempora noras." But it seems not to have been noticed that this is the only instance of the superlative of *mollis* in the *A.* (24 instances), surely a fact affecting the tone.

26. Austin on 4.423: "How groping these two were: Aeneas would have done far better to go in person to Dido immediately after his decision to leave, instead of looking for ways and means to tell her; and if Dido had gone in person to him now, she might yet have won him back." Otis, *Virgil* 268 (on Aeneas' final speech to Dido): "He should have avoided excuses and taken his share of the blame"—quoted by Highet 72, who slyly asks: "What was Dido's share of the blame?" Such comments are an unconscious tribute to the power of Virgil's fiction: a critic may speak in this way only if he remains aware that he is speaking not of decisions humanly possible but of literary decisions, that he is complaining, in effect, not of Aeneas' behavior but of Virgil's.

27. Similarly Servius: "blanditiis circumuenire." See *TLL* s.v. 1850.29.

28. T. E. Page is an honorable exception. Pease, after Conington: "The verb denotes an indirect rather than a direct approach. . . . Rand . . . notes that it is used of a worshipper who implores." Austin: "literally, 'to canvass,' a good [!] word here, but Page is wrong in thinking that it 'hints at cunning and treachery'; the sense of pleading or persuading is uppermost, as in Hor. C. 1.35.5 'te pauper ambit sollicita prece / ruris colonus.' " This is essentially Wunderlich's interpretation (see Heyne); but cf. Nisbet and Hubbard on Hor. *Carm.* 1.35.5: "*ambit*: the word suggests the ingratiating blandishments of a canvasser or office-seeker." Williams: "*ambire*: 'approach,' 'try to win over,' *blanditiis circumvenire* (Servius); cf. *Aen.* 7.333, Hor. *Odes* 1.35.5." Conington (Boston, 1880; published posthumously by J. A. Symonds) translates "ambire" as "approach," A. Mandelbaum (Berkeley, 1971) as "face"; J. W. Mackail (London, 1908) is evasive, R. Humphries (New York, 1951) and C. Day Lewis (Oxford, 1952) exactly right, "get round." Neither Otis nor Klingner comments on "ambire."

29. Fordyce (on 7.333): "*ambire*: the metaphor is derived from political canvassing and usually conveys, as it does here, a suggestion of cajolery: that suggestion is not absent in iv. 283 f. 'quo nunc reginam ambire furentem / audeat adfatu' (Aeneas is wondering how to break his news to Dido)

or even from Hor. *Od.* 1.35.5 f. 'te pauper ambit sollicita prece / ruris colonus.' " The fact that "ambire" is "in the mouth of Aeneas' enemy Juno" (Austin) does not alter its meaning.

30. See p. 32.

31. See p. 48.

32. See p. 48.

33. Klingner 445–46: "Wenn sie dabei *optima* genannt wird, so hat man zu bedenken, dass dieses Wort nicht herablassend, sondern eher aufblickend gemeint ist, mit entschiedener Verehrung. Anchises, Latinus und Evander werden damit geehrt, Aeneas so genannt, *pater optime* sagt man." But a woman in love does not want "Verehrung," not, certainly, in the first instance: she wants a like response from her lover.

34. Conington: "kindest of friends"; Mackail: "in her kindness," also "benignant," "gracious"; Humphries simply omits "optima"; Day Lewis: "generous"; Mandelbaum: "gracious"; Williams, *Tradition and Originality in Roman Poetry* 385: "his dear Dido." Austin: " 'Dido, his best'.... *Optima* is heart-breaking in its context.... It means what it says, that Dido was all the world to him." But cf. Cartault I 317: "l'excellente Didon— *optima Dido* 291, c'est tout ce qu'il trouve à en dire"; Pease: "Is it not, perhaps, in the (slightly disparaging) sense of 'that excellent woman, Dido'?" Ancient readers too may have felt some difficulty: DServ.: "pro adhuc optima."

35. 4.298: "omnia tuta timens": a deep-seated human sense of experience. See Henry.

36. See Heinze 287 n. 1; Campbell, *Posthomerica XII* 178. In structure, as in reference and tone (although the tone is now more intense), this simile corresponds to the simile of the stricken deer, 4.68–72: "uritur" (68), "saeuit" (300); "totaque uagatur / urbe furens" (68–69), "totamque incensa per urbem / bacchatur" (300–301); "qualis coniecta cerua sagitta" (69), "qualis commotis excita sacris / Thyias" (301–2); "quam . . .–que" (70–71), "ubi . . . –que" (302–3). See below, n. 59.

37. Highet 134: "with a hiss of hatred"; see D. Feeney, "The Taciturnity of Aeneas," *CQ* n.s. 33 (1983) 207.

38. Cartault I 350: "305 perfide, 366 perfide, 421 perfidus; de même dans la bouche d'Ariane, Catulle, LXIV, 132 perfide, 133 perfide, 174 perfidus"; also Highet 222. That is, "perfide" is found in the same metrical position in the first line of Ariadne's lament and Dido's first speech, and "perfide" at the beginning of the second line of Ariadne's lament and Dido's second speech.

39. 4.314: "mene fugis?" Cf. Sappho 1.21: καὶ γὰρ αἰ φεύγει, ταχέως διώξει (but see A. Giacomelli, "The Justice of Aphrodite in Sappho Fr. 1," *TAPA* 110 [1980] 135–42); Anacreon 417.1–2 Page: πῶλε Θρηικίη, τί δή με / . . . / νηλέως φεύγεις . . . ;; Theocr. 6.17: καὶ φεύγει φιλέοντα καὶ οὐ φιλέοντα διώκει; *E.* 2.60: "quem fugis, a! demens?"; *A.* 9.199–200:

"mene ... / Nise, fugis?" Norden on *A.* 6.466: "Das Motiv ist aus der alten Lyrik ... über die alexandrinische Poesie ... in die lateinische Erotik gekommen." In the Underworld their roles are reversed and it is Aeneas who puts the question, 6.466: "quem fugis?"

40. For the idea of this passage Virgil is indebted to Apollonius 1.896–98 (Hypsipyle to Jason, who is about to sail away): μνώεο μήν, ἀπεών περ ὁμῶς καὶ νόστιμος ἤδη, / Ὑψιπύλης· λίπε δ᾽ ἥμιν ἔπος, τό κεν ἐξανύσαιμι / πρόφρων, ἤν ἄρα δή με θεοὶ δώωσι τεκέσθαι (note the echo of Nausicaa's farewell to Odysseus, *Od.* 8.461–62: χαῖρε, ξεῖν᾽, ἵνα καί ποτ᾽ ἐῶν ἐν πατρίδι γαίῃ / μνήσῃ ἐμεῖ᾽); for its tenderness, to Catullus 61.209: "Torquatus ... paruulus" (Ursinus); 214–15: "sit suo similis patri / Manlio" (Fedeli, *Il carme 61 di Catullo* 114: "in tal modo il *paruolus Torquatus* attesterà la pudicizia della madre." To the passages cited by Fedeli and Pease here add Macrob. *Sat.* 2.5.3 [Augustus]: "idem cum ad nepotum turbam similitudinemque respexerat qua repraesentabatur Agrippa, dubitare de pudicitia filiae erubescebat"); the pathos is Virgil's own. In the case of Jason and Hypsipyle, there was a son, Euneos, king of Lemnos (*Il.* 21.41); and Hypsipyle did not kill herself. The Hypsipyle passage seems first to have been noticed by Kvičala, *Vergil-Studien* 147–48.

41. Cf. 4.221 (noting the plural): "oblitos famae melioris amantis"; 281: "dulcis ... terras"; 395: "multa gemens magnoque animum labefactus amore" ("labefactus amore" is a very strong expression; cf. 8.389–90: "notusque medullas / intrauit calor et labefacta per ossa cucurrit"; Lucr. 4.1114: "membra uoluptatis dum ui labefacta liquescunt"; *labefactus* is found only once elsewhere in Virgil, *G.* 2.264: "labefacta mouens robustus iugera fossor"); 448: "magno persentit pectore curas"; 6.455: "dulcique adfatus amore."

42. See Heinze 36–37; Klingner 464–65.

43. See Feeney's excellent discussion, *CQ* n.s. 33 (1983).

44. Or 189 lines; Highet 332.

45. Book 8, 219 lines; Highet 333.

46. "Memin*isse* ... El*isse*": the assonance calls attention to the strange name. Dido uses it herself as she prepares for death, 4.610: "di morientis Elissae"; and it occurs, for the third and last time, at the beginning of Book 5: as Aeneas puts out to sea he looks back at the walls of Carthage, 3–4: "moenia respiciens, quae iam infelicis Elissae / conlucent flammis." Mackail on 4.335: "In none of these cases is any special reason for the variation apparent; but it is to be observed that the name Dido is only used in its uninflected form"—a nonexplanation (Virgil was not at the mercy of his own technique) accepted by Austin and Williams ("It does not seem that there is any difference other than metrical preference in the use of the two names") and, cautiously, by Pease.

47. 4.340–43: "*me* si fata *meis* paterentur ducere uitam / auspiciis et sponte *mea* componere curas, / urbem Troianam primum dulcisque *meorum* / reliquias colerem"—unobtrusive Virgilian rhetoric, beautifully controlled.

48. "Phoenissam": emphatic and ungenerous, reinforcing the effect of "Elissae" (335); 347–48: "si te Karthaginis arces / Phoenissam Libycaeque aspectus detinet urbis." Note the sudden accumulation of foreign names.

49. But Aeneas is telling the truth, however unconvincingly: 6.695–96: "tua me, genitor, tua tristis imago / saepius occurrens."

50. 4.360: "desine meque tuis incendere teque querelis"; the intensity of the rhetoric expresses the intensity of the emotion. See Feeney, *CQ* n.s. 33 (1983) 209–10.

51. Helen is the only woman in Homer—and Helen is virtually a goddess—who is visited or spoken to by a deity (Aphrodite, *Il.* 3.389–94). Calypso's case is special, obviously. Athena does not appear to Penelope, as she does to Odysseus, but she twice puts an idea into her head, *Od.* 18.158–59 (= 21.1–2): τῇ δ᾽ ἄρ᾽ ἐπὶ φρεσὶ θῆκε θεὰ γλαυκῶπις Ἀθήνη, / κούρῃ Ἰκαρίοιο, περίφρονι Πηνελοπείῃ, and prevents her from recognizing Odysseus, 19.479: τῇ γὰρ Ἀθηναίη νόον ἔτραπεν. Athena appears to Nausicaa and speaks to her, but in a dream and disguised, 6.22: εἰδομένη κούρῃ ναυσικλειτοῖο Δύμαντος. When Nausicaa and her handmaids are about to return to the city, Athena again intervenes, and the ball is thrown into the water (see above, p. 19). See also Heinze 188, 307–8.

52. "Scilicet is": cf. Lucr. 1.377, 2.710, 4.773, 6.995; "quietos": cf. Lucr. 5.168, 6.73.

53. See Feeney, *CQ* n.s. 33 (1983) 209–10.

54. See Clausen, *A. Persi Flacci Saturarum Liber* (Oxford, 1956) xx, adding Meleager 72.1–4 Gow-Page (= *A.P.* 5.184).

55. See Feeney, *CQ* n.s. 33 (1983) 210.

56. See *TLL* s.v. *collabor* 1572.63. A. 4.664: "conlapsam aspiciunt comites" (death of Dido); 6.226: "conlapsi cineres" (funeral pyre of Misenus); 8.584: "conlapsum in tecta ferebant" (Evander, like Dido, in a dead faint); 9.434: "ceruix conlapsa recumbit" (death of Euryalus); 9.708: "conlapsa ruunt immania membra" (death of Bitias); 9.753: "conlapsos artus" (death of Pandarus); G. 3.485: "morbo conlapsa" (plague, death of animals). Cf. A. 11.805–6 (of the fatally wounded Camilla): "concurrunt trepidae comites dominamque ruentem / suscipiunt." The form *suscipiunt* does not occur elsewhere in Virgil.

57. Austin: "here, as Pease remarks, it presumably refers to the beautiful African marbles which are so often mentioned by the poets; but it is curiously otiose." Paratore (*Eneide. Libro 4.* [Rome, 1947]): "Nota ... il tocco di molle opulenza orientale, ben adatto a questo momento di doloroso languore della regina."

58. The repetitions are suggestive—"fletus" (437), "fletibus" (439), "flatibus" (442), "nullis" (438), "ullas" (439), "obstant" and "obstruit" (440)—and no doubt deliberate.

59. Cf. "antiquam ... ornum" (2.626), "annoso ... quercum" (4.441); "instant / eruere ... certatim" (2.627–28), "eruere ... certant" (4.443); "concusso uertice" (2.629), "concusso stipite" (4.444).

60. Virgil was concerned to establish a verbal connection with 2.610–12: "Neptunus muros magnoque emota tridenti / fundamenta quatit totamque a sedibus urbem / eruit" (and with "eruere," 4.443; see n. 59; cf. also Catull. 64.108: "eruit"). Neptune uproots the city with his trident as if it were a great tree; cf. *G.* 2.209–10 (the plowman): "antiquasque domos auium cum stirpibus imis / eruit"; *A.* 5.449: "radicibus eruta pinus." Cf. also "Neptunus" (2.610), "Neptunia" (625); "auulsaque saxis / saxa" (608–9), "iugis auulsa" (631). The tree-simile here is related to its context as it is not in 4.441–46.

61. Heinze 250: "Landschaftliche Schilderungen gibt Virgil nur wenig; aber die wenigen ausführlichen sind Imitationen . . . vom Vorbild geht er aus, nicht von der eigenen Anschauung. Die Schilderung des Seesturms in I vermeidet fast geflissentlich jeden Zug, der auf eigene Beobachtung schliessen lassen könnte. Der Stoff der Gleichnisse, soweit sie Naturvorgänge heranziehen, ist überwiegend entlehnt: selbst ein so auffallendes und gesuchtes, wie den Vergleich eines schwankenden Gemüts mit dem von der Wasserfläche eines Beckens zurückgeworfenen zitternden Sonnenlicht übernimmt Virgil unbedenklich (VIII 22, Apollon. III 754)." See above, pp. 61–62. But cf. Austin on 2.626–31: "Homer has many tree-similes . . . and Virgil himself has others. . . . But no literary ancestry is needed here; Virgil must often have watched the felling of a tree in his country days (as his *agricolae* itself suggests)." And on 4.441, "Alpini," the related simile, Cartault II 895: "il y a là un souvenir de l'enfance passée dans la Cisalpine"; Pease: "may be a suggestion of the observations of the poet's youth in the Po valley"; Austin: "The following simile is no doubt from Virgil's own observation; *Alpini* suggests this, and the detail confirms it." Possibly; but the adjective no more indicates autopsy than it does in *E.* 10.47: "Alpinas, a! dura niues et frigora Rheni." There is, however, a reference to Virgil's own experience—a reference that puzzled ancient readers; cf. DServ.: "quidam alnos poetica consuetudine pro populis accipiunt"—in *E.* 6.62–63: "tum Phaethontiadas musco circumdat amarae / corticis atque solo proceras erigit alnos." According to all other accounts (see Roscher s.v. 2192) Phaethon's sisters, weeping over their brother's charred body on the banks of the Eridanus, were changed into poplars, weeping tears of amber; but Virgil remembered the alder-fringed Po, the mythical Eridanus, of his youth (*G.* 2.451–52). Perhaps he regretted his youthful originality, for he later took pains to "correct" it, *A.* 10.189–91: "namque ferunt luctu Cycnum Phaethontis amati, / populeas inter frondes umbramque sororum / *dum canit* et maestum Musa *solatur amorem*" (cf. *E.* 6.61, 46).

62. As noticed by Heyne: "Similia ex Homero Iliad. δ, 482 sq. et Apollonio IV, 1682 sq. loca laudant Macrob. V, 11, Ursinus, Guellius et Cerda; sed ad occisos, non ad urbis excidium, instituta, verborumque ornatu cum h.l. neutiquam comparanda."

63. "Mortem orat; taedet *c*aeli *c*onuexa tueri" (4.451)—like the Trojan

women who have grown weary of wandering over the sea, "urbem orant; taedet pelagi perferre laborem" (5.617).

64. A hypermetric line, the final syllable of which is elided into the following line, here over a full stop at the end of a speech; the nearest parallel is *A.* 7.470–71. For a complete list of hypermetric hexameters, chiefly a Virgilian phenomenon, see J. Soubiran, *L'élision dans la poésie latine* (Paris, 1966) 466–67.

65. As, with equal precision, she echoes the opening; above, n. 38. Catullus 64.201, "funestet seque suosque," while not hypermetric, is nevertheless arresting; see D. O. Ross, Jr., *Style and Tradition in Catullus* (Cambridge, Mass., 1969) 63–64. The only commentator on Virgil or Catullus who notices this relationship is Pease: "So Ariadne's curse included Theseus and his race (Catull. 64.201: *seque suosque*)."

66. On suicide in Greek tragedy see B. Seidensticker, "Die Wahl des Todes," *Fondation Hardt, Entretiens* 29 (1982) 108–44.

67. Cf. *A.* 4.496–97: "lectumque iugalem, / quo perii"—the marriage bed on which she "died of love," and on which she will now die. *Lectus* occurs nowhere else in Virgil; see *TLL* s.v. *genialis* 1806.73.

68. Cf. Parthenius Περὶ ἐρωτ. παθ. 2.2: ἡ κόρη φωρᾶταί τινα τῶν Τρωϊκῶν λαφύρων ἔχουσα καὶ τούτοις μετὰ πολλῶν δακρύων ἀλινδουμένη and Clausen, "Virgil and Parthenius," *HSCP* 80 (1976) 179.

69. Vian on Quint. Smyrn. 7.343 (p. 213) identifies this as "un thème alexandrin," citing Ap. Rhod. 4.26, Parthenius Περὶ ἐρωτ. παθ. 2.2, Prop. 4.3.30, and *A.* 4.659.

70. Seidensticker, *Fondation Hardt, Entretiens* 29 (1982) 113: "Bezeugt sind für die griechische Tragödie fast ausschliesslich Schwert und Strick. . . . Für Männer ist das Schwert üblich; bei Frauen überwiegt der Strick." See also E. Fraenkel, "Selbstmordwege," *Philologus* 87 (1932) 470–73 = *Kl. Beiträge* I (Rome, 1964) 465–67; and Stevens on Eur. *Andr.* 811.

71. See Heinze 137 n. 2 and above, n. 56.

72. DServ.: "non induxit occidentem se sed ostendit occisam. et hoc tragico fecit exemplo, apud quos non uidetur quemadmodum fit caedes, sed facta narratur" (Pease).

73. Cf. 4.640: "Dardaniique rogum capitis"; 646–47: "rogos ensemque . . . / Dardanium"; 658: "Dardaniae . . . carinae"; 661–62: "crudelis . . . / Dardanus."

74. This description recalls that of the sacking of Priam's palace in 2.486–88; see above, p. 25.

75. The frequency of initial spondaic words—651, 653, 655, 657, 658— is unparalleled in Book 4; see Norden, pp. 435–36.

76. *CIL* I², p. 192. See E. Fraenkel, "Vrbem Quam Statuo Vestra Est," *Glotta* 33 (1954) 157–58 = *Kl. Beiträge* II (Rome, 1964) 140–41; G. Williams, *Tradition and Originality in Roman Poetry* 261–62. No doubt Virgil was thinking too of epitaphs composed in the form of elegiac distichs, a very

old practice; see P. Friedländer and H. Hoffleit, *Epigrammata* (Berkeley, 1948) 70; Cicero *Tusc.* 1.49.117, *De sen.* 20.73: "Solonis quidem sapientis elogium est" (the *elogium* or elegiac distich, which Cicero translates, is preserved by Plutarch, *Solon* 1). Cf. *E.* 5.42–44; Ov. *Met.* 2.327–28; *Culex* 411–14 (the only instance of the word in verse); Ov. *Am.* 2.6.61–62; Prop. 4.7.85–86; and see *TLL* s.v. *carmen* 465.74.

77. See above, p. 31.

78. See above, p. 40.

79. The wish is expressed at the beginning of the nurse's speech in Euripides and Ennius, and near the middle of Ariadne's lament.

80. Dryden, Preface to *Sylvae* (1685).

81. See Norden, pp. 393–98.

82. See Ross, *Style and Tradition in Catullus* 51–53.

83. *Heu nimium* is not found before Virgil and first occurs in the *A.* here, 6.189, and 11.841: "heu nimium, uirgo, nimium crudele luisti / supplicium" (cf., however, Hor. *Carm.* 1.2.37: "heu nimis longo satiate ludo"); then in Ovid (*Fasti*), *Ciris*, Lucan, Statius (*Theb.*), Silius; see *TLL* s.v. *heu* 2673.56. *A nimium*, on the other hand, is idiomatic and as old as Plautus; see *TLL* s.v. *ah* 1442.78. *A* is found 9 times in the *E.*, only twice in the *G.* ("a nimium," 2.252), and never in the *A. Heu*, by contrast, is found 34 times in the *A.* ("in erster Linie der hohen Dichtung angemessen"; J. B. Hofmann, *Lat. Umgangssprache* [Heidelberg, 1951³] 14), 5 times in the *G.*, and only once in the *E.*, in 9.17, where it is repeated in a moment of extreme pathos: "heu, cadit in quemquam tantum scelus? heu, tua nobis / paene simul tecum solacia rapta, Menalca!" The double interjection *heu heu* is found in *E.* 2.58: "heu heu, quid uolui misero mihi?" and 3.100: "heu heu, quam pingui macer est mihi taurus in eruo!"; but *heu heu* seems to be Virgil's imitation of Theocritus 4.26–27: φεῦ φεῦ βασεῦνται καὶ ταὶ βόες, ὦ τάλαν Αἴγων, / εἰς ᾿Αίδαν and 5.86, the two *Idylls* with which he was most concerned while writing *E.* 3. And it is probably not coincidental that *heu heu*, like φεῦ φεῦ in the *Idylls*, occurs only twice in the *E.* See Appendix 1 on line 47.

V. ARCADIA REVIEWED

1. Since myrtle was good for spear-shafts (*G.* 2.447), Virgil, to make his point, defines *myrtus* as *pastoralis*. The adjective occurs only twice in Virgil, here and in 7.513, "pastorale . . . signum, " of a shepherd's horn sounding to battle.

2. *Lumen* is not found elsewhere in Virgil with the genitive (cf. "splendor aquai"); *sicut* ("sicut . . . ubi") is not found elsewhere in Virgil (but "sicut . . . cum" three times in Lucretius), nor is *peruolito*, a Lucretian verb (cf. 4.203: "perque uolare"). On "radiantis . . . lunae" see below, n. 46. It should also be noted that the form *alituum* occurs five times in Lucretius but only

here in Virgil. Here again is an instance of twofold imitation—or, rather, threefold: cf. Ennius *scen.* 292 V.² = 150 J.: "lumine sic tremulo terra et caua caerula candent." By inverting the Ennian phrase Virgil has rendered it more musical; cf. *A.* 7.9: "splendet tremulo sub lumine pontus."

3. ἠὲ λέβητι / ἠέ που ἐν γαυλῷ: rhetorical elegance combined with exquisite homeliness. The preposition is to be understood with λέβητι; a detail of technique as old as Homer, *Od.* 12.27: ἢ ἁλὸς ἢ ἐπὶ γῆς (unique?) and found occasionally in other poets (Wilamowitz on Eur. *Her.* 237 cites ten instances, from Homer, the *Scutum*, Alcman, Pindar, Aeschylus, Sophocles, Euripides); but the Hellenistic poets seem to have employed it as a deliberate elegance. See O. Schneider on Nicander fr. 70.4: "in semel posita secundoque demum verbo iuncta praepositione posteriores epici quandam quaesivisse videntur quasi elegantiam"; Pfeiffer on Callim. fr. 714.3, adding *Hymn* 3.172, 246. From Hellenistic poetry it was transferred to Latin; see F. Leo, *Analecta Plautina* I (Göttingen, 1896) 42–44. (42: "apud latinos vetustiores perpauca sunt") = *Ausgew. Kl. Schriften* I (Rome, 1960) 116–18; and Clausen on Persius 1.131, adding *G.* 4.80; Ov. *Met.* 6.190, 488, 10.213, 13.937, 14.176; Stat. *Theb.* 4.607–8, 6.902, 9.324, 801, 10.714, 12.315.

Amid the gear in the Cyclops' cave Odysseus and his men found pails, γαυλοί, *Od.* 9.223: γαυλοί τε σκαφίδες τε, τετυγμένα, τοῖς ἐνάμελγεν. The word occurs only once in Homer, and only once, significantly, in Apollonius. And Apollonius emphasizes its homeliness by contrasting it with λέβης, in the *Odyssey* the silver basin in which guests wash their hands before meals. *Labrum* is as plain a word as γαυλός; tolerable in the *G.*, 2.6: "spumat plenis uindemia labris," but not, without embellishment, in the *A.* Virgil therefore made *labrum* a poetic plural (in the *G.* it is simply a plural) and adorned it with an epithet, 8.22: "labris . . . aenis"; 12.417: "labris splendentibus." He does not use the word elsewhere.

4. See above p. 52.

5. Conington: "It must be owned that the comparison is more pleasing when applied . . . to the fluttering heart of Medea than to the fluctuating mind of Aeneas"; Cartault II 638: "elle convient moins aux réflexions graves, aux calculs profonds d'un conducteur de peuples; c'est le type de l'emprunt dépaysé"; V. Pöschl, *Die Dichtkunst Virgils* (Innsbruck, 1950) 239: "Hier fügt es sich der Stimmung mit jener inneren Musikalität ein, die das Geheimnis Virgils ist." Heinze 250 seems to approve neither of Apollonius' simile ("so auffallendes und gesuchtes") nor of Virgil's using it. Williams, Gransden, and Fordyce are noncommittal.

6. The phrase is Eden's. Eden (following M. Coffey, "The Subject Matter of Vergil's Similes," *BICS* 8 [1961] 71) was right to look for a Homeric antecedent; but Virgil was not thinking—certainly not in the first instance—of *Od.* 20.1 ff., where the sleepless Odysseus is likened to a snarling bitch standing guard over her litter.

7. As noticed by Vian on *Arg.* 3.751–52 (*Argonautiques Chant III* [Paris, 1961]), and more elaborately on 3.744 (1980). Cf. Knauer on 8.26–30.

8. See Vian on Quint. Smyrn. 1.194.

9. 43: "litoreis ingens inuenta sub ilicibus sus": a remarkable line, beginning with a new adjective and ending with an Ennian rhythm (see Fordyce on 7.592); note also the interlocking word order. For a similar combination of the new and the old cf. 71–72 (p. 66).

10. "Caeruleus . . . caelo": Ennian wordplay, *Ann.* 49 V.²: "caeli caerula templa."

11. When Jason enters the Phasis, he pours libations of pure sweet wine into the river from a golden cup to Earth and the gods of the place, *Arg.* 2.1273: Γαίῃ τ᾿ ἐνναέταις τε θεοῖς.

12. Cf. also *G.* 4.321: "mater, Cyrene mater," cited here by Conington, but only because of "some doubt about the pointing." See above, p. 11.

13. See E. Norden, *Ennius und Vergilius* (Leipzig, 1915) 161–62. Norden points out (162 n. 2) that "teque" implies the preceding invocation of another deity, as in Virgil, but that "Nymphae, Laurentes Nymphae" is Virgil's own invention ("sprachlich und sachlich durchaus Vergils eigene Schöpfung").

14. Quoted by Conington. See below, nn. 26, 76.

15. See Knauer 242–43.

16. Arend 138–39: "Wenn er aber die Reise zu Euander schildert, der fern von der Kultur ein einfaches Leben führt—er will ja die kleine Ansiedlung in Kontrast stellen zu dem Rom seiner Zeit (vgl. 8,98–100)—so folgt er stark dem homerischen Stile und wählt von den vielen Besuchsszenen der Odyssee gerade die zum Vorbild, in der Homer ausdrücklich das patriarchalische Leben im Gegensatz zur Pracht am Hofe des Menelaos schildert: den Besuch bei Nestor (γ 1 ff.)." But the river voyage itself—under shadowy trees, cleaving the green woods on the calm and level water ("placido aequore," 96: see Norden, p. 455); only here and in 88–89, "mitis ut in morem stagni placidaeque paludis / sterneret aequor," does Virgil use *aequor* of a river—is not Homeric; Virgil being the first epic poet to describe the special pleasure of traveling by ship (Arend 136–37).

Arend 127 observes that Apollonius, to establish the Homeric reference of his poem, gives one example of typical scenes in Homer: one sacrificial banquet, 1.403–35; one chariot ride, 3.869–75; one arming scene, 3.1225–32; one dressing scene, 3.828–35; one sleep scene, 4.1141–45. Virgil seems to have followed Apollonius in this practice, or at least to have been aware of it: thus he has one sacrificial banquet, 8.175–83. (Dido's banquet; the only other banquet scene in *A.* is notably un-Homeric, perhaps for contrast); one sleep scene, 8.367–74; one dressing scene, 8.457–60—all three, it will be noticed, in Book 8.

17. 97: "sol medium caeli conscenderat igneus orbem," as when Telemachus and Athena arrive at Pylos, *Od.* 3.1–2: Ἥλιος δ᾿ ἀνόρουσε, λιπὼν περικαλλέα λίμνην, / οὐρανὸν ἐς πολύχαλκον. Similarly, Aeneas arrives "at the dark river-mouth in a pomp of sunrise" (Conington), 7.25–26:

"iamque rubescebat radiis mare et aethere ab alto / Aurora in roseis fulgebat lutea bigis," as when the ship bearing Odysseus approaches Ithaca, *Od.* 13.93–94: εὖτ᾽ ἀστὴρ ὑπερέσχε φαάντατος, ὅς τε μάλιστα / ἔρχεται ἀγγέλλων φάος Ἠοῦς ἠριγενείης. See Arend 135, Knauer 243–44, 250.

18. See Appendix 9.

19. 110: "audax . . . Pallas"—the reckless valor that will lead to his death at the hands of Turnus. On *audax* (*audacia*) see pp. 84–85.

20. As Nestor's son Peisistratus comes forward to greet Telemachus and Athena, *Od.* 3.36: πρῶτος Νεστορίδης Πεισίστρατος ἐγγύθεν ἐλθὼν (Arend 139).

21. In the place of honor, as Evander seats Aeneas, 177–78: "praecipuumque toro et uillosi pelle leonis." Knauer compares *Od.* 14.50 (Eumaeus seating Odysseus): ἐστόρεσεν δ᾽ ἐπὶ δέρμα ἰονθάδος ἀγρίου αἰγός. Cf. also *Od.* 14.519–20 (Eumaeus): ἐν δ᾽ ὀΐων τε καὶ αἰγῶν δέρματ᾽ ἔβαλλεν. / ἔνθ᾽ Ὀδυσεὺς κατέλεκτ᾽; *A.* 8.367–68 (Evander): "Aenean duxit stratisque locauit / effultum foliis et pelle Libystidis ursae." It would be beneath the dignity of an ideal hero to sit or sleep on lamb or sheep or goatskins (Arend 149).

The adjective *Libystis* is Callimachean, fr. 676.1: ζορκός . . . Λιβυστίδος, where see Pfeiffer; it occurs once in Apollonius (4.1753, where see Livrea), and twice in Virgil, in the same phrase, "pelle Libystidis ursae," here and in *A.* 5.37, where Acestes is described hurrying down from the mountaintop to greet the Trojans, but not elsewhere in Latin. I owe the following observation to one of my students, Abby Westervelt: "In Ap. Rhod. 1.321–25 Acastus and Argus are described hurrying down to the shore to join the gathering of the Argonauts; Argus wears a bull's hide reaching to his feet, with the black hair still upon it, 324–25 δέρμα δ᾽ ὁ μὲν ταύροιο ποδηνεκὲς ἀμπέχετ᾽ ὤμοις / Ἄργος Ἀρεστορίδης λάχνῃ μέλαν. Nowhere in Homer is such an outfit described (cf. *Il.* 10.177–78 ὁ δ᾽ ἀμφ᾽ ὤμοισιν ἑέσσατο δέρμα λέοντος /αἴθωνος μεγάλοιο ποδηνεκές . . .). It is probable that Virgil had this passage in mind in describing Acestes, for both passages have a feature in common—the description of a novel form of attire." Valerius Flaccus evidently thought so, 1.484–86: "Ecce per obliqui rapidum compendia montis / ductor ouans laetusque dolis agnoscit Acastum / horrentem iaculis"; cf. *A.* 5.35–37: "At procul ex celso miratus uertice montis / aduentum sociasque rates occurrit Acestes, / horridus in iaculis." See below, n. 49.

22. A curiously elaborate line (Eden: "almost impossible to translate . . . into English accurately without being grotesque"). Virgil seems to be thinking of Dido's luxurious banquet, 1.639–40: "arte laboratae uestes ostroque superbo, / ingens argentum mensis" (*laboratus* is not found elsewhere in Virgil); 1.701–2: "Cereremque canistris / expediunt" (*canistra* is not found elsewhere in the *A.*). See above, n. 16.

23. See Appendix 10.

24. See below, nn. 26, 76. See also A. H. McDonald, "The Style of Livy," *JRS* 47 (1957) 166.

25. 1.7.5: "ferox uiribus." In Dionysius of Halicarnassus 1.39.2 (see below, n. 28) Cacus is simply a local robber.

26. 1.7.10: "Ioue nate, Hercules, salue." Cf. *A.* 8.301: "salue, uera Iouis proles." Cf. also Livy 1.7.10 (Carmenta): "ueridica interpres deum . . . cecinit"; *A.* 8.340: "uatis fatidicae, cecinit."

27. See p. 81.

28. It is told not only by Livy and Virgil but also by Prop. 4.9, Dion. Hal. 1.39, and Ovid *Fasti* 1.543–82. For a comparison of the versions of Livy, Virgil, and Dion. Hal. see V. Buchheit, *Vergil über die Sendung Roms, Gymnasium,* Beihefte 3 (Heidelberg, 1963) 118–19; for discussion, F. Münzer, *Cacus der Rinderdieb* and J. Fontenrose, *Python* (Berkeley, 1980²), 339–43.

29. See G. Thome, *Gestalt und Funktion des Mezentius bei Vergil* (Frankfurt am Main, 1979) 28–30; also Heinze 214.

30. Cf. *A.* 8.475–76 (the Etruscan encampment at Caere): "opulentaque regnis . . . castra," where commentators should cite Livy, especially 2.14.3: "Porsennam discedentem ab Ianiculo castra opulenta, conuecto ex propinquis ac fertilibus Etruriae aruis commeatu." Livy likes to apply this adjective to the Etruscans: 2.50.2, 5.22.8, 9.36.12, 10.16.6. Virgil uses *opulentus* only once elsewhere (as Conington notes), of Juno's temple in Carthage, 1.447: "donis opulentum et numine diuae."

31. See p. 92.

32. Aeneas, like Hercules, is a stranger, an *aduena*: 10.460–61: "per patris hospitium et mensas, quas aduena adisti, / te precor, Alcide"; 10.515–17: "Pallas, Euander, in ipsis / omnia sunt oculis, mensae quas aduena primas / tunc adiit." Virgil applies the term *aduena* only to Hercules (10.460) and Aeneas (4.591, 7.38, 10.516, 12.261); cf. Livy 1.2.1 (Aeneas), 1.7.9 (Hercules). Aeneas, like Hercules, is a victim of Juno's hatred: 1.3–4: "iactatus et alto / ui superum, saeuae memorem Iunonis ob iram"; 10–11: "tot adire labores / impulerit"; 667–68: "frater ut Aeneas pelago tuus omnia circum / litora iactetur odiis Iunonis acerbae"; 8.291–93: "ut duros mille labores / rege sub Eurystheo fatis Iunonis iniquae / pertulerit." "Impulerit" and "pertulerit" are unique forms in Virgil, and each is emphatically placed. Cf. Buchheit, *Vergil über die Sendung Roms* 123.

33. On Virgil's characterization of Mezentius see H. C. Gotoff, "The Transformation of Mezentius," *TAPA* 114 (1984) 191–218.

34. See Eden xxiii n. 1.

35. See Appendix 9.

36. Eden: "*lautis* . . . here makes its unique appearance, not only in Virgil, but in all poetry, epic or lyric, of the high style." Fordyce: "The point of the epithet *lautis* . . . contrasted with *pauperis* is clear: the Carinae, on the western end of the Esquiline, was in later times a fashionable residential

quarter, where Pompey, Antony, and Quintus Cicero among others had houses. But the adjective, which begins as a colloquialism and usually has a familiar, sometimes a disparaging tone, is surprising in this context." It was meant to be surprising in this context. The emotions of the modern reader will be even more complicated here than were those, as they may be imagined, of the ancient reader; for the modern reader knows that the Roman Forum, Evander's cow pasture, became again, with the lapse of time, a cow pasture, the Campo Vaccino. See M. R. Scherer, *Marvels of Ancient Rome* (New York, 1955) 65, plates 31, 55.

37. Evander's love for his son, here expressed at length, was indicated in his speech of welcome to Aeneas, 8.168: "frenaque bina *meus* quae nunc habet aurea *Pallas*." This simple style of reference connotes intimacy and affection: so Catullus refers to Cinna, 95.1: "mei Cinnae"; Virgil to Gallus, *E.* 10.2: "meo Gallo"; and Horace to Maecenas, once only, near the end of their long friendship, *Carm.* 4.11.19: "Maecenas meus"; see E. Fraenkel, *Horace* 416–17; *TLL* s.v. *meus* 917.67. In the *Aeneid*: 1.231 (Venus): "meus Aeneas"; 2.522 (Hecuba): "meus ... Hector"; 3.489 (Andromache): "mei ... Astyanactis"; 10.902 (Mezentius): "meus ... Lausus."

38. A speech of 29 lines not counting 8 preceding.

39. A speech of 92 lines not counting 13 preceding and 42 following.

40. Gransden on Erulus (563): "this mythical king, not elsewhere attested ... and endowed with three lives, recalls the triple-bodied Geryon slain by Hercules. ... So Nestor recalled (*Il.* 11.672) his slaying of Itymoneus, who is not mentioned elsewhere." It only remains to add that such learned imitation of Homer is in the Alexandrian tradition.

41. See Norden, pp. 376–78.

42. All the more dramatic for being unique in Virgil. *Vulnero*, as might be expected, is frequent in Caesar and Livy, nor is it avoided by Ovid (*Met.* 1.717, 8.65, 11.372, 15.769, and six times elsewhere); it is, however, avoided by almost every other poet—by Lucretius, Catullus, Horace, Propertius, Lucan (but found in the spurious line 6.187), Persius, Seneca, Valerius Flaccus, Statius, even Silius, and Juvenal. Tibullus uses it once (1.2.26). The metaphorical sense first appears in Cicero, *Catil.* 1.17: "quorum mentis sensusque uulneras."

As a further indication of the structure cf. 568: "amplexu"; 569: "nate, tuo"; 581: "te, care puer"; 582: "complexu."

43. See above, pp. 49–50.

44. As Jason passes through the city, he is met by the aged priestess of Artemis, who kisses his hand and wishes to speak to him; but the crowd sweeps him on, and she is left behind by the side of the road—as the old are left behind by the young (315–16: οἷα γεραιὴ / ὁπλοτέρων).

45. See p. 95.

46. The verb *radio* is found only twice before Virgil, and only twice in Virgil, and in all four places as a present participle: Cic. *Arat.* 172 of the

constellation Aquarius, Lucr. 4.213 of the stars reflected in water, *A.* 8.23 of the moon reflected in water (see above, p. 61) and here. In a typical arming scene there will be a reference to the glitter of the hero's weapons; see T. Krischer, *Formale Konventionen der homerischen Epik, Zetemata* 56 (Munich, 1971) 36–38. Here "arma . . . radiantia" is an imitation of *Il.* 18.617 (Thetis): τεύχεα μαρμαίροντα παρ᾽ Ἡφαίστοιο φέρουσα; but the suggested contrast of light and shadow—"radiantia quercu"—is Virgil's own, e.g., *A.* 6.136–37: "latet arbore opaca / aureus . . . ramus"; 9.373–74: "et galea Euryalum sublustri noctis in umbra / prodidit immemorem radiisque aduersa refulsit." On arming scenes, or rather the lack of them, in the *Aeneid* see Arend 131–32.

47. 618: "expleri nequit atque oculos per singula uoluit." Cf. Catull. 64.267–68: "quae postquam cupide spectando Thessala pubes / expleta est"; Lucr. 4.1102: "nec satiare queunt spectando corpora coram"; *A.* 8.265–66: "nequeunt expleri corda tuendo / terribilis oculos"; 1.713: "expleri mentem nequit ardescitque tuendo." There are no other instances of *expleo* used of sight (*TLL* s.v. 1717.6).

48. 620: "terribilem cristis galeam flammasque uomentem." See below, n. 80.

49. An imitation, as Heyne noticed, of Ap. Rhod. 4.123–26: μεθ᾽ ἱερὸν ἄλσος ἵκοντο, / φηγὸν ἀπειρεσίην διζημένω ᾗ ἔπι κῶας / βέβλητο, νεφέλῃ ἐναλίγκιον ᾗ τ᾽ ἀνιόντος / ἠελίου φλογερῇσιν ἐρεύθεται ἀκτίνεσσιν; Jason and Medea discover the Golden Fleece hanging on an immense oak tree in a sacred grove—like a cloud reddening with the fiery beams of the rising sun. Homer's brief simile describing the fiery splendor of Achilles' shield—*Il.* 18.610 (Hephaestus): τεῦξ᾽ ἄρα οἱ θώρηκα φαεινότερον πυρὸς αὐγῆς—seems to have put Virgil in mind of Apollonius' simile; a reminiscence prompted perhaps by Apollonius' description of Jason's mantle, his "shield" (see below, n. 55), in 1.725–27 (see Vian, p. 84 nn. 1 and 2). W. A. Camps, *An Introduction to Virgil's Aeneid* (Oxford, 1969) 102–3, suggests that Virgil was thinking also of the oak leaves and golden shield which the senate voted to Augustus in 27 B.C.; possibly, but imitation of Homer and Apollonius is a sufficient explanation. Valerius Flaccus apparently recognized the source of Virgil's simile, 8.461–62 (Medea): "qualis erat cum Chaonio radiantia trunco / uellera uexit." See above, n. 21.

50. Arend 131: "Wir hören zwar, wie er [Aeneas] die neuen Waffen bewundert und prüft und danach—bezeichnenderweise—die Bildwerke auf ihnen betrachtet (8,619 ff.). Dazu hatte Achill keine Zeit, ihn reizten die Waffen nur noch mehr zu rasendem Kampfe (T 16)." K. Reinhardt, *Die Ilias und ihr Dichter* (Göttingen, 1961) 405: "Der Schild des Achilleus enthält nicht den geringsten Hinweis auf Achills Wesen, Taten und Zukunft. Vom Wogen und Toben des ihn umbrandenden Geschehens und seiner Bedeutung bleibt er unberührt."

51. G. E. Lessing, *Laokoon*, Werke 6 (Munich, 1974) 120: "Homer malet

nämlich das Schild nicht als ein fertiges vollendetes, sondern als ein werdendes Schild."

52. But relative position within individual scenes is indicated, to suggest life and movement, as is (though not in Homer) the central scene; see R. F. Thomas, "Virgil's Ecphrastic Centerpieces," *HSCP* 87 (1983) 176–80.

53. There is no mention of Hellenistic influence in Williams, Eden, Fordyce, or Klingner; in Gransden merely a suggestion (p. 161). But see Heinze 398–99 and P. Friedländer, *Johannes von Gaza* ... (Leipzig, 1912) 19: "Die unhomerische Weise, dass der Schild als fertig, nicht als werdend gegeben wird, hat Lessing mit ungerechtem Tadel gegen den Römer stärker als nötig hervorgehoben, und andere haben nach dem Ursachen gefragt. [Heinze 392 n. 1] Aber bevor man von innen her begründet, muss gesagt werden, dass seit Hesiod solche Beschreibungen durchaus ruhend waren, dass sich also Vergil hier nur im Einklang mit aller nachhomerischen Dichtung befindet."

54. *Il.* 18.490–540 is conventionally paragraphed as two scenes, the city at peace and the city at war, of 19 and 32 lines respectively; but since there is no introductory formula in 509, Homer evidently intended that these lines should constitute one scene, introduced by the formula ἐν δὲ δύω ποίησε πόλεις in 490. Cf. Lessing, *Laokoon*, p. 126: "Wo diese Eingangsworte nicht stehen, hat man kein Recht, ein besonderes Gemälde anzunehmen; im Gegenteil muss alles, was sie verbinden, als ein einziges betrachtet werden, dem nur bloss die willkürliche Konzentration in einem einzigen Zeitpunkt mangelt." (Thus, on a smaller scale, *A.* 8.635–41, 714–28.) And even with the scene so divided, a very considerable asymmetry remains: 7, 19, 32, 9, etc.

55. See Vian on 723 (p. 83 n. 2): "Apollonios se souvient de la scène 'typique' de l'armement du guerrier."

56. Lines 671–74 may be regarded as transitional, and there is a final scene of 15 lines (714–28), the triple triumph of Augustus, centering on Augustus (720: "ipse"). See also R. F. Thomas, *HSCP* 87 (1983) 179. Whatever the precise analysis of this scene, Virgil's intention is clear.

57. On the shield of Eurypylus in Quint. Smyrn. 6.200–291 there are eighteen scenes (the labors of Hercules): 8, 4, 8, 3, 4, 5, 4, 4, 5, 4, 7, 4, 9, 5, 10, 3 –, 3 +, 3. The first seven scenes on the shield of Heracles, unlike the rest of the description, seem to show some concern for symmetry (*Scutum* 161–215): 6, 10, 13, 6, 4, 4, 7.

58. *Il.* 18.483: ἐν μὲν γαῖαν ἔτευξ᾽; 490: ἐν δὲ δύω ποίησε; 541: ἐν δ᾽ ἐτίθει; 550: ἐν δ᾽ ἐτίθει; 561: ἐν δὲ τίθει; 573: ἐν δ᾽ ἀγέλην ποίησε; 587: ἐν δὲ νομὸν ποίησε; 590: ἐν δὲ χορὸν ποίκιλλε.

59. 144: ἐν μέσσῳ δ᾽ ἀδάμαντος ἔην; 154: ἐν δὲ Προΐωξίς τε Παλίωξίς τε τέτυκτο; 161: ἐν δ᾽ ὀφίων κεφαλαὶ δεινῶν ἔσαν; 178: ἐν δ᾽ ἦν; 191–92 ἐν δ᾽ ... ἐν δὲ καὶ; 197: ἐν δὲ; 201: ἐν δ᾽ ἦν; 207: ἐν δὲ; 216: ἐν δ᾽ ἦν.

60. *Arg.* 1.730: ἐν μὲν ἔσαν; 735: ἐν δ᾽ ἔσαν; 742: ἐξείης δ᾽ ἤσκητο; 747: ἐν δὲ βοῶν ἔσκεν; 752: ἐν δὲ δύω δίφροι πεπονήατο; 759: ἐν καὶ

Ἀπόλλων Φοῖβος ὀιστεύων ἐτέτυκτο; 763: ἐν καὶ Φρίξος ἔην; *Europa* 44: ἐν μὲν ἔην; 50: ἐν δ' ἦν; 55–56: ἀμφὶ δὲ δινήεντος ὑπὸ στεφάνην ταλάροιο / Ἑρμείης ἤσκητο.

61. See R. F. Thomas, *CQ* n.s. 33 (1983) 109–10.

62. 1.32: ἔντοσθεν; 39: τοῖς δὲ μετὰ; 45: τυτθὸν δ' ὅσσον ἄπωθεν. Cf. *A.* 8.635: "nec procul hinc"; 642: "haud procul inde"; 646: "nec non"; 652: "in summo"; 663: "hic"; 666: "hinc procul"; 671: "haec inter"; 675: "in medio"; also 1.469: "nec procul hinc"; 474: "parte alia."

63. Cf. Quint. Smyrn. 6.200–91 (above, n. 57).

64. 630: "fecerat"; 637: "addiderat"; 665: "extuderat"; 710: "fecerat"; 726: "finxerat"—all pluperfect except 666: "addit," apparently *metri gratia*, with "extuderat" in the line preceding.

65. As Virgil indicates, 630: "fecerat et." Servius: "dicendo autem 'et' ostendit multa alia fuisse depicta." Heyne: "*Fecerat et*, inter cetera, quae poeta memorare non vult." Cf. Ov. *Met.* 13.493: "plura quidem, sed et haec laniato pectore dixit." In ecphrases before Virgil all the scenes on the object in question are described; nowhere is it suggested that description has been less than complete. Cf. however Quint. Smyrn. 5.97–98: ἄλλα δὲ μυρία κεῖτο κατ' ἀσπίδα τεχνήεντα / χερσὶν ὑπ' ἀθανάτης πυκινόφρονος Ἡφαίστοιο; 6.292–93: ἄλλα δ' ἄρ' Ἀλκείδαο θρασύφρονος ἄσπετα ἔργα / ἄμπεχεν Εὐρυπύλοιο διοτρεφέος σάκος εὐρύ.

66. 645: "sparsi rorabant sanguine uepres"; cf. Ap. Rhod. 1.750–51 (the fourth scene on Jason's mantle): τῶν δ' αἵματι δεύετο λειμὼν / ἐρσήεις. Apollonius likes the adjective ἐρσήεις, as Virgil may have noticed: 1.751, 881, 2.1004, 4.970, where see Livrea, 1172, 1302. *Roro* is found only twice before Virgil, in Lucr. 2.977: "lacrimis spargunt rorantibus ora," and 3.469: "lacrimis rorantes ora genasque"; in Virgil, here, *A.* 11.8: "rorantis sanguine cristas"; 12.512: "capita et rorantia sanguine portat"; and 3.567: "rorantia uidimus astra."

67. 649–50: "illum indignanti similem similemque minanti / aspiceres." There are two traditional features of ecphrastic style represented here: *similis* (ἐοικώς) with the present (usually) participle, and the indefinite second person of the potential subjunctive (in Greek the optative). Thus *Il.* 18.548: ἀρηρομένῃ δ' ἐῴκει; *Scutum* 215: ἰχθύσιν ἀμφίβληστρον ἀπορρίψοντι ἐοικώς (cf. Theocr. 1.41–42: κάμνοντι τὸ καρτερὸν ἀνδρὶ ἐοικώς. / φαίης κεν; *Il.* 3.219–20: ἀΐδρεϊ φωτὶ ἐοικώς. / φαίης κε); 228 (Perseus): σπεύδοντι καὶ ἐρρίγοντι ἐοικώς; 314: Ὠκεανὸς πλήθοντι ἐοικώς; Ap. Rhod. 1.739 (Zethus): μογέοντι ἐοικώς; 764 (Phrixus): ἐξενέποντι ἐοικώς; Quint. Smyrn. 6.211 (the Nemean lion): ἀποπνείοντι δ' ἐῴκει; 231 (Heracles): μάλα σπεύδοντι ἐοικώς; *A.* 5.254 (Ganymede): "anhelanti similis." Cf. A. Traina, "Laboranti Similis," *Maia* 21 (1969) 71–78.

68. Heinze 396: "die Handlung stockt selbst während der Schildbeschreibung nicht völlig, da wir uns Aeneas als Beschauer zu denken haben, der *rerum ignarus imagine gaudet* und dann weiterschreitet *attollens umero famamque et fata nepotum*."

69. See above, pp. 17–18.

70. With the defeat of the Gauls, Livy says, Rome experienced a radical rebirth: "uelut ab stirpibus laetius feraciusque renatae urbis" (6.1.3); see T. J. Luce, *Livy* (Princeton, 1977) 3–4.

71. R. Syme, *History in Ovid* (Oxford, 1978) 2: "For Livy the culmination of Roman history was the end of the Civil Wars and the triple triumph celebrated in 29 B.C. (in Book CXXXIII). What follows is an epilogue."

72. So Horace *Carm.* 1.37.6–8: "dum Capitolio / regina dementis ruinas / funus et imperio parabat." Syme, *The Roman Revolution* 297–98: "Actium became the contest of East and West personified, the birth-legend in the mythology of the Principate. On the one side stood Caesar's heir with the Senate and People of Rome, the star of the Julian house blazing on his head; in the air above, the gods of Rome, contending against the bestial divinities of Nile. Against Rome were arrayed the motley levies of all the eastern lands, Egyptians, Arabs and Bactrians, led by a renegade in un-Roman attire. . . . Worst of all, the foreign woman."

73. Fordyce, p. 270: "the crowded space of history between 392 and 31 B.C. is awkwardly bridged by an underworld scene presenting Catiline and Cato." Such criticism arises from a failure to appreciate the dramatic character of the ecphrasis and Virgil's intention here. Aeneas has already had a vision of Roman history in which many worthies appeared, among them the hero of the Gallic invasion, who does not appear here, 6.825: "referentem signa Camillum."

74. 638: "Romulidis," borrowed from Lucr. 4.683: "Romulidarum arcis seruator candidus anser."

75. 654: "Romuleoque recens horrebat regia culmo." Commentators object to this line as being out of place (Gransden is a notable exception): "an awkward interruption of the account of Manlius and the Gauls" (Eden); see also G. Binder, *Aeneas und Augustus* (Meisenheim am Glan, 1971) 186 n. 2. The original *casa Romuli* stood on the Palatine, but there was a replica on the Capitoline. And to this latter Camillus refers in his magnificent speech, which Virgil certainly had read, in Livy 5.53.8: "si tota urbe nullum melius ampliusue tectum fieri possit quam casa illa conditoris est nostri"; cf. Seneca the Elder *Contr.* 1.6.4: "nudi hi stetere colles, interque tam effusa moenia nihil est humili casa nobilius: fastigatis supra tectis auro puro fulgens prae-lucet Capitolium"; 2.1.5: "colit etiamnunc in Capitolio casam uictor omnium gentium populus."

76. See Ogilvie on Livy 5.49.7. The first pentad of Livy's history (Books 1–5) was completed by 27 B.C.; see T. J. Luce, "Livy's First Decade," *TAPA* 96 (1965) 238.

77. See R. F. Thomas, *HSCP* 87 (1983) 176–80. As Thomas points out (177), Homer's shield has no centerpiece. But Nonnus, who imitates Homer with his usual prolixity, supposed it was earth: *Il.* 18.483: ἐν μὲν γαῖαν ἔτευξ᾽, ἐν δ᾽ οὐρανόν, ἐν δὲ θάλασσαν; *Dionys.* 25.386–90: θαύματα

μαρμαίροντα, τά περ κάμεν οὐρανίη χεὶρ / ἀσπίδα δαιδάλλουσα
πολύχροον, ἧς ἐνὶ μέσσῳ / ἐν μὲν γαῖαν ἔτευξε περίδρομον, ἀμφὶ δὲ
γαίη / οὐρανὸν ἐσφαίρωσε χορῷ κεχαραγμένον ἄστρων, / καὶ χθονὶ
πόντον ἔτευξεν ὁμόζυγον.

78. On *caeruleus* (713) see above, p. 65; *niueus* (720) refers to the marble of the actual temple.

79. The phrase is found only once elsewhere, of Anchises in 3.527. Earlier in Book 8 Aeneas speaks to Pallas "puppi . . . ab alta" (115). Cf. also 4.554: "Aeneas celsa in puppi"; 5.775 (Aeneas): "stans procul in prora pateram tenet." Arend 131: "Er zeichnet ja auch sonst gern den Aeneas durch erhöhten Platz aus (vgl. 8,115. 541; 2,2; 5,44; 12,564). Und den Kaiser mit der Opferschale sieht man nicht zufällig auf der Ara Pacis und der Trajanssäule."

80. There are, in all, twelve instances of *uomo* in the *Aeneid*. As in Homer, warriors literally vomit blood: 9.349, 414, 11.668; Cacus vomits fire: 8.199, 259 (and smoke, 252–53: "faucibus ingentem fumum . . . euomit"; see Norden, p. 115 n. 1); 5.682: "stuppa uomens tardum fumum." There is only one other instance in Virgil, G. 2.462, of the rich man's house spewing out a wave of early-morning callers. The metaphor originates with Pindar *Pyth.* 1.21–22 (Aetna): τᾶς ἐρεύγονται μὲν ἀπλάτου πυρὸς ἁγνόταται / ἐκ μυχῶν παγαί (cf. A. 3.576). Cf. Ennius *Ann.* 142 V.²: "et Tiberis uomit in mare salsum."

81. This grave and beautiful last line, which may qualify, for the modern reader, Virgil's praise of Augustus, was condemned in antiquity as superfluous and undignified, and neoteric: "hunc uersum notant critici quasi superfluo additum nec conuenientem grauitati eius; namque est magis neotericus" (DServius). The term *neoteric* was generally applied in a disparaging sense to poetry after Homer (see Wiseman, *Cinna the Poet* 51; A. Cameron, *HSCP* 84 [1980] 136); and in this respect Virgil's critics were, perversely, right: such a verse could never have been composed by Homer. Cf. C. Becker, "Der Schild des Aeneas," *WS* 77 (1964) 125: "Ein solcher Vers wäre in der Ilias weder hier noch an einer anderen Stelle denkbar, er würde der Unmittelbarkeit, der 'Natürlichkeit' dieser Epik völlig widersprechen; für das Neue, das die Schildbeschreibung oder vielmehr die ganze Aeneis in der Dichtung bedeutet, ist er um so charakteristischer."

VI. THE DEATH OF TURNUS

1. Note the following line: "at Caesar, triplici inuectus Romana triumpho." Such moments are rare: Horace *Carm.* 1.37.30–32: "inuidens / priuata deduci superbo /non humilis mulier triumpho"; Dante, *Inferno* 15.123–24: "e parve di costoro / quelli che vince, non colui che perde."

2. See Clausen, *HSCP* 68 (1964) 144–47 = Commager, *Virgil*, 84–88.

3. See Stanford ad loc.

4. See A. E. Astin, *Scipio Aemilianus* (Oxford, 1967) 263–64.

5. So portrayed in Cicero's *Somnium Scipionis*. No doubt Cicero idealized Scipio, but it is unlikely that he misrepresented him entirely.

6. See Astin, *Scipio Aemilianus* 153.

7. See ibid. 77 f., 282 ff.; F. W. Walbank, *A Historical Commentary on Polybius* III (Oxford, 1979) 722–25; E. Fraenkel, *Horace* 302–3.

8. On *pulcherrimus* see above, p. 23.

9. See above, p. 67.

10. On this scene see Heinze 188–89, Arend 146.

11. See C. Wirszubski, "*Audaces*: A Study in Political Phraseology," *JRS* 51 (1961) 12–22.

12. *Pro Sest.* 86: "oportere hominum audacium, euersorum rei publicae, sceleri legibus et iudiciis resistere" (quoted by Wirszubski, *JRS* 51 [1961] 14 n. 13).

13. See *TLL* s.v. 1025.84: "inde a Cic., Verg."

14. But in 11.438 Turnus likens Aeneas to Achilles, by implication casting himself in the role of Hector.

15. Priests in Homer do not take part in battle; see Conington on *A.* 6.484, Stanford on *Od.* 9.198. But they do in Virgil; see Norden on *A.* 6.484: "Derselben nachhomerischen Vorstellung folgt Vergil selbst auch 10,537 ff. 11,429. 768 ff. 12,258." Apollonius respects the Homeric inhibition and neither of his two priests takes part in battle: Idmon is killed by a wild boar in the land of the Mariandyni, and Mopsus dies after stepping on a poisonous serpent in the Libyan desert; though Mopsus, as Norden remarks, had combined his priestly vocation with that of the warrior in the battle of the Lapiths and Centaurs, Ov. *Met.* 12.455–56: "nec tu credideris tantum cecinisse futura / Ampydicen Mopsum: Mopso iaculante...."

16. 9.50: "cristaque tegit galea aurea rubra." An adjective seldom found in epic poetry, *ruber* is, however, found four times in the *A.*: notably here and in 12.89: "rubrae cornua cristae" (cf. 9.270: "cristasque rubentis"), of the plume on Turnus' helmet; in 8.686 of the Red Sea, an established epithet; and in 12.247: "rubra ... in aethra," an imitation of Enn. *Ann.* 435 V². The adjective as applied to the plume suggests blood and may be meant to recall Virgil's initial description, 7.785–88: "cui triplici crinita iuba galea alta Chimaeram / sustinet Aetnaeos efflantem faucibus ignis; /tam magis illa fremens et tristibus effera flammis / quam magis effuso crudescunt sanguine pugnae." Cf. Hor. *Epod.* 17.51: "cruore rubros ... pannos"; *Carm.* 3.13.7: "rubro sanguine"; *E.* 10.27: "sanguineis ebuli bacis minioque rubentem"; *G.* 2.430: "sanguineisque inculta rubent auiaria bacis"; *A.* 10.272–73: "cometae / sanguinei lugubre rubent"; and finally, of Turnus in his *aristeia*, 9.732–33: "tremunt in uertice cristae / sanguineae."

17. "turbidus" (9.57), an adjective applied oftener to Turnus than to any other warrior: 10.648, 12.10, 671 (cf. also 12.685). Turnus had been led

by Iris to think that, in Aeneas' absence, he could surprise and take the camp by storm, 9.13: "turbata arripe castra."

18. By La Cerda and Heyne: "Apollonium I, 1243 sq. ante oculos habuisse et ornasse videtur; respectu etiam ad Homerum habito"; but *Il.* 11.547–57 or 17.658–66, which Heyne cites, have only a general connection with Virgil's simile; see Knauer ad loc. La Cerda also notes that "saeuit in absentis" is an imitation of Varius Rufus fr. 4.3 M.: "saeuit in absentem" (Virgil had already imitated line 6 of this passage in *E.* 8.88); an observation not found in Heyne or subsequent commentators.

19. Heyne may be misleading: "Comparatio lupi cum pugnantium rabie satis frequens." There are four places in Homer where warriors (but not single warriors) are compared to wolves (but not attacking sheepfolds), all in the *Iliad*: 4.471–72 (the Trojans and Achaeans): οἱ δὲ λύκοι ὥς / ἀλλήλοις ἐπόροσαν; 11.72–73: οἱ δὲ λύκοι ὥς / θῦνον; 16.156–57 (the Myrmidons): οἱ δὲ λύκοι ὥς / ὠμοφάγοι; and 16.352–53, which is rather different (see below). Cf. *A.* 2.355–56 (the Trojans): "inde, lupi ceu / raptores." With "lupi raptores" W. Schulze, *Kleine Schriften* (Göttingen, 1966[2]) 222 compares Lycophron 147: ἁρπακτῆρας . . . λύκους. The phrase seems to have its origins in Homer: *Il.* 16.352–53 (the leaders of the Danaans): ὡς δὲ λύκοι ἄρνεσσιν ἐπέχραον ἢ ἐρίφοισι / σίνται; 355: αἶψα διαρπάζουσιν ἀνάλκιδα θυμὸν ἐχούσας; 24.262 (only Priam's unworthy sons are left to him): ἀρνῶν ἠδ᾽ ἐρίφων ἐπιδήμιοι ἁρπακτῆρες; cf., however, Leonidas of Tarentum 81.4 Gow-Page (= *A. Pl.* 190): ἁρπακτῆρος . . . λύκου, on which Gow-Page comment: "again of wolves (no doubt hence) Lyc. 147." As in the *A.*, there is only one plural wolf-simile in the *Arg.*, 2.123–29: the Argonauts are provoked into attacking the Bebrycians, as, on a winter's day, gray wolves attack a sheepfold. But Quintus of Smyrna compares Odysseus, as he emerges from the Wooden Horse, to a famished wolf attacking a sheepfold, 13.44–46: ὡς δ᾽ ὅταν ἀργαλέῃ λιμῷ βεβολημένος ἦτορ / ἐξ ὀρέων ἔλθῃσι λύκος χατέων μάλ᾽ ἐδωδῆς / ποίμνης πρὸς σταθμὸν εὐρύν.

20. Cf. the scholiast on *Arg.* 1.1243–48a Wendel: κυρίως οἱ ποιηταὶ τὸν λέοντά φασι θῆρα, ὡς καὶ Καλλίμαχος· θηρὸς ἀερτάζων δέρμα κατωμάδιον (fr. 597, where see Pfeiffer); also *LSJ* s.v. θήρ. Similarly, in *A.* 9.551, "fera" = a lion; a simile that may owe something to *Arg.* 2.26–29.

21. *Od.* 6.130–34: βῆ δ᾽ ἴμεν ὥς τε λέων ὀρεσίτροφος, ἀλκὶ πεποιθώς, / ὅς τ᾽ εἶσ᾽ ὑόμενος καὶ ἀήμενος [= "uentos perpessus et imbris"], ἐν δέ οἱ ὄσσε / δαίεται· αὐτὰρ ὁ βουσὶ μετέρχεται ἢ ὀΐεσσιν / ἠὲ μετ᾽ ἀγροτέρας ἐλάφους· κέλεται δέ ἑ γαστὴρ / μήλων πειρήσοντα καὶ ἐς πυκινὸν δόμον ἐλθεῖν. Cf. also *Il.* 12.299–301 (Sarpedon compared to a lion attacking a sheepfold): βῆ ῥ᾽ ἴμεν ὥς τε λέων ὀρεσίτροφος, ὅς τ᾽ ἐπιδευὴς / δηρὸν ἔῃ κρειῶν, κέλεται δέ ἑ θυμὸς ἀγήνωρ / μήλων πειρήσοντα καὶ ἐς πυκινὸν δόμον ἐλθεῖν.

22. Cf. *E.* 5.60: "nec lupus insidias pecori"; *G.* 3.537: "non lupus insidias explorat ouilia circum"; 4.435: "auditisque lupos acuunt balatibus agni."

23. *Il.* 15.586–88: ἀλλ᾽ ὅ γ᾽ ἄρ᾽ ἔτρεσε θηρὶ κακὸν ῥέξαντι ἐοικώς, / ὅς τε κύνα κτείνας ἢ βουκόλον ἀμφὶ βόεσσι / φεύγει πρίν περ ὅμιλον ἀολλισθήμεναι ἀνδρῶν; *A.* 11.809–12: "ac uelut ille . . . / continuo in montis sese auius abdidit altos / occiso pastore lupus magnoue iuuenco, / conscius audacis facti."

24. Cf. Lucr. 1.473–74: "amoris / ignis, Alexandri Phrygio sub pectore gliscens." The association of *glisco* and *uiolentia* may have been suggested by Lucretius, who uses *glisco* five times, 3.480–82: "clamor singultus iurgia gliscunt, / et iam cetera de genere hoc quaecumque sequuntur, / cur ea sunt, nisi quod uemens uiolentia uini . . . ?" Cf. also Livy 2.23.2: "inuidiamque eam sua sponte *gliscentem* insignis unius calamitas *accendit*." This is the only instance of *glisco* in Virgil.

25. Virgil's single imitation of "Homeric" practice: Books 3, 5, 7, 9, 10, 16, and 17 of the *Iliad* begin with similes; on the division of the Homeric poems into books see Pfeiffer, *History of Classical Scholarship* 115–16. It can hardly be accidental that the first and last books of Quintus of Smyrna's poem begin with similes.

26. 9.339–43 (Euryalus), 9.792–96 (Turnus), 10.454–56 (Turnus), 10.723–29 (Mezentius), 12.4–9 (Turnus).

27. By far his longest speech; see Highet 337.

28. 12.48–49: "quam pro me curam geris, hanc precor, optime, pro me / deponas." The rhythm of line 48 (three successive diaereses) is curious, and the acknowledgment of Latinus' position seems perfunctory; elsewhere in *A.* (there are no instances ι᾽ *E.* or *G.*) "optime" is qualified, "pater optime," "optime regum," or the like. Turnus adds "pater" almost as an afterthought, it seems, in line 50.

29. *Aegresco*, a Lucretian verb (see *TLL* s.v.), is not found elsewhere in Virgil, and the Lucretian gerund (see Munro on Lucr. 1.312) is suggestive.

30. Cf. also Lucr. 5.964: "uiolenta uiri uis"; 1226: "uis uiolenti per mare uenti"; 1270: "uiolentis uiribus."

31. *Il.* 6.77–79, 17.513; cf. *A.* 11.283–92.

32. *Il.* 20.332–39.

33. See Krischer, *Formale Konventionen der homerischen Epik* 23–26; M. M. Willcock, "Battle Scenes in the *Aeneid*," PCPS 209, n.s. 29 (1983) 87–99.

34. See Heinze 210 n. 2.

35. Aeneas' encounters with Magus and Tarquitus are both modeled on that of Achilles with Lycaon, *Il.* 21.97–135.

36. See Heinze 221; Willcock, PCPS 209, n.s. 29 (1983) 93.

37. 12.511–12: "curruque abscisa duorum / suspendit capita et rorantia sanguine portat," where Knauer cites no parallel. On decapitation in Homer see C. Segal, *The Theme of the Mutilation of the Corpse in the Iliad*, Mnemosyne, Suppl. 17 (1971) 20–22.

38. Hector's angry heart urges him to cut off Patroclus' head and set it

on the palisade (18.176–77). Cf. Segal, *Mutilation of the Corpse* 22: "the degree of brutality is extraordinary. . . . There is nothing else quite like it in the *Iliad*." Cf. Livy 3.5.9: "intentos in castra Romana Aequos legatique caput ferociter ostentantes," with Ogilvie's note.

39. The phrase "ora uirum" is not found elsewhere in the *Aeneid*.

40. Translated above, p. 71. Compare also *A.* 3.626–27 (the cave of Polyphemus): "uidi *atro* cum membra *fluentia tabo* / manderet et *tepidi* tremerent sub dentibus artus." See J. Glenn, "Mezentius and Polyphemus," *AJP* 92 (1971) 138–40.

41. In the briefest of similes, *Il.* 5.299: λέων ὥς; elsewhere in the *Iliad* Aeneas is compared to a ram (13.492) and, with Hector, to a hawk (17.755). Even Jason is compared, though not in the Homeric mode, to a lion; see Livrea on Ap. Rhod. 4.1338. There is only one other lion-simile in Apollonius, 2.26–29.

42. See Pöschl, *Die Dichtkunst Virgils* 167–68.

43. See Heinze 210.

44. See above, n. 26.

45. 12.753: "uiuidus Vmber": a curious adjective in this context; cf., perhaps, *A.* 10.609–10: "non uiuida bello / dextra uiris animusque ferox." The Umbrian was not an especially ferocious breed, and later at any rate seems to have been known for keenness of scent rather than courage; see Grattius *Cyn.* 171–73.

46. Presumptuous as interfering with the order of things, here the fated, and fatal, conclusion of the duel.

47. 12.874: "talin possum me opponere monstro?" See above, p. 38.

48. See Willcock, *PCPS* 209, n.s. 29 (1983) 90–91.

49. See Krischer, *Formale Konventionen der homerischen Epik* 23–24.

50. Cf. *Il.* 3.330–38 (Paris), 11.17–45 (Agamemnon), 16.131–41 (Patroclus), 19.369–88 (Achilles).

51. *A.* 11.486–90 (Turnus), 12.87–94 (Turnus), 430–34 (Aeneas). Arend 131 was mistaken in asserting that Aeneas has no arming scene.

52. See above, p. 75.

53. See Krischer, *Formale Konventionen der homerischen Epik* 24. The glitter of the warrior's armor is a feature of the arming scene.

54. See above, p. 64. Apollonius is also indebted to Homer *Il.* 11.61–64 (note the repetition, 62: ἀναφαίνεται; 64: φάνεσκεν) and 22.25–31. Not unrelated, and no less extreme, is the transformation of Homer represented by Jason's mantle; see above, p. 79.

55. Hence the perplexity (or silence) of commentators. Eden: "It was significantly Lucifer which rose at the end of the night of the sack of Troy (*A.* 2.801), and this guiding star was Aeneas' mother's." Gransden: "although Virgil's comparison is with Pallas, Venus watches over the convoy because it contains her own beloved son Aeneas."

56. A small point, but Virgil, like Apollonius, names the star (Homer nowhere does): ἅ τε Σείριος Ὠκεανοῖο, "Oceani perfusus Lucifer unda."

57. Cf. Livy 2.5.5 (Brutus and his traitorous sons): "et qui spectator erat amouendus, eum ipsum fortuna exactorem supplicii dedit."

58. 10.454–56, an imitation of *Il.* 16.487–89 (the death of Sarpedon), the only Homeric simile in which a lion attacks and kills a bull.

59. The main reference is to the death agony of Sarpedon, *Il.* 16.504–5; other grim details have been assembled from elsewhere; see Knauer ad loc.

60. On such figures in Homer see J. Griffin, "Homeric Pathos and Objectivity," *CQ* n.s. 26 (1976) 161–87.

61. For the contemporary political significance of this scene see P. Zanker, "Der Apollontempel auf dem Palatin, Ausstattung und Sinnbezüge nach der Schlacht von Actium," *Analecta Romana Instituti Danici*, Suppl. 10 (1983) 27–31.

62. 10.499: "quae Clonus Eurytides multo caelauerat auro"—a final Homeric touch. See Stanford on *Od.* 8.373; cf. *A.* 5.359, 9.303–5.

63. Pallas is called "puer" only here and in Evander's farewell, "care puer" (8.581).

64. This line occurs twice in the *Aeneid*, here and in 11.831 (of the death of Camilla), and is an imitation of a passage that occurs twice in the *Iliad*, 16.856–57 (of the death of Patroclus) and 22.362–63 (of the death of Hector): ψυχὴ δ᾽ ἐκ ῥεθέων πταμένη Ἀϊδόσδε βεβήκει, / ὃν πότμον γοόωσα, λιποῦσ᾽ ἀνδροτῆτα καὶ ἥβην. Conington on *A.* 11.831: "Serv. remarks that Camilla, like Hector, dies young, and so unwillingly. So Patroclus and Hector, *Il.* 16.856 foll., 22.362 foll., doubtless imitated by Virg." It only remains to add that such deliberate and precise imitation of Homer is an Alexandrian practice.

65. See above, pp. 96–97.

66. See above, p. 91.

67. See Clausen, *ICS* 2 (1977) 220.

68. See above, pp. 96–97.

69. Cf. the words of Evander spoken over the body of his son:

"non haec, o Palla, dederas promissa parenti,
cautius ut saeuo uelles te credere Marti.
haud ignarus eram quantum noua gloria in armis
et praedulce decus primo certamine posset."

(11.152–55)

70. "nec minus ille / exsultat demens" (10.812–13). For the force of *exsulto* cf. *A.* 2.470, 386; 10.550, 643–44; 11.648.

71. First noticed by La Cerda. See also T. R. Glover, *Virgil* (New York, 1912²) 223; E. A. Hahn, "Note on Vergil's Use of Anchisiades," *CW* 14 (1920) 3–4. The patronymic is applied twice to Aeneas in the *Iliad*, 17.754, 20.160; that it has no emotional connotation is shown by 23.296. Cf., however, *Od.* 1.29–30: μνήσατο γὰρ κατὰ θυμὸν ἀμύμονος Αἰγίσθοιο, / τόν

ῥ᾽ Ἀγαμεμνονίδης τηλεκλυτὸς ἔκταν᾽ Ὀρέστης—a suggestive and striking use of the patronymic (Ἀγαμεμνονίδης is not found elsewhere in Homer) which Virgil may have noticed; cf. *A.* 4.471–73.

72. See Gotoff, *TAPA* 114 (1984) 201 n. 26.

73. Whom he refers to earlier in his speech as "pius Aeneas" (170).

GENERAL INDEX

a, neoteric interjection, 60

Abandoning former occupations a symptom of lovesickness in Hellenistic poetry, 12

Achilles: crest of, 131n8; shield of, 76–79

Actium, Battle of: and Augustus, 81–82; second great crisis of Republic, 80–81. *See also* Gallic invasion of 390 B.C.

aduena, of Aeneas and Hercules, 154n32

aedifico, of shipbuilding, 139n34. See also *intexo*

Aeneas: and Augustus, 81–82; claims a distant kinship with Evander, 69, 119–20; compared to an ancient oak, 50; compared to Apollo, 22–23; "dux Troianus," 24; emotional response to murals of Trojan War in Carthage, 16–18; encounters mother in forest, 15–16; epiphany of, 26; and fall of Troy, 32; and the fatal hunt, 23–24; guilty of atrocities, 91; and Hercules, 72; hesitates to kill, 99; his love for Dido unexpressed, 47–48; his troubled mind compared to light reflected by water, 61–62; a Homeric warrior, 90; kills Lausus unwillingly, 99–100; kills Turnus, 98–99; never compared to a lion, 92; *pietas* of, 90, 99, 100, 166n73; prominent part in fall of Troy as Virgil's innovation, 32; "pulcherrimus," 23; reluctantly tells his story to Dido, 32; a Roman Stoic, 49; sacred obligation to Evander, 100; shield of, 76, 80–82; speeches

to Dido, 48. *See also* Dido; Evander; Turnus

Agamemnon, sleepless with worry, 64

Allecto, 84, 85

Alliteration, 42, 142n3

Amata, death of, 9

Ambiguity in Latin poetry, 24, 37, 42

ambire, 45–46

Anchisiades, 100

Anna, 43, 50

antrum, 134n40

Aonius, 129n59

Apollonius Rhodius: gives one example of typical scenes in Homer, 152n16; sentimentalizes Homer, 64, 96

Ara Maxima, 70

Ariadne, 20, 40–41, 53, 59

aristeia: double, a Virgilian tour de force, 92; Homeric, 94–95; Virgil's imitation of Homer, 95

Arruns, 88

Asclepiades, 5

Atlas, 31

audax, audacia, 85, 90, 93

Augustan conception of Roman history, 80–81

Augustus: and Aeneas, 81–82; at Battle of Actium, 81–82; and Romulus, 80–81

Bucolic diaeresis, 102, 113–114; preceded by feminina caesura, 21

Cacus, 69–71; transformed into a monster by Virgil, 71

Caecilius Epirota, Q., ca. 26 B.C., lectures on Virgil and other New Poets, 4

Callimachus: attitude to Homer, 10;
central figure for New Poets, 9;
erudition of, 9; his imagination
nourished on books, 9; poetics of,
2–3, 7; relation to Hesiod, 3;
speaking for a minority, 125n4;
style of, 10

Calvus: date of death, 126–27n23; his
miniature epic *Io*, 12

Camilla, 61; death of, 88, 147n56,
165n64

Camillus, 81

Campo Vaccino, 154–55n36

Carthaginians alien to heroic world,
30

casa Romuli, 81

Cassandra, 35, 39

Catiline, 80, 81

Cato, 80, 81

Cinna, 4; erotic character of his
Zmyrna, 7–8; obscurity of his
Zmyrna, 3; publication of his
Zmyrna greeted by Catullus, 6–7;
still alive when Virgil arrived in
Rome, 5. *See also* Parthenius

concubitus, 101

conlapsus, 50

Cornelius Gallus: in *Eclogue* 10, 44; his
miniature epic on the Grynean Grove,
11; pupil of Parthenius, 7

Cremona, 3

Cresius, 44

crinitus, 108

Culex, character and date of, 1

culpa, 25, 42

Cupid, substituted for Ascanius (Iulus),
28

Cynthius, Callimachean epithet of
Apollo, 3

Dante, 160n1

Decapitation in epic, 91, 92

deuenio, 24

Dictaeus, 44

Dido: compared to Diana, 18;
compared to a Maenad, 46;
compared to a mortally wounded
deer, 43–44; curses Aeneas and his
descendants forever, 52–53; Elissa
her old Phoenician name, 46, 48; an
Epicurean, 49; epiphany of, 22; and
the fatal hunt, 23–24; generosity of,
26; her limited experience of the
supernatural, 48–49; her past, 15–
16; holds banquet for Trojans and
Carthaginians, 28–29; last speech of,
57–58; loquacity of, 48; "optima
Dido," 45, 46; "Phoenician Dido,"
43; pronounces curse on self, 42;
pronounces own epitaph, 58;
"pulcherrima," 23; "regina," 46;
restless and frightened, 41; senses
deception, 46; Sidon's high-descended
daughter, 28, 57; sleepless with
passion and anger, 63; and Sychaeus,
42, 50; thinks of death, 50; tragic
form of her death, 53–57; urgent,
passionate nature of, 23, 49; wedding
of, 23–25; wounded by love, 40, 41.
See also Aeneas

Donatus, 125n3, 129n57; *Life* of Virgil,
3, 4

Drances, 89

Dryden, John, 60, 150n80

Ecphrasis: choice of scenes from Trojan
War traditional in, 131–32n12;
color-words in, 81; dramatic
ecphrasis Virgil's innovation, 17;
history of, 17; medial position in, 81;
phrases introducing scenes in, 79;
symmetry of scenes in, 79; traditional
features of style, 158n67

elogium of Appius Claudius Caecus, 58

Envy, a Callimachean motif, 7, 129n59

Epic poet intervenes in own fiction, 24,
25

Epyllion, 6, 14; containing story within the story, 12. *See also* Miniature epic
Eros, 41
errabundus and similar formations, 114
Eryx, 110
euersor, 85
Euphorion, 6
Eurotas, the, 20
Eurydice, death of, 8
Evander, 65; emotional speech to Pallas, 73–75; entrusts Pallas to Aeneas, 94; loquacity of, 48; modeled on Nestor, 48, 74; points out principal monuments of Pallanteum to Aeneas, 72; tells story of Hercules and Cacus, 69, 71–72. *See also* Aeneas
expleri, of sight, 156n47

Fall of Troy, amplitude and variousness of tradition, 138n22
fluenta, 133n30
flumen, of tears, 130–31n7
furtiuus, 135n44

Gallic invasion of 390 B.C., first great crisis of Republic, 80–81. *See also* Actium
γαυλός, Homeric hapax, 151n3
glisco, 163n24
Golden line, 60

Hearing (reading) more important than seeing, 10, 51
Hercules, 67; and Cacus, 69–70; Cacus story becomes popular in reign of Augustus, 71
ἐρσήεις, 158n66
Hesiod, his encounter with the Muses, 3
heu nimium, 150n83
Homeric etiquette, 67–69
Hunting in pastoral poetry, 44
Hypermetric hexameters, 53

Imitation, 10, 12, 15–16, 18–21, 30, 38, 40–41, 51, 87, 101, 111–12, 129n55, 132n15, 135n43, 140n39, 140n40, 145n38, 149n65, 156n49
infigo, used metaphorically, 41
Interrelated similes in *Aeneid*, 22, 23, 51, 52, 134n34, 145n36, 147n59
intexo, texo, of shipbuilding, 139n34. *See also aedifico*
Iopas: song of, 29; taught by Atlas, 31, 109

Jason, 23, 30, 75; compared to Apollo, 21; compared to a lion, 164n41
Julia, daughter of Augustus, 106, 146n40
Juno, 15, 16, 24–25, 43, 85
Juturna, 93; recognizes *monstrum*, 94

Kissing in epic, 136n11
Κυδώνιος, 44

labi, lapsus, inlabi, of snakes, 141–42n53
Landscape, description of, 51
Laocoon, 35–36; death of, 38–39
Latin poetry, criticism of, 64–65, 135n2, 141–42n53
Lausus, 99–100
lautus, 154–55n36
λεπτός, λεπταλέος, in literary sense, 3. See *tenuis*
Libystis, 153n21
Lion-similes, in Homer and Apollonius Rhodius, 87–88, 92; in Virgil, 88, 92–93
Loss of hair by women a result of passion, 101
Love-at-first-sight, a motif of Hellenistic poetry, 28

Maecenas, 13
Mantua, relative insignificance of, 3
Marlowe, Christopher, 138n29

Marriageable age for Roman girls, 106

Medea: age of, 19, 106; compared to Artemis, 19–20; compared to a deer startled by hunters, 44–45; at first sight of Jason, 23; her troubled mind compared to a sunbeam reflected by water, 62–63; kisses her bed, 56, 59; sleepless with passion, 62; wedding of, 24; wishes Jason had never come, 59; wishes she were dead, 42

mene fugis?, a motif of Greek poetry, 145–46n39

mercari, 140n40

Metaphor of love's burning wound, 41

meus connoting intimacy, 155n37

Mezentius, 72; transformed into a monster by Virgil, 71; wounded by Aeneas, 99

Milton, John, ix–x, 131n8

Miniature epic, 6, 11, 12, 40. *See also* Epyllion

monstrum, defined, 38

Nausicaa, compared to Artemis, 18–19

neotericus, 160n81

Nestor, 48, 68–69; prolixity of, 75

New Poets (*Poetae noui*), 4

niueus, 104

obstupesco, of love-at-first-sight, 136n7

Odysseus, 12, 16, 27, 32

opulentus, 154n30

Orpheus song of, 10, 30

Pallanteum: future site of Rome, 65; not pastoral Arcadia, 66

Pallas, 67; dies a hard and bloody death, 97; reckless young prince, 84–85, 153n19; sword-belt of, 98; a virginal figure, 96. *See also* Evander

Parthenius: brought to Rome as prisoner of war, 6; Cinna's mentor, 5; delicacy and restraint of his narrative imitated by Virgil, 8–9; his handbook Περὶ ἐρωτικῶν παθημάτων, 7; his poem on the incestuous passion of Byblis, 7–8; imitation of Callimachus, 8; instructed Virgil in Greek, 5; poet and scholar, 6

paruulus, 47

Pasiphae, 11, 66

Phaeacians, 30

Philitas, 5, 6

Poetae noui (New Poets), 4

Polemical poem in the Callimachean manner, 7

Preposition understood from following phrase, 151n3

proluo, 136–37n13

Quarrel of Odysseus and Achilles, 137n17

Quintus of Smyrna, independent of Virgil, 138n27

radians, 155–56n46

Rivers symbolizing kinds of poetry, 7

Roman education, 4

Romulus, 70, 80–81

ruber, 161n16

rumino, 101–2

Sannazaro, 66

saucia, of woman wounded by love, 40, 41

Scipio Aemilianus, 84

Servius (DServius), 45–46, 131n8, 133n31, 134n33, 137n18, 138n22, 139n34, 141–42n53, 142n1, 143n10, 145n34, 148n61, 149n72, 158n65, 160n81, 165n64

Shakespeare, William, 32

Sidney, Sir Philip, 66

Silenus, 10; song of, 10–11

Silvanus, grove of, 75–76

Sinon, 34–35; his elaborate and persuasive speech, 36
sinuo, 141–42n53
spelunca, 134n40
Suicide in Greek tragedy, 56
Superstition, 69

Tasso, 127n36
Telchines, 2
Telemachus, 67–68
tenuis, in literary sense, 3. *See also* λεπτός
Tiberinus, the river-god, 65, 66
Tricolon: with anaphora, 49; diminuendo with anaphora, 137–38n20; inverted, 31; Sinon's speech an extensive tricolon crescendo, 36
Triphiodorus: independent of Virgil, 138n27; a more imaginative poet than Quintus of Smyrna, 35
Troilus, 10
Troy, compared to an ancient tree, 51
Turnus, 61; "audax," 84–85; a brilliant figure, 86; compared to a lion, 88; compared to various animals, 92–93; compared to a wolf, 86–87; deliberately kills Pallas, 96–98; duel with Aeneas, 93–94; identifies self with Achilles, 85; killed by Aeneas, 98–99; pleads for his life, 94; "pulcherrimus," 23, 84; savagery of, 92; "turbidus," 161–62n17; violent nature of, 89

uiolentia, uiolentus, 89–90
Umbro, a warrior priest, 86
uomo, used metaphorically, 82
uulnero, used metaphorically, 155n42

Valerius Probus, his criticism of Virgil, 132n13
Varius Rufus, L., 4, 5
Varro of Atax, 5
Venus, 15–16, 23, 28, 76
Virgil: the *Aeneid* and Callimachean poetics, 14; and Catullus, 4, 41, 45, 59, 60, 102; and Cinna, 4–5; doubts about the *Aeneid,* 13–14; family and education of, 3–4; his literary career misunderstood, 1, 12–13; his miniature of a miniature epic, 12; his periods normally not exceeding four lines, 75; humanity of, 45, 83; imitates two or more poets simultaneously, 20, 51, 62, 64, 66, 115; likes to quote or imitate self, 12, 87, 88; pastoral translation of Callimachus, 2; rejects epic poetry, 1; response to the New Poetry, 10. *See also* Parthenius

Wolf-similes, in Homer, 162n19; in Virgil, 87–88
Wooden Horse: ambiguous description of, 33, 34, 37; described in terms of shipbuilding, 139n34; and Lucretius, 32–33; a *monstrum,* 37, 38; problem for modern poet, 32
Wordsworth, William, 9–10

INDEX OF PASSAGES CITED

Accius
  Philocteta
    fr. 558–59 R.³: 121
Aeschylus
  Agamemnon
    825: 139n33
Anacreon
  417.1–2 Page: 145–46n39
Antiphilus of Byzantium
  35.1–2 G.-P.: 139n33
Apollodorus
  Bibliotheca
    2.2.2: 101
  Bibliotheca, epitome
    3.32: 131n10
Apollonius Rhodius
  Argonautica
    1.13–14: 118
    1.65–66: 109
    1.144–45: 109
    1.307–10: 21
    1.309: 133n30
    1.315–16: 155n44
    1.324–25: 153n21
    1.472–74: 137n16
    1.496–502: 30
    1.723–24: 109
    1.739: 158n67
    1.750–51: 158n66
    1.764: 158n67
    1.790–91: 135n2
    1.792: 135n2
    1.827–29: 135n2
    1.896–98: 146n40
    1.1064–66: 8
    1.1243–49: 87
    2.257–58: 109
    2.512: 110
    2.1273: 152n11

    3.286–87: 41
    3.356–61: 119–20
    3.443–44: 23
    3.446–47: 23
    3.529–30: 110
    3.744–60: 62
    3.773–77: 42
    3.798–801: 143n13
    3.876–86: 19
    3.956–61: 96
    3.1008: 135n2
    3.1022–23: 135n2
    3.1265–66: 112
    4.12–13: 45
    4.26: 56
    4.26–33: 59
    4.123–26: 156n49
    4.207–8: 111
    4.989: 110
    4.1025–28: 106–7
    4.1131: 134–35n41
    4.1151: 128n42
    4.1165–69: 24
    4.1682–86: 51
Aristophanes
  Frogs
    215–16: 134–35n41
Asclepiades
    12.3 G.-P.: 130–31n7
Aulus Gellius
    9.9.12–17: 132n13

Bion
  Epitaphium Adonidis
    19: 132–33n21

Callimachus
  Aetia
    fr. 1.21–28 Pf.: 2

Callimachus (*cont.*)
  fr. 2.1–2 Pf.: 2
  fr. 67.1–3 Pf.: 109
  fr. 75.24–26 Pf.: 20
  fr. 110.52 Pf.: 105
  fr. 612 Pf.: 9
  fr. 676.1 Pf.: 153n21
  fr. 701 Pf.: 109
  Hymns
    1.47: 143n16
    2.32–34: 22
    2.108–12: 7
    3.81: 143n20
    3.110–12: 22
    3.170–73: 21
    3.212–13: 132n17
    5.94–95: 128n43
Calvus
  Io
    fr. 9 M.: 12
Catullus
  5.1: 45
  8.7: 134n35
  58b.4: 104
  61.27–30: 129n59
  61.79: 133n25
  61.90–91: 133n25
  61.209: 146n40
  61.214–15: 146n40
  64.10: 139n34
  64.75: 102
  64.89: 20
  64.108: 148n60
  64.112–13: 113
  64.132–33: 47
  64.171–72: 59
  64.200–201: 53
  64.201: 149n65
  64.249–50: 41
  64.267–68: 156n47
  66.52: 105
  68.55–56: 130–31n7
  68.70–71: 136n3
  68.139: 143n11

83.6: 45
95: 6
95.1: 155n37
111.3: 143n11
Cicero
  De officiis
    1.18.61: 131–32n12
  De oratore
    2.357: 142n4
  De senectute
    20.73: 149–50n76
  In Catilinam I
    17: 155n42
  Philippics
    2.28.68: 90
    2.64: 142–43n9
    5.7.19: 90
    12.11.26: 90
  Post reditum ad Quirites
    25: 142–43n9
  Pro Sestio
    86: 161n12
  Prognostica
    fr. 3.3 Soubiran: 104
  Verrines
    2.2.13: 139n34
Columella
  6.6.1: 102
Cornelius Gallus
  Epigram
    6–7: 126n19
Corpus Inscriptionum Latinarum
I², p. 192: 58

Dictys Cretensis
  4.9: 131n10

Ennius
  Alexander
    65–66 V.² = 43–44 J.: 139n34
    76–77 V.² = 72–73 J.: 139n33
  Annales
    49 V.²: 152n10
    54 V.²: 66

142 V.²: 160n80
477 V.²: 139n34
Medea exul
246–47 V.² = 208–9 J.:   59
253–54 V.² = 215–16 J.:   142n3
254 V.² = 216 J.:   40
Scenica
31 V.² = 28 J.:   108
92 V.² = 87 J.:   141n50
292 V.² = 250 J.:   150–51n2
Varia
18 V.²: 129n59
Euripides
Alcestis
175:    54
176–79:   55
183:    55
Rhesus
304:    103
616–18:   103
Troades
11:    139n33

Festus
De uerborum significatu
p. 146.32 L.:   38
p. 314.15 L.:   131–32n12

Hesiod
Catalogue
fr. 129.24 M.-W.:   101
fr. 133.4–5 M.-W.:   101
[Hesiod]
Scutum
215:    158n67
228:    158n67
314:    158n67
Homer
Iliad
1.255–56:   140n40
1.474:   137n15
3.219–20:   158n67
4.182:   143n13
4.471–72:   162n19

5.4–6:   95
5.51–52:   109
6.132–33:   134–35n41
6.410–11:   143n13
6.448–49:   84
7.132–35:   74
10.1–12:   64
10.177–78:   153n21
10.437:   103
10.500–501:   131n10
11.72–73:   162n19
11.670–72:   75
12.299–301:   162n21
13.389–91:   51
15.586–88:   163n23
16.138:   131n8
16.156–57:   162n19
16.352–53:   162n19
16.355:   162n19
16.473–74:   112
16.856–57:   165n64
18.483:   159–60n77
18.548:   158n67
18.610:   156n49
18.617:   155–56n46
20.215:   119
21.50–52:   131n10
22.309–10:   88
22.362–63:   165n64
23.307–8:   109
24.262:   162n19
Odyssey
1.29–30:   165–66n71
1.47:   84
1.123–24:   68
1.130–31:   68
1.170–72:   68
1.338:   29
3.1–2:   152–53n17
3.36:   153n20
3.37–40:   68
3.71–74:   69
3.113–14:   138n22
3.333:   118

Homer, *Odyssey (cont.)*
  4.244:   139–40n36
  5.294:   142n54
  6.22:   147n51
  6.102–9:   18–19
  6.130–34:   162n21
  6.229–35:   27
  6.233–34:   109
  6.237:   23
  7.78:   16
  8.75:   137n17
  8.367–69:   137n15
  8.448:   109
  8.461–62:   146n40
  8.480–81:   109
  8.488:   109
  9.69:   142n54
  9.223:   151n3
  10.126–27:   111
  10.130:   112
  12.27:   151n3
  13.93–94:   152–53n17
  13.356–57:   66
  14.50:   153n21
  14.519–20:   153n21
  17.518–19:   109
  18.158–59:   147n51
  19.479:   147n51
  20.72:   109
  21.1–2:   147n51
Homeric Hymn to Aphrodite
  174–75:   134n32
Horace
 Carmina
  1.2.37:   150n83
  1.35.5–6:   144–45n29
  1.37.6–8:   159n72
  1.37.30–32:   160n1
  3.13.7:   161n16
  4.11.19:   155n37
 Epode 17
  51:     161n16
 Sermones
  1.5.16:   136–37n13

  1.10.81:   129n56
  1.10.85:   129n56
  2.4.26–27:   136–37n13

Leonidas of Tarentum
  81.4 G.-P.:   162n19
Livy
  1.2.3:   71
  1.7.5:   154n25
  1.7.10:   154n26
  1.7.15:   70–71
  2.5.5:   165n57
  2.10.11:   66
  2.14.3:   154n30
  2.23.2:   163n24
  3.5.9:   163–64n38
  5.37.7:   127–28n37
  5.49.7:   81
  5.53.8:   159n75
  6.1.3:   159n70
Lucan
  2.421–23:   127–28n37
Lucretius
  1.473–74:   163n24
  1.473–77:   33
  1.1031:   130–31n7
  2.354:   130–31n7
  2.977:   158n66
  3.296–98:   90
  3.469:   158n66
  3.480–82:   163n24
  3.521–22:   89
  4.203:   150–51n2
  4.211–13:   62
  4.683:   159n74
  4.1048–49:   142n4
  4.1102:   156n47
  4.1114:   146n41
  4.1120:   142n4
  5.964:   163n30
  5.1226:   163n30
  5.1270:   163n30
  5.1297:   139n34

Lycophron
147: 162n19
342: 139n33

Macrobius
Saturnalia
1.24.11: 129n61
2.5.3: 146n40
5.17.18: 127n24
5.22.12: 140n39
Martial
14.195: 126n10
Moschus
Europa
44–45: 115
51: 116

Nonnus
Dionysiaca
25.386–90: 159–60n77

Ovid
Amores
1.13.31–32: 105
Fasti
3.658: 116
Heroides
12.33: 132n15
16.112: 139n34
Metamorphoses
1.610–11: 116
1.612: 116
1.632–34: 129n55
4.681–82: 131–32n12
7.748–50: 143n11
11.302: 106
12.455–56: 161n15
13.493: 158n65
Tristia
1.3.18: 130–31n7
[Ovid]
Amores
3.5.17–18: 102

Parthenius
Περὶ ἐρωτικῶν παθημάτων
2.2: 149n68
11: 7–8
Persius
Prologus 1: 136–37n13
6.31: 139n34
Pindar
Pythian 1
21–22: 160n80
Plautus
Epidicus
34–36: 121
Pliny
Naturalis Historia
13.62: 139n34
Propertius
4.4.21: 136n7

Quintus of Smyrna
2.101: 105
5.97–98: 158n65
5.537–38: 143n13
6.211: 158n67
6.231: 158n67
6.292–93: 158n65
9.155–56: 131n10
12.19–20: 137n17
12.83: 110
12.358–59: 141n51
12.389–90: 141n45
12.575: 142n54
13.44–46: 162n19

Sappho
1.21: 145–46n39
Seneca the Elder
Controuersiae
1.6.4: 159n75
2.1.5: 159n75
Sophocles
Ajax
817–18: 57

Sophocles (*Cont.*)
Electra
   718–19:   141n48
Oedipus Tyrannus
   1241–43:   53–54
   1249–50:   55
   1263–64:   56
Philoctetes
   314–15:   140n40
Trachiniae
   912–13:   54
   915–18:   54
   919–20:   55
   929–31:   56
Statius
Thebaid
   4.590–91:   130–31n7
Suetonius
Augustus
   7.2:   81
Supplementum Hellenisticum
   984.2:   105

Theocritus
   1.41–42:   158n67
   2.19:   101
   2.82:   132n15
   2.89:   101
   4.26–27:   150n83
   6.17:   145–46n39
   7.39–41:   5
   11.72:   12
   24.129:   109
Theognis
   785:   132n19
Triphiodorus
   37:   131–32n12
   63–64:   139n34
   216:   139–40n36
   247–48:   141n51
   279–80:   140n40
   288–89:   141n51
   310–15:   37–38
   452–53:   142n54

   664–65:   138n22

Valerius Flaccus
   1.484–86:   153n21
   8.461–62:   156n49
Varius Rufus
De morte
   fr. 2 M.:   136–37n13
   fr. 4.3 M.:   162n18
Virgil
Aeneid
   1.3–4:   154n32
   1.10–11:   154n32
   1.204:   61
   1.231:   155n37
   1.279:   86
   1.315:   15
   1.328:   15
   1.338–39:   15
   1.364:   16
   1.364–65:   24
   1.402:   136n3
   1.407–9:   16
   1.447:   154n30
   1.456:   80, 130n2
   1.461–62:   16
   1.464:   17
   1.465:   130–31n7
   1.467–68:   17
   1.469–70:   103
   1.473–74:   131n10
   1.475:   17
   1.481:   17
   1.485:   17, 130–31n7
   1.489:   105
   1.493:   131–32n12
   1.496:   23
   1.498–504:   18
   1.500–501:   132n17
   1.561:   135n2
   1.572:   135n2
   1.588–93:   26
   1.595–96:   27
   1.607–10:   28

1.613: 28
1.639–40: 153n22
1.651: 28
1.667–68: 154n32
1.685–88: 136n11
1.701–2: 153n22
1.709: 29
1.713: 156n47
1.714: 28
1.718–19: 29
1.738–39: 29
1.740–41: 108
1.741: 31, 109
1.742–46: 29
1.747: 30
1.751–52: 31
1.603: 49
2.1: 138n23
2.3: 32, 46
2.5–6: 32
2.10–11: 32
2.13–20: 33
2.29–30: 34
2.38: 34
2.52–53: 34
2.64: 140–41n43
2.103–4: 140n40
2.112–13: 139n34
2.186: 139n34
2.195–98: 36
2.201–2: 38
2.208: 141–42n53
2.223–24: 39
2.225–26: 141–42n53
2.228–29: 39
2.234–40: 36–37
2.235–36: 141–42n53
2.240: 141–42n53
2.241–45: 37
2.250: 142n54
2.258–59: 141n47
2.271: 130–31n7
2.343: 48
2.355–56: 162n19

2.361–62: 138n22
2.363: 51
2.374–75: 112
2.486–88: 25, 31
2.522: 155n37
2.610–12: 148n60
2.626–31: 51
3.12: 82
3.19: 117
3.222–23: 118
3.489: 155n37
3.555: 130–31n7
3.567: 158n66
3.626–27: 164n40
3.674: 130–31n7
3.716: 138n23
3.718: 40
4.1–2: 40
4.2–3: 142n3
4.4–5: 41
4.5: 40
4.9: 41
4.15–19: 41–42
4.23: 42
4.24–26: 42
4.27: 43
4.28–29: 42
4.55: 43
4.66–67: 41
4.68–73: 43
4.83–85: 136n11
4.133: 133n25
4.138–39: 22
4.141: 23
4.143–50: 23
4.163: 134–35n41
4.165–66: 23, 24
4.166–68: 24
4.169–72: 25
4.221: 45, 146n41
4.279: 136n7
4.281: 45, 146n41
4.283: 45
4.283–84: 144–45n29

Virgil, *Aeneid* (cont.)

4.291: 45
4.292: 45
4.293–94: 144n25
4.296: 46
4.298: 145n35
4.300–303: 46
4.305–6: 47
4.314: 145–46n39
4.317–18: 47
4.328–29: 47
4.331–32: 47
4.333–36: 48
4.334: 46
4.335: 46
4.340–43: 146n47
4.345–46: 48
4.347–48: 147n48
4.360: 147n50
4.361: 48
4.368–70: 49
4.379–80: 49
4.382–84: 49
4.387: 49
4.391–92: 50
4.423: 144n25
4.424: 57
4.425–26: 52
4.433: 50
4.441–49: 50
4.451: 148–49n63
4.457–58: 50
4.460–61: 50
4.496–97: 149n67
4.507: 54
4.522–29: 52
4.522–32: 63
4.554: 160n79
4.579–80: 111
4.581: 112
4.607: 53
4.610: 146n46
4.625–29: 53
4.640: 149n73

4.645–47: 54
4.646–47: 149n73
4.648–51: 55
4.651–58: 58
4.658: 149n73
4.659: 55
4.659–65: 56
4.661–62: 149n73
4.664: 147n56
4.665–71: 57
4.689: 41
4.790–91: 49
5.3–4: 146n46
5.35–37: 153n21
5.37: 153n21
5.254: 158n67
5.391–92: 110
5.449: 148n60
5.617: 148–49n63
5.682: 160n80
5.704–5: 109
5.775: 160n79
6.24–30: 113
6.57: 134–35n41
6.86–87: 61
6.89: 85
6.136–37: 155–56n46
6.226: 147n56
6.455: 144n24, 146n41
6.456: 48
6.460: 46
6.466: 145–46n39
6.515–16: 139n33
6.638: 134n38
6.695–96: 147n49
6.699: 130–31n7
6.825: 159n73
7.9: 150–51n2
7.11–12: 139n35
7.25–26: 152–53n17
7.41–42: 14
7.55: 84
7.136–38: 65
7.333–34: 46

7.409:   84
7.451:   139n35
7.467:   85
7.469:   85
7.475:   85
7.513:   150n1
7.738:   130–31n7
7.750–60:   86
7.785–88:   161n16
7.789–92:   115
7.817:   61
8.19:   61
8.22:   151n3
8.22–27:   61
8.36–38:   65
8.43:   152n9
8.64:   65
8.71–73:   65
8.88–89:   152n16
8.96:   152n16
8.97:   152–53n17
8.102–3:   117
8.110:   153n19
8.112–14:   67
8.115:   160n79
8.115–19:   67
8.134–42:   119
8.168:   155n37
8.175–83:   69
8.177–78:   153n21
8.188–89:   70
8.195–97:   92
8.195–98, 205:   71
8.230–32:   137–38n20
8.252–53:   160n80
8.265–66:   156n47
8.270–71:   82
8.273–79:   118
8.291–93:   154n32
8.301:   154n26
8.340:   154n26
8.359–69:   72
8.367–68:   153n21
8.389–90:   146n41

8.475–76:   154n30
8.481–88:   71
8.514–17:   94
8.560–84:   73–74
8.584:   147n56
8.587–91:   95
8.590:   75
8.596:   75
8.597:   75
8.616:   76
8.618:   156n47
8.620:   156n48
8.622–23:   76
8.626–29:   79
8.629:   130n2
8.638:   159n74
8.645:   158n66
8.649–50:   158n67
8.654:   159n75
8.678–81:   82
8.704–5:   108
8.711–13:   83
8.714:   160n1
8.724–26:   121
8.730:   80
8.730–31:   82
9.2–3:   84
9.13:   161–62n17
9.50:   161n16
9.59–66:   86–87
9.126:   84
9.199–200:   145–46n39
9.270:   161n16
9.373–74:   155–56n46
9.434:   147n56
9.470–72:   92
9.516:   112
9.565–66:   88
9.609–10:   131n10
9.638–39:   108
9.708:   147n56
9.732–33:   161n16
9.742:   85
9.753:   147n56

Virgil, *Aeneid* (cont.)

9.777:   29

9.813–14:   130–31n7

10.46–47:   134–35n41

10.74–76:   85

10.132–33:   134–35n41

10.148–50:   76

10.151:   89

10.189–91:   148n61

10.261–62:   82

10.272–73:   161n16

10.333–35:   91

10.441–43:   96

10.442–43:   100

10.460–61:   154n32

10.467–73:   97

10.475:   112

10.482–89:   98

10.499:   165n62

10.515–17:   154n32

10.531–33:   91

10.586–87:   131n10

10.609–10:   164n45

10.705–6:   97

10.781–82:   98

10.800:   99

10.810:   99

10.812:   100

10.812–13:   165n70

10.822:   100

10.902:   155n37

11.8:   158n66

11.37–38:   130–31n7

11.68–69:   96

11.110–11:   92

11.152–55:   165n69

11.170:   166n73

11.177–79:   100

11.326:   139n34

11.346:   89

11.354:   89

11.376:   89

11.805–6:   147n56

11.809–12:   163n23

11.841:   150n83

12.4–9:   88

12.45–46:   89

12.48–49:   163n28

12.89:   161n16

12.107:   95

12.247:   161n16

12.417:   151n3

12.497:   92

12.511–12:   163n37

12.512:   158n66

12.545:   85

12.601–4:   9

12.751:   164n45

12.786:   93

12.861–68:   93

12.874:   164n47

12.903–4:   94

12.932–34:   99

12.947–52:   98–99

Eclogues

1.1–2:   3

1.3:   144n24

2.58:   150n83

2.60:   145–46n39

2.61:   134–35n41

2.69:   12

3.100:   150n83

5.60:   162n22

6.1–8:   1

6.45–60:   11

6.47:   101, 115

6.50:   101

6.51:   101

6.54:   101

6.55–56:   44, 66

6.55–58:   114

6.58:   102

6.62–63:   129n55, 148n61

6.65:   129n59

6.68:   129n55

6.87:   11

8.41:   132n15

9.17–18:   150n83

9.28:   3
9.35–36:   4
9.60:   133n22
10.2:   155n37
10.12:   129n59
10.27:   161n16
10.47:   148n61
10.55–60:   44

Georgics
1.377:   127n27
2.6:   151n3
2.209–10:   148n60
2.264:   146n41
2.430:   161n16
2.498:   84
2.506:   136–37n13
3.2:   129n59

3.6:   13
3.10–16:   13
3.11:   129n59
3.41:   13
3.46–47:   14
3.153:   116
3.344:   143n18
3.485:   147n56
3.537:   162n22
4.321:   152n12
4.339:   133n22
4.435:   162n22
4.457–61:   8

[Virgil]
Culex
8–9:   1

Designer:	Barbara Llewellyn
Compositor:	Auto-Graphics, Inc.
Text:	10/12 Sabon
Printer:	Braum-Brumfield, Inc.
Binder:	Braum-Brumfield, Inc.